A Start in Freedom

A START
IN FREEDOM

Sir Hugh Foot

30338

HARPER & ROW, PUBLISHERS

NEW YORK AND EVANSTON

Contents

Illustrations

The Cartoons

The extracts on pages 22 and 23
are reprinted by kind permission
of the *Evening Standard*

Introduction

I T is a very long time since I arrived in Jerusalem fresh from Cambridge at the age of twenty-one to take up my first post— and straight away walked into one of the bloodiest communal riots which even the Holy Land had ever known.

Since then I have survived many risks and scrapes and mistakes and certainly I have had much more luck than I deserved.

I was first of all fortunate to serve my apprenticeship in riot and rebellion in Palestine before the last war. That was a good preparation for later excitements and I learnt some useful lessons. I learnt to work with Arabs and Jews—and I learnt to respect rebels. I often idly wished to be on their side of the barricades instead of on the side of authority. And I learnt to hate violence. And then in the war years in Trans-Jordan and Libya and in Cyprus I learnt to work with many different peoples — Arab Ministers and officials, and Arab villagers in the hills east of Jordan, and bedouin in the magnificent deserts between Amman and Aqaba, and the brave Senussi in Cyrenaica, and Greeks and Turks in Cyprus.

By the time the war was over and I went to new countries, in the West Indies and in West Africa, I was of an age to take responsibility, for eight years as a Colonial Secretary and ten years as a Governor. It was a period when earlier ground-work was rewarded, when a great transformation was being achieved —the transition from colonies to new independent nations. It was a time of fulfilment. All the countries in which I served are now governing themselves. Since the last war more than six hundred million people in the British Commonwealth have attained independence, and the number of member countries in the United Nations has more than doubled, from fifty-one to one hundred and thirteen. Surely one of the most revolutionary changes of our age.

Then, having worked with different peoples in Arabia and Africa and the West Indies in preparation for self-government and independence, I was again fortunate when I left Cyprus in

1960 to go to the United Nations. There I met the representatives of peoples I had known before in their previous colonial existence. Some of them were my old personal friends. I met them in their new status as delegates speaking for independent States.

There I met Prime Minister Sir Abubakr Balewa, of Nigeria, whom I had first known as an eloquent and fiery back-bencher from the North when we served together years ago in the Nigerian Legislative Council.

I heard Archbishop Makarios address the General Assembly. I had last seen him when I shook hands with him and Vice-President Kutchuk as I left Cyprus in 1960 on Independence Day.

When the Jamaican flag went up at one of those frequent and simple ceremonies, which always greatly moved me, of raising the flags of new nations outside the United Nations Building, Prime Minister Sir Alexander Bustamante was there, an elegant and striking figure in his grey morning coat and top hat. I had known him first as the leader of the Jamaica Labour Party in the turbulent days of 1945, and subsequently worked with him in daily association when he was the first Chief Minister of Jamaica.

And at the United Nations I met, as well as old friends, a new generation of Africans and Asians—some of them too young to have held responsibility in the days of British administration, but many of them nevertheless familiar with British institutions and strongly influenced by British traditions and methods.

I was fortunate therefore not only in the time I entered the Colonial Service but also in the opportunity to work with many different people in many different countries, and then to go to the centre of it all in New York. And finally, having been a delegate at the United Nations, I have been most fortunate of all to graduate to the service of the United Nations organisation itself.

When I came back from Cyprus someone suggested that I should write a book. I impatiently replied that I wanted to do something, not write anything. My reminiscences seemed to be entirely unimportant. I was not concerned with the past. But during my time at the United Nations, as I spoke of our colonial record and our aims and methods, I began to feel that there had been some coherence and some pattern, and some significance for the future, in my experience of three decades of overseas administration. I began to think that I should try to put down something of what I had seen and learnt, and give some account of how we worked to give colonial peoples a good start in independence.

When I say "we" I mean those of us who worked overseas in the Colonial Administrative Service. When I have been speaking to American audiences I have suggested that they should look twice at the battered figure they saw before them. For never again might they see a British Colonial Governor. We are becoming increasingly rare. Soon, except in a few scattered islands and outposts, there will be none of us left. I am one of the last of an almost extinct species.

So my story is partly an account of the last few decades of the Service to which I belonged, the decades in which with gathering momentum there emerged so many new nations from the greatest empire of history. We were rowing on a flood tide. It was much stronger than we were. But we rowed with it, not against it. At first we did not realise its force; we sometimes misjudged its pace, and did not fully understand its world-wide effect. But we had long believed that the way to train people in the exercise of responsibility was to give it to them. We worked with and for the people. We respected their aspirations and we believed in their sincerity and ability. We realised, perhaps dimly at first, that we were fortunate enough to have a hand in one of the greatest enterprises of our generation—the creating of new nations.

We did not doubt that the colonial peoples should become free to govern themselves, but we never imagined or pretended that all the problems of any new nation could be neatly solved in advance. Obviously independence creates new problems, and new dangers. And some problems are better tackled after independence than before. Nearly all the new nations face towering difficulties and terrible dangers. We of the British Colonial Service never claimed that we could do more than help to give the new nations the best possible start in governing themselves. How did we go about it? How far did we succeed?

Those are the questions I shall try to answer by going back over my own experience—and it is very much a personal story

13

Introduction

I have to tell—but what I have to say will be worth while only if it suggests some guidance for the future. The theme of my story is that what we managed to achieve was not an end but a beginning.

There are some people who regard the results of our work with doubt and misgiving, or downright dislike and disapproval. They look on the new nations with irritation or even contempt, and speak of their activities in the United Nations in particular as irresponsible, dangerous, misguided. They think of the granting of independence either as a mad mistake or as a good riddance, with one new country after another walking the plank into a sea of troubles.

My hope is that by telling my own story I shall make some small contribution to understanding the new nations and to a sympathy for their aims and needs and, above all, to a greater readiness to help them in their manifold difficulties. They desperately need our understanding and sympathy and help. As U Thant said in his first Annual Report:

"The present division of the world into rich and poor countries is, in my opinion, much more real and much more explosive than the division of the world on ideological grounds."

In spite of past mistakes and present vacillations Great Britain has an immense fund of good-will and respect in the world. It would be tragic if we threw it away. Our relations with the new nations are much more important now than when we had a direct responsibility for their welfare and progress. A good working understanding with the new nations, whose peoples make up two-thirds of the population of the world, should surely be one of the main purposes of our future policy.

It is the future that matters; that is why I have called this book "A Start in Freedom".

1st of January 1964
New York

Hugh Foot

14

A Start in Freedom

CHAPTER I

Making a Start

"Better is the end of a thing than the beginning thereof."
ECCLESIASTES VII. 8

ONE of the advantages of the Colonial Service, we were told, was that you could be transferred from one territory to another. Certainly it was an advantage to gain experience in different parts of the world, but I never asked for a transfer—and whenever I was moved I thought that my masters had made an extraordinary and unforgivable error. I remember my indignation in 1943 when, having just passed my higher Arabic examination, I was transferred to Cyprus where Arabic was scarcely spoken at all. I remember too how depressed I was at first to leave Cyprus and then Jamaica and then Nigeria—and my fury when in the war I was ordered back from North Africa to Amman.

But once I had reluctantly extracted myself from one territory it was always exciting to face adventures in another, to leave old mistakes behind, to look forward to working with a new team, to get to know a new people, to make an entirely new start; these were thrilling prospects. My most vivid recollections are of arrivals in half a dozen very different countries, in Arabia, in Africa and in the West Indies.

Having spent my first few years overseas in Palestine, and after a short interval in London, I was posted at the beginning of the second world war to Trans-Jordan. I travelled by the Orient Express through wavering and frightened countries all the way from Calais to Istanbul, and then on again by train through the grandeur of the Taurus mountains into Syria on my way to be Assistant British Resident under Sir Alec Kirkbride in Amman.

Three years later, at the beginning of 1943, I drove amidst the crowded transport of the Eighth Army from Alexandria through the Western Desert, past the battlefield of Alamein, on past battered Tobruk and Derna, to join the Military Administration of Cyrenaica.

In 1947, after my first few years in Jamaica, I arrived in Nigeria. After the cold night stop in the war-damaged Tripoli airport, we set out on the long flight south and I woke in the aircraft to see the sun come up over the vast curve of the Sahara; and later that morning I entered the new world of Africa south of the great desert through the gates of the walled city of Kano.

What a joy to go back to Jamaica in 1951, to recognise all the familiar landmarks as we sailed into Kingston Harbour on a brilliant sunlit morning, past the ancient capital of Port Royal, to look up to the commanding beauty of the Blue Mountains rising steeply over the Liguanea plain. Our old friend Donald MacGillivray, who had been acting as Governor, was there to receive us, and a host of other friends. Guards of Honour, bands and bunting at the landing stage and smiling welcomes on every side, as we made our way to Kings House for the swearing-in ceremony. We rejoiced in our great good fortune, and felt like coming home.

How different was our return to Cyprus late in 1957. Sylvia and I and our eight-year-old youngest son Benjamin flew from London to Malta, and then on in the Commander-in-Chief's plane to the uncertainties of an island distracted by violence. We stepped out of the plane on a rainy morning onto a windy runway at Nicosia to a damp welcome from Service chiefs and a few officials, without a Cypriot in sight.

But of all arrivals in new countries it is my arrival in August 1929 to take up my first post in Palestine which stands out most clearly in my mind. My mother drove me from our home in Cornwall to the station in Plymouth, and I went to London to join the British India ship which was to take me to Port Said. Then along the Suez Canal to Kantara, where I waited in the deserted and fly-blown station café for the train which left at midnight to travel over the Sinai desert on its way to Jerusalem.

Early the next morning I eagerly lifted the blind to catch my first sight of the Holy Land, in the plains of Gaza, and my excitement rose as the train went on first through the orange groves of the plain and then, the track winding its way up through the hills of Judea, to the railway station at Jerusalem. There was no one there to meet me, and in the glare of the bright sunlight I stood disconsolate on the platform.

I soon discovered why no one was at the station. It was a time of tension and expected disorder. An uneasy peace had lasted for the previous decade. But now intense feeling had arisen between the Arabs and the Jews in the dispute over the Wailing Wall. The Jews wept at the Wall for the loss of King Solomon's temple. The Arabs claimed the Wall as part of the holy Haram ash Sharif. It was a dispute which aroused fierce religious passions on both sides and at any moment, I was told, fanatical feeling might explode into violence.

On Friday, after the noon-day prayers, the explosion came. I was at the Government Offices overlooking the Damascus Gate, and I shall not forget the distant clamour, like the remote roar of a football crowd, as the mob poured out of the Mosque of Omar and pressed through the narrow streets of the Old City. And then I saw the crowd come out through the Damascus Gate. It was wild with a chanting frenzy, which I was to get to know well in subsequent riots.

Then all was confusion and commotion. Kingsley Heath, a senior Police Officer, alone gallantly but quite ineffectively charged the crowd on his horse—and I was astonished that he did not come down on the steep asphalt. And a little later Tesseyman, another Police Officer, came in breathlessly with his revolver hot and blood down the side of his uniform to report that killing and burning had started in the Jewish quarters. Soon afterwards I saw in Hebron where the mob had gone from one end of the long street to the other killing everyone, man, woman and child, as it went. By that time I had been given a rifle and a uniform and for the next month or two I was a bewildered but excited amateur policeman. Within a week of my arrival in Jerusalem I had been caught up in the violence and hatred which have divided the Holy City and surrounded the Holy Land ever since.

So it was that in my first few days in my first post I began to

realise what I was later to learn better—how barren is partition, how senseless is cruelty and hatred, how much terrible
damage can be done when men are divided by fear and malice,
and how evil the results of violence can be.

CHAPTER II

Raw Material

"Look unto the rock whence ye are hewn, and to the hole of
the pit whence ye are digged."*

ISAIAH LI. 1

BEFORE I go on, let me stop to try to give some rough picture
of my background and my family. What kind of young man
was it who unsuspectingly walked into violence and conflict in
Palestine in the summer of 1929? Why was he there at all?
What had he learnt from his Methodist home and his Quaker
school and from four mis-spent years at Cambridge? And,
since the predominant influence in his life had always been his
family, what kind of family was it?

When, as Governor of Cyprus, I came home at the beginning
of 1958 for consultations in Whitehall I wrote this letter to the
Daily Mail:

"Sir—I read in the *Daily Mail* this morning an article by
Kenneth Allsop about my father and my family in which it
is said that I 'was always considered the slightly out-of-step
hearty in the intellectual menage'.

This is the culmination of a whispering campaign put
about, I am sure, by my brothers.

They say to any newspaperman who will listen that I am
a sort of wild half-wit brought up on the Cornish moors with
the gypsies. They suggest that I was shuffled off overseas at
an early age because I was clearly unfit to follow their
pursuits of the law and politics.

I wish to protest about all this. I was, I think, the only one
of the five brothers to win a scholarship to my school. I got
exactly the same university degree as all of them—second-
class Honours. Like them I was President of the Union. The

* This was one of my father's favourite texts. "Pit and Rock" became a family
motto and password.

only difference was that I went to Cambridge and they all went to Oxford.

I would thank them to remember that, except for our father, who is, as we all know, head and shoulders above all of us, we are intellectually equal—all second-class stuff.

And as to the gypsies—well, I like gypsies. And who wouldn't make for the moors when the alternative was to endure the insufferable superiority of four Oxford brothers."

My brother John replied with greater vehemence, and the correspondence attracted some attention. It achieved the distinction of a special article in *Time* magazine. Some people took it seriously and said what a pity it was that brothers should be so sadly at loggerheads. Others thought that with Cyprus in crisis it was scarcely the time for pursuing family jests in public. No doubt they were right, but my brothers as well as myself find it difficult to resist the temptation to have a go at one another.

A year or two ago my brother Michael writing in the *Evening Standard* said:

"Put the point crudely: Sir Hugh was never considered the brightest of the brood. Ideas he took ready-made, usually straight from his father's commonplace books. And no one could dispute: he *did* go to Cambridge of his own volition.

He picked up bad habits that never entirely left him. Over the years it became increasingly evident that he had acquired strange tastes and was ready to indulge in pastimes which the rest of us wouldn't be seen dead at—such as rowing, playing polo, dressing up in Goering-like uniforms and enjoying it, and occasionally even—at a pinch—placing some trust in the word of Tory Prime Ministers."

Earlier in the article Michael wrote:

"Sir Hugh started his career in the Colonial Service as an administrative officer in Palestine. Later he became, inter alia, Assistant British Resident in Trans-Jordan, Chief Secretary of Nigeria, Captain-General of Jamaica, and Governor and Commander-in-Chief in Cyprus.

One common feature may be discerned in the modern

history of all these territories. All of them, after a suitable period of unrest, riot and rebellion, have been removed from the aegis, direct or otherwise, of the British Parliament.

Working himself out of one job after another and hauling down the flag at increasingly impressive ceremonial occasions, Sir Hugh has moved on elsewhere to apply the same infallible touch.

Possibly this is the reason why the *Evening Standard* may welcome his latest appointment as a chief British spokesman at the United Nations. The hope may be born in the Beaverbrook breast that Sir Hugh may perform his famous improved version of the Samson act there.

Certainly it would be a mistake to underrate his talents. He lays hold of the pillars with brawny arms. The temple crashes. But, lo and behold, the modern Samson emerges unscathed, with his muscles flexed in readiness for some fresh feat of constructive demolition."

But finally he relented sufficiently to say:

"Way back at his father's knee and beneath his mother's gentle eye unsuspected by his suspicious brothers, Sir Hugh had grasped the point about our convulsive Commonwealth. One man is as good as another. Each has an equal right to control his own destinies. How would they learn responsibility? Give it to them; it's the only way.

As for colour, who cares? No one but the stupidest snob and, for all his sartorial aberrations, Sir Hugh was never that.

All in all, a credit to the family, and I can't say fairer than that, can I!"

When they quoted my brother Dingle or my brother Michael against me in the Fourth Committee of the United Nations, I used to reply that in my family none of us took any responsibility whatever for the utterances of the others. We liked to work to the rule "let not the left Foot know what the right Foot doeth".

All this, and the fact that we have been scattered most of our lives, does not take away from the fact that we are a very close family. We lived for a number of years when I was a boy near the village of St. Cleer on the edge of the Cornish moors. We were a self-sufficient family, five brothers and two sisters, and we had and needed few outside friends. We were united in our devotion to our parents—and in a sneaking respect for each other.

My mother was the centre and inspiration of our lives, working and planning for us all the time, uncompromising in her strict adherence to Methodist and Liberal principles, always long suffering and compassionate. Others might be sick or tired or temperamental. It never entered her head, or ours, that she could be any such thing. Human failings were for us, not for her. Never complaining, never short tempered, she made us all laugh at ourselves and at each other. My picture of her is as she sang in a high, clear voice seldom quite in tune in our family pew in the Chapel at Callington or slipped away to take her Sunday School class, or at her place at our crowded dining table with tears in her eyes as she helplessly laughed at the nonsense we talked. And at night when she at last abandoned her efforts to get us to go to bed she would give us all a brisk nod at the door of the library with a final comprehensive loving rebuke. She set us all an example of devotion and gaiety.

She never openly approved of Michael's desertion to the Labour Party, and when Michael was Labour candidate for Devonport in 1945 she gave him no sign of support until the eve of the poll. As he was addressing his final rally a message came that there was an urgent package from his mother. He stopped speaking and a parcel was handed up to the platform. He was for a moment undecided, but there were shouts from the crowd telling him to open it. When he did so there emerged a large Cornish pasty. It was a family peace offering. Michael was the only member of the family to win in the election of 1945. My father beaten in Tavistock; Dingle, who had been Member for Dundee for fourteen years, beaten too; John beaten in Bodmin. As the news of defeats came in to our home one after another late that night there was only Michael's win in Devonport to lighten the general gloom. My father used to say proudly that our family had lost more parliamentary elections than any family in England.

When we lived at St. Cleer my father would stride out early

in the morning to walk down over the moor and along the narrow lanes to Liskeard, declaiming poetry as he walked, there to catch his train to Plymouth where he had a growing solicitor's practice. He had already entered Westcountry politics, and had been narrowly defeated in the Totnes Division in 1910. It was not until 1922 that he entered the House of Commons as Liberal Member for South-East Cornwall (and Sir John Simon sent him a telegram: "Dear Foot, Congratulations on your magnificent feat"). By 1931 he had become Minister of Mines in the Ramsay MacDonald Coalition Government, but he soon resigned from the Government, together with the independent Liberal Ministers. The law and politics would have been enough for most men. But he preached in the Cornish chapels on Sundays, and had already started collecting one of the greatest private libraries in England. And when he came back late in the evenings from Plymouth he had time to play cricket with us in the back field and to read to us under the big lamp in the crowded main room of our thickly-populated home. He was teaching himself French and read to us *Les Miserables*, translating as he went. Later on I earned a shilling an hour teaching him my schoolboy Greek so that he could read the New Testament in the original. It was difficult to know what progress he was making, for once he had got a phrase or a word of the text he knew the rest of the chapter by heart.

And when he was not reading to us he did a prodigious amount of reading of his own—poetry, history and biography. He could concentrate on his reading with all the pandemonium of the family going on round him and would look up occasionally to join in any argument amongst his children which interested him. He was the finest speaker and preacher I have ever heard. When I arrived back in London one evening on one of my many returns from Cyprus for consultation, I learnt that he was to speak at the National Liberal Club in an hour's time with his friend, Lord Birkett. I changed quickly and hurried to the dinner. It was the last time I heard him speak in public. He was then eighty years of age. He had slowed up a little; his speaking mannerisms were more pronounced; he could not resist over-loading his speaking with innumerable quotations. But what a delight it was to hear the magic of his oratory once more. What humour, especially when he was telling a story in Westcountry dialect, what timing, what elegance and music in his speech.

He took a tremendous interest and unreasonable pride in the activities of his offspring. When Michael wrote *The Pen and the Sword* he was overjoyed that one of his sons should have ventured into literature and history. When I was in Cyprus he followed every development with the keenest anxiety, and it was a special satisfaction to him that shortly before he died in 1960 a settlement in Cyprus was achieved.

We on our side would go to him for guidance and for encouragement. Once when I finally returned from Cyprus I was offered a commercial job at any salary I liked to state. I was not attracted by the prospect, but I went to him to tell him of the offer. He said he would think about it, and next day at breakfast he said: "I have thought about that offer. If you accepted it your enemies would know what to say, but your friends wouldn't."

And one day when the situation in Cyprus was at its worst and seemed to be in hopeless bloody deadlock, I received a telegram from my father which said: "See Second Corinthians four verses eight and nine." I turned from my anxieties to look it up and found this text to encourage me in my adversity: "We are troubled on every side, yet not distressed; we are perplexed but not in despair; persecuted but not forsaken; cast down but not destroyed." I sent back this telegram: "See Romans five verses three and four." "And not only so, but we glory in tribulations also; knowing that tribulation worketh patience; and patience, experience; and experience, hope." My father's opinion of my biblical knowledge was rightly low. The fact that I had been able to cap his text made him shake his head in wonder for long afterwards.

To return to the charges my brothers make against me, I do not deny them. My elder brother Dingle was clearly cleverer than I was. He did not seek to disguise the fact. I suffered for a short time from going to the same preparatory school with him, and I made up my mind then that I would escape from the comparisons which close association with him made inevitable. I would not follow him to the same Public School so I persuaded my parents to send me to Leighton Park, a Quaker school, instead. When he was at Oxford, I went to Cambridge. Like him I was destined for the law and politics and I did law in my last two years at Cambridge. But just when there was a danger that I would follow in his footsteps I escaped again. I left home politics and the law to my brothers, turned my back on home and family and set out for a lifetime of voluntary exile.

I plead guilty too to an affection for gypsies. When we were living on the edge of the Bodmin moor and I was about ten years old I used to escape to the gypsy encampments. There in their tents I learnt how to make clothes pegs and broom handles. Sitting with the gypsy children round their fire I felt their contempt for the settled life of people who lived in the comfort and complacent security of houses. And I remember the feeling of intense moral indignation when my mother objected to my bringing my small gypsy friends home to tea. This struck me as gross discrimination, an intolerable social injustice.

At Cambridge again I escaped. I became an enthusiastic member of the Lady Margaret Boat Club, one of the toughest organisations in the University. It was a brutish life we led. We met early in the morning for a training run. We rowed every afternoon. We dined together in Hall at night. Female society was entirely excluded and despised. The language was startlingly foul. When we were not in training, vast quantities of beer were consumed. I had promised my grandfather (for a financial reward) not to drink till I was twenty-one, and so, as the only teetotaller in the Boat Club (until the moment I was twenty-one), it was my special duty to see that fellow members of the Club who were unable to get to bed were assisted to do so. My devotion to the Boat Club remains, but I cannot pretend that, apart from the exuberance of intense physical fitness and the occasional joy of being in an eight rowing perfectly together, I had much to show for the long hours I spent on the River Cam.

What did arise from my rowing activities was the thought of escape from the prospect of a life-time in my father's law office. It was fashionable for rowing Blues to go to the Sudan Political Service. The Blues governing the blacks was the jibe. So, although I could not claim the supreme qualification of being a Blue, I put my name down in my last year as an applicant for that Service. My motives were vague and not particularly creditable. I knew little about the Sudan. I had some desire for escape and adventure. It would be pleasant to earn money on my own as soon as possible. I was attracted, too, by a picked Service with a fine tradition. But I had no high motive, no dedication, no missionary enthusiasm, and certainly no thought at that time of self-government or independence for peoples under British administration. I casually informed my father what I had done. I passed the first few interviews, and then one day I was summoned to London to see the Colonial Office Appointments Department. I was told that there was a vacancy for a Junior Assistant Secretary in Palestine. Would I like to be considered for it, and abandon my Sudan application? A decision must be made at once since the Palestine vacancy could not wait. I went out into London and had a noisy dinner with some of my Cambridge friends. None of them could tell me anything about the relative attractions or disadvantages of the Sudan and Palestine. Nevertheless, the Palestine offer was a bird in the hand. I went back to the Colonial Office the next morning. Yes, I would go to Palestine. And so within two months of leaving Cambridge I was on my way to become the most junior member of the British Administration in Jerusalem.

My time at Cambridge had not been wholly devoted to rowing. In my first year I pompously set myself the aims of rowing in the Lady Margaret First May Boat and being elected President of the Union and getting a First in History. Unfortunately I put them in that order. I did less and less work as my four years at Cambridge proceeded. I failed to get a First. Having got what is known as a two-one in the first part of my Tripos in History, I then sank to a two-two when I switched to Law in my last two years. I gave up much of my time to University politics and I became President of the Cambridge University Liberal Club and, in my last term, President of the Union.

As President of the Liberal Club I received Lloyd George when he came to speak at our annual dinner. After the first world war he had been reviled by my family as a traitor to the true Liberal cause, but when I met him at Cambridge and had breakfast with him on the morning following the dinner I came under the charm of his wit and his imagination. I remember being struck by the fact that he seemed healthier and happier than ordinary mortals. His terrific zest for life and the quickness of his good humour delighted us—even those of us who were not at our best at breakfast.

Another grand figure who came to Cambridge in those days was the first Lord Birkenhead. After a dinner at which he consumed what we undergraduates thought was an enormous quantity of wine he made the most eloquent and devastating speech I ever heard in the Union. At one point when he was in full spate there was a faint interruption from the back of the crowded benches opposite to him. The great man stopped short. We were all terrified by the ominous silence which followed. "Stand up, Sir" ordered Lord Birkenhead, and at the back of the Debating Hall a small figure rose in a tattered gown looking as if he wished he could sink into the floor. There was another dreadful silence. Then Lord Birkenhead exploded. "Sit down, Sir, the insignificance of your appearance is sufficient answer to the impudence of your interruption." The anxious tension was broken; the whole House roared its delight.

When I came up to Cambridge the best known names in the Union were those of the present Archbishop of Canterbury (A. M. Ramsey of Magdalene) and the present Foreign Secretary (R. A. Butler of Pembroke). As freshmen we listened to them speak, and in our time, they were followed at the Union by a red-headed orator from Christ's called Patrick Devlin, a round bustling energetic figure from Clare, Geoffrey Crowther, and an ambitious wing forward from Magdalene, Selwyn Lloyd. Another well-known Union figure was Gilbert Harding of Queens'. Gilbert never became President of the Union. Indeed, he never seemed to set himself any definite target. He was restless, dissatisfied with himself, unreliable in everything except in friendship—but how much better company he was than most of his contemporaries!

At one time he used to wear a black cape and a wide hat. Wherever he moved there was jest, eloquence and controversy. Wherever he went there was argument, strong language and outbursts of uproarious laughter. He had a deep guffaw which I can hear now. Sometimes there were wild disputes—for all his life Gilbert was inclined to flare up into violent personal quarrel. Afterwards he would often go through torments of remorse, but they did not last long.

I organised with him and others a campaign against admission of women to the Union. This was not a serious anti-feminist move. We treated it as a joke—and left the pompous arguments to the other side. A plebiscite on the issue was to be taken. We raised a small amount of money for our campaign, enough to print and despatch to every member of the Union a restrained and respectfully worded appeal setting out the arguments (I cannot remember what they were!) for maintaining the ban on the women. We arranged that our appeal would be delivered to every voter on the day of the poll. We also sent to each voter at the same time on the same day a dirtily-stencilled appeal purporting to come from the other side. The tone of this second appeal was unpleasantly superior, the grammar was deliberately bad—and we made a special point of mis-spelling the names on the envelopes in a way best calculated to irritate the recipients. We won the poll easily.

Since those days I have been overseas. I did not follow Gilbert's activities closely, but whenever I came home I would go to see him in Weymouth Street, and we would go out to eat and talk together.

I often tried to persuade him to come to see me wherever I was overseas. I specially wanted him to come to Cyprus. But he was too sick to come, and anyhow flying was bad for his asthma.

Only once he came to visit me, and that was when I was Governor of Jamaica. He wouldn't fly so he came out and went back on a banana boat. That gave him only one night in Jamaica with us. He sent me word from the boat saying that Nancy Spain and another newspaper woman were on the boat. Could he bring them to dinner at Kings House? Of course. So we sat down that night, Sylvia and I and Gilbert and Nancy Spain and the other visiting journalist and an A.D.C. We had not met for a long time and we talked far into the night. I remember being impressed yet again with Gilbert's astonishing memory for detail. He told us one story that night of a football match in the days when he was a schoolmaster in Cyprus years before. He could remember the name of every player on the field.

When at last we went to bed Sylvia said that I had been rude to our other guests who couldn't get a word in edgeways as we told one story after another of Cambridge and since. But Nancy Spain got her own back. She wrote a stinker in her paper under the headline "Who wouldn't be a Governor?" and gave a lurid description of wild nights at Kings House as "the corks popped under the stars in the tropical night".

Politics and public speaking were an increasing part of my life at Cambridge. I had done some speaking while I was still at school. And at Cambridge, as well as speaking in the Union and the Liberal Club, I went off one summer speaking from a travelling van in the Liberal Land Campaign. I went with Selwyn Lloyd. In those days he was a Liberal—he had been my predecessor as President of the Liberal Club. It was good practice to speak in the squares and street corners of Devonshire villages, occasionally to quite large and noisy crowds but more often to a mere handful of curious villagers. When we arrived in a village or country town, we would put down the side of our van and Selwyn and I would take it in turns to speak first to an empty street or square, endeavouring to collect a crowd. It was useful speaking experience to have to attract a crowd—and equally good for us no doubt when our listeners decided to disperse, leaving us holding forth to a salutary solitude. I went later to the United States as one of a three-man Cambridge University debating team, as three of my brothers did representing Oxford. The other members of our team were Lionel Elvin, now Head of the Department of Education at London University, and Alan King Hamilton, now a distinguished barrister. We travelled through the Middle West and West of the United States for four months debating in some forty colleges and speaking at innumerable other occasions. Again good experience; American Colleges were, and still are, wonderful audiences, lively, curious and critical.

American College debating was serious and formal by our standards. Our American opponents were out to win the debates by the accumulated weight of solid arguments for which points were allotted by the judges. We were more light-hearted and we liked to reply at once to the previous speaker without waiting for the rebuttals at the end of the debates (made after an interval to consult card-indexes of previously prepared replies to the anticipated arguments). We were more anxious to score as we went along—and our opponents were shocked that we didn't seem to care whether we won or lost.

Those few months gave me a liking for speaking in America, and in subsequent years whenever I have had leave from my posts in Arabia or Africa or the West Indies I have sought permission to go off on speaking tours in the United States. It is hard work. Travelling every day and some nights too, meeting new people, giving all you have got in speaking and answering questions and then, more often than not, attending late receptions when you are dog tired. But the American audiences and hosts make it a delight in spite of the hard going. Such genuine and generous hospitality and such anxiety to learn about new problems and distant countries and such an intense desire, specially amongst the young Americans, to play some personal part in understanding and helping the outside world—a much healthier attitude in America in these matters, I am sad to say, than in present-day England.

To interest, arouse and hold an audience. To persuade, convince people and move them to agreement, concern or indignation. To stir them from their lethargy or complacency. These things can be done by writing and speaking. The writing, it often seems to me, is r ually so well done in books, magazines, newspapers. But the sta... .ard of public speaking is dreadfully low in America, and England too—and getting worse. So many speeches these days are merely readings from prepared texts, surely an insult to any audience. The art of oratory is now almost lost. I have heard a few real orators—Lloyd George, Birkenhead, Winston Churchill, Aneurin Bevan, Paul Henri Spaak of Belgium, Sir Abubakr Balewa of Nigeria, Norman Manley of Jamaica, and some of the French-speaking Africans at the United Nations. At Cambridge in the crowded debates in the Union I first felt the thrill of hard-hitting debate.

When I moved up to be President of the Union in 1929 my

father and mother came to Cambridge for the Change of Officers debate. Norman Birkett was to be one of the speakers. At the last moment he sent word that he could not come. John Leathem, the retiring President, came to me that afternoon to beg that my father should speak in his place. He had no time to prepare, and he had never spoken in the Union before. But he agreed. How anxious I was that night as I called on him to speak. I should not have worried. In a few minutes he had the House listening intently, and then laughing, and that night he made one of the finest speeches I ever heard him make.

My brothers and I claim that we hold a record. There have never before been four brothers Presidents of the Union at Oxford and Cambridge—and it was a special treat when I was home from New York a year or two ago to sit in the gallery of the Oxford Union to hear my son speak, and later to see him occupying the President's Chair. I was nervous, as I am whenever I hear one of the family. But he had the quality of good timing and communicating a sense of mounting excitement and the urgency of true eloquence. I was not surprised to hear him quoting Edmund Burke. He had something in his accent of my brothers and my father too. A wonderful thing to hear one's father speaking in the voice of one's son.

I have put down these random recollections of my family and my upbringing to give some idea of the kind of raw material I was when I embarked on a career in the Colonial Service. I do not deny Michael's accusation that I learnt bad habits at Cambridge, or that I wasted much of my time there. But I had some assets for the career I so casually adopted. I was physically very fit. I had learnt some history and a little law. I had picked up some experience of politics and public speaking. Most important of all, in spite of many diversions, I had not altogether forgotten what I learnt from my mother and my father. I had not properly digested the family diet of noncomformity, but I had the beginnings of a hatred of tyranny and privilege and injustice and cruelty. I was irresponsible no doubt, but I have often said—and I realised it more as I grew older—that of all the privileges of my life the greatest privilege of all was to have been brought up in a good liberal, Methodist home.

A few days before he died at the end of 1960 my father gave

me a small volume of Edmund Burke's *Speeches on American Independence*. I knew the speeches from my school days when I had stolen many quotations from my father's commonplace books. I could quote several passages of the speeches by heart. The book was my father's last gift to me, and I value it as a sort of political testament. The famous Burke quotations which I knew so well as a boy have always been in my mind:

> "Magnanimity in politics is not seldom the truest wisdom; and a great empire and little minds go ill together."

> "We view the establishment of English colonies on principles of liberty as that which is to render this kingdom venerable to future ages. In comparison of this, we regard all the victories and conquests of our warlike ancestors, as of our own times, as barbarous vulgar distinctions, in which many nations, whom we look down upon with little respect or value, have equalled if not excelled us. This is the peculiar and appropriated glory of England."

> "Slavery they can have everywhere. It is a weed that grows in every soil . . . freedom they can have from none but you. This is the commodity of price of which you have the monopoly . . . Deny them this participation of freedom and you break the sole bond which originally made and must still preserve the unity of empire."

"Magnanimity in politics", "the establishment of English colonies on principles of liberty", and "the participation of freedom"—these are some of the principles I learnt from my father. I have not had reason to doubt them. I have had some small part in putting them into practice. They seem to me as true today as ever.

CHAPTER III

The Arab Rebellion in Palestine

"The Imperial Ministers pursued with prescriptive laws and
ineffectual arms the rebels they had made."

EDWARD GIBBON

ONE of the worst sins in public life, I am sure, is to lead ordinary people to expect something which may not be possible. It
used to make me angry in the United Nations when the Afro-
Asians drew up grandiose resolutions which would raise
peoples' hopes in Africa and elsewhere without any early
prospect of satisfying them by practical action. My Afro-Asian
friends would reply privately (and there was much in what they
said) that their resolutions were not promises but expressions
of international opinion and that strongly-worded resolutions
were all they could do, short of instigation to violence, to bring
home to the world the intensity of their feelings and their
determination to end political slavery in Africa. I shall come
back later on to the question of United Nations action on
African issues. Diplomats may have to lie for their countries,
but they are usually speaking only to other diplomats. Politicians sometimes speak not for Governments but for their
parties or only for themselves. But an official can only speak for
his Government. He has an absolute obligation never to raise
false hopes. He must never make a promise to the people
unless he is absolutely sure it can be carried out.

The failure of British administration in Palestine was inevitable. The double sin had been committed of raising false
hopes both with the Arabs and with Jews. The hopes were false
because they were conflicting. The Arabs who fought with
Great Britain in the first world war to throw off the yoke of the
Turkish Empire were led to believe that they were fighting for
their freedom. The Jews were led to believe by the Balfour
Declaration in 1917 that they would win a national home for

35

the Jewish people in Palestine. Relying on British assurances they too fought and worked with us. But Palestine was populated and owned by Arabs.

Other nations share the responsibility with us. The United States in particular urged us on in the pursuit of policies which were bound to lead to conflict. But the main responsibility was ours. It is true that when the Balfour Declaration was made and indeed for many years afterwards no one, other than a few Jewish visionaries, thought of a Jewish State in Palestine. The Balfour Declaration promised support for a Jewish National Home *in* Palestine. It was just, but only just, possible to imagine a Jewish National Home in an Arab country progressing towards self-government and eventual independence. Later on various plans of cantonisation or condominium were broached. But by prevarication and procrastination and basically by the fundamental dishonesty of our original double dealing we had made disaster certain. In the narrow compass of the Holy Land we had unleashed two hopes, two forces, two nationalisms. In 1915 we supported King Feisal's desert rising. In 1917 we signed the Balfour Declaration. The surprising thing is that it was twenty years after those actions before the Arabs revolted and almost another decade before the Jews turned to violence and rebellion. By trying to please both Arabs and Jews we lost the respect and friendship of both and eventually earned the contempt of the world by an ignominious withdrawal. We left those who had relied on our promises to fight it out amongst themselves.

I pray that we shall not make the same terrible error again —in southern Africa for instance.

I had left Palestine long before the Jewish revolt took place. But I was in charge of the Samaria District through most of the Arab rebellion of 1936 to 1939. Let me go back to recall those events, now so little remembered.

How difficult it is now to picture the peaceful Palestine of thirty years ago. The resounding failure of the British Mandate, the blood and fury in which the State of Israel was created and all the subsequent conflicts and tensions of the Middle East have intervened. So has the great constructive effort in Israel itself, and the continuing misery of a million Arab refugees. We see Jerusalem still divided by the no-man's-land of enmity which runs like a scar through the Holy City. But for a while, before all these crowded events took place, Palestine was a quiet backwater.

In the years following the first world war the first British High Commissioner, Sir Herbert Samuel, had worked wonders. He had overcome all the early obstacles and set the standards and created confidence. His combination of political and administrative judgment and his absolute fairness in his dealings with Arabs and Jews alike enabled the Mandated territory to make a good beginning with a sound administrative machine and some signs of understanding between the different communities—Moslem, Christian and Jewish. He was followed as High Commissioner by Field Marshal Lord Plumer. He consolidated what Sir Herbert Samuel had initiated, and the strength of his forthright personality dominated everyone round him.

The story was told that an Arab political leader had said to the Field Marshal that if the Government took certain action the Arabs could not be responsible for the consequences. Lord Plumer had looked first astonished and then furious, blown out his white moustache and immediately ended the interview, saying "I am responsible".

So great had been the authority of Lord Plumer that all troops were withdrawn from the country. The Palestine Gendarmerie was disbanded and public security left to the civil police, of which most of the senior officers were British but nearly all the lower ranks Palestinians. When he left Palestine in 1928 there were some grounds for believing that the first two High Commissioners, the brilliant political administrator and the bluff, shrewd soldier, had in ten years established the British Mandate on a sound working basis.

The Arabs were still utterly opposed to the Balfour Declaration but the immigration of Jews in the decade after 1918 had been small and had dwindled to almost nothing in Lord Plumer's time. Moreover, Jewish capital and enterprise, particularly in the agricultural settlements, had brought obvious benefits. No one could see how the future would develop, but orderly and efficient administration seemed for a while to offer reasonable prospects of peaceful progress.

The country was administered by a small band of British officials, and the system of government was that of any other British administered territory. The High Commissioner acted through a central Secretariat, under a Chief Secretary, which carried out his orders and directed the various technical Departments and the District Administration. The District Administration was responsible in the three Districts for dealings with the people and for day-to-day administration. The total number of British administrative officials both in the Secretariat and the District Administration did not at that time exceed twenty, and in this small team I was last arrived and much the most junior.

The four first High Commissioners were all outstanding men. After Sir Herbert Samuel and Lord Plumer came Sir John Chancellor. He had been a Colonial Governor for more than twenty years and was the most experienced man of his generation in the practical field of Colonial administration. And he was followed by General Sir Arthur Wauchope, who was High Commissioner for the fateful years I now want to describe.

Sir Arthur was a bachelor soldier, short and wiry, and consumed by restless energy, not altogether unlike General Ken Darling who served with me in Cyprus twenty-five years later. General Wauchope had been wounded in the legs and his short temper was famous. He used to infuriate senior officials by interfering in the smallest details, and he had a disconcerting habit when he had been given an answer on a question of fact of asking the same question of someone else immediately afterwards. The Secretariat was bewildered by a flood of orders, notes and enquiries from the High Commissioner on every conceivable subject—and his spelling was astonishingly erratic.

But though he sorely tried Heads of Departments we junior officers were devoted to him. When he came to our Districts we knew that he would listen to us. We stored up suggestions and requests for him, and on these he would often give immediate decisions. Many were the subjects on which we had waited months for answers which were settled in a short drive with him. We had the additional satisfaction of picturing the irritation in Jerusalem when the High Commissioner returned and told those at headquarters what he had decided.

Once, I remember, when he was on tour in the Tulkarm District he was talking to me in his eager, engrossed way, with a circle of Army officers and senior officials round us. He looked up from our conversation and impatiently said to all around us, "Go away." The large group of very important persons looked put out but moved off obediently. He continued his earnest conversation with me. Then he suddenly looked up and said, "Go further away." Again the senior officers and officials moved away, looking half sheepish and half angry. After another few minutes of intense conversation the High Commissioner looked up again and shouted, "Go right away!"

Sir Arthur accumulated an enormous store of information and himself initiated many schemes of development. He was specially interested in agriculture and his energy led to many far-reaching agricultural improvements. He liked to be called "the friend of the fellah" (*fellah* meaning Arab cultivator). He became completely absorbed in Palestine and all its problems and exercised a strong political hold on the country with both Arabs and Jews. If anyone could have saved Palestine from disaster I believe that he would have done so. But the destiny of Palestine was not to be decided within its borders. Forces were building up in Germany under Hitler which made his task increasingly difficult and took decisions out of his hands. At the end he saw all his constructive work swept away by violence, and he left Palestine broken-hearted.

I have served under many chiefs, and I have been fortunate in many of them, but I have never served under a chief whom I more loved and admired. More than anyone else I have ever met, he had the capacity for giving his whole self to the service of the people under his charge.

The Chief Secretaries who served under Sir John Chancellor and Sir Arthur Wauchope were picked men. All of them went on to the top to be Governors—Sir Harry Luke to Fiji, Sir Hathorn Hall to Uganda, Sir Mark Young to Hong Kong and Sir William Battershill to Cyprus.

Under them there was an administrative team made up of a strange assortment of unusual men, mostly left behind by the military administration after the war. There were a few Arabs and Jews in the administration, notably the principal Arab adviser Ruhi Bey Abdul Hadi in the central Secretariat, and Norman Bentwich, the brilliant Jewish Attorney-General. But nearly all the senior officials were English—with a mixture of Scots and Irish (the Irish were strongest amongst the Police officers, many of whom had served in the Irish Black and Tans and subsequently in the Palestine Gendarmerie). The leadership was good and the scratch team of administrative officers intelligent and hard working.

Yet it was an oddly narrow life we lived in Jerusalem in the early 1930s as we tried to forget the explosion of the 1929 riots. No one could say what the eventual aim was. Municipalities and local councils were encouraged and Arabs and Jews invited to serve on official boards, but there was no talk of legislatures or elections. It was direct, authoritarian, bureaucratic, straightforward administration at its best—and at its worst. The Supreme Moslem Council on the one hand, under the crafty Mufti of Jerusalem, Haj Amin el Husseini, had to be kept quiet, and the persistent, nagging Jewish Agency pacified on the other. But it was as much as the officials could do to keep up with day-to-day problems. Higher policy and ultimate aims could wait their turn. Sufficient unto the day was the administration thereof.

In this corner of the old Ottoman Empire and against the grand backdrop of Jerusalem, the life of the official community was separate from the life of the people of the country, and very suburban. The day at the office was followed by tennis at the Club, with a small group of regulars playing bridge there later in the evening over their whiskies and sodas. Cricket and mixed hockey at week-ends, or bathing expeditions to Jaffa on Sundays. A rare, middle-aged dance, and, by way of social excitement, an occasional invitation to lunch or dinner at Government House.

When I first reported for duty in the summer of 1929, I went on my arrival to see the Acting High Commissioner, Sir Harry Luke. As I came through the Private Secretary's office I saw a long way off in the huge domed white room a small figure at a big desk. The Acting High Commissioner looked tiny and lost in such a vast setting. He was a round little figure, as unlike the standard picture of a colonial administrator as it was possible to imagine. He was, as I later discovered, a scholar, a writer, an expert on the Near East, sensitive and articulate, and wonderfully good company, but strangely miscast, it seemed, in the role of pro-consul dealing with a situation so rough and so dangerous. An odd successor to Pontius Pilate.

When the 1929 riots were over he was attacked unfairly, as we thought, by the counsel for the Jewish Agency at the Enquiry for his failure to control the situation leading up to and during the riots, and soon afterwards he was transferred to be Deputy Governor in Malta. He was made the scapegoat.

Before he left he was the principal guest at the St. Andrew Dinner. It used to be the custom in many colonial territories for the Governor to attend the St. Andrew Dinner every year, and usually to make it the occasion to deliver a policy statement specially directed to the officials of the territory. No one seemed to know how or why this custom had grown up—perhaps because Scots made up a good proportion of the Services, and they were usually the most vocal and critical amongst the officials. On St. Andrew's night they were likely to be more belligerent than usual, and sometimes Governors have found them an awkward audience. On this occasion it was scarcely expected that Sir Harry Luke, whose transfer had just been announced, would have much to say. He was not a popular figure among the ordinary run of officials and he had little in common with tough engineers from the Public Works Department and other Scots from the various Departments.

The time came for him to speak. There was a polite round of applause. And then a strange thing happened. I am sure that it was not rehearsed or planned. But the applause continued and swelled, and then the whole company started to cheer. They had served under him through a very rough time. They did not know their guest of honour well, nor did they understand him, but they had watched him in the ordeal he had endured before the Commission of Enquiry. They had come to respect him and they now saw him being sacrificed under partisan attack. They felt a sudden surge of sympathy and loyalty. There was also a feeling of pent-up defiance and anger against those who come when danger is over to find fault. They wanted to demonstrate both the solidarity of the Service and their indignation at an unfair attack on their chief. The din grew. Some kilted figures jumped shouting on their chairs. The cheering mounted to a crescendo. When at last it died down, Sir Harry Luke was too moved to speak.

After the 1929 riots the Administration settled down again to its busy but humdrum existence, the only outward outcome of the disorders being the presence of two battalions of British troops, one in Jerusalem and one in Haifa.

This was a special comfort to me, for all the officials were older than I was and the subalterns became my friends. How much we objected, by the way, to the strictness, and what we regarded as the puritanical pettiness, of the Lieutenant-Colonel who commanded a battalion of the Northamptonshire Regiment in Jerusalem—who later became better known as Field Marshal Lord Montgomery.

In the early 1930s the stream of Palestine events flowed along calmly. There was little to give warning of the rapids which we approached, or of the terrible cataract beyond. The 1929 riots had been fierce and bloody but they had arisen from religious more than political stresses. The experiment of establishing a home for the Jews in Arab Palestine under the Balfour Declaration seemed, extraordinary as it might appear, to be settling down fairly well.

After a year or two in the Jerusalem Secretariat I escaped to become the youngest member of the team of some ten officials who administered the Districts. I went first to Haifa. Then, at the age of less than twenty-five, while my neighbouring Assistant District Commissioner was on leave, I found myself for six months in charge of both the Galilee and Samaria Districts. By 1932 I was established as the Assistant District Commissioner in charge of Samaria, a District which extended from Ramallah just north of Jerusalem to the plain of Jezreel south of Nazareth, and from the Jordan to the Mediterranean. In my District there were three hundred Arab villages and a handful of Jewish settlements in the coastal plain—soon to expand and multiply. I had with me in Nablus a doctor, Dr. Bill Bigger, so much loved by the Arabs that he was safe in his travels through the District even when the Arab rebellion was at its height; a Police Officer, Michael Fitzgerald, another

Irishman, thoughtful and able; and "Phifi" Taylor, an engineer, who was as eccentric as he was energetic. The four of us, with occasional visits from a Judge, ran the District. We were left much to ourselves. The District Commissioner for Haifa came rarely to visit us and more infrequently the High Commissioner would make a day's tour, but for weeks and months at a time we were left to get on with our job.

I was lucky enough to stay in Nablus for nearly six years.

For a while I went in to Jerusalem once a week to the New-man Missionary School to prepare for my examinations in Arabic. And whenever I could at week-ends I would drive in my enormous open Buick to Haifa, where I was courting Sylvia Tod, whom I married in 1936. But nearly all my time was spent in the villages. There were three Arab District Officers under me and for two or three days every week I would ride with one of them and an Agricultural Officer through the Samaria hills or over the Tulkarm plain. Towards evening we would decide which village would make a good place to stop for the night and ride in unannounced, but always we were welcome. It took several hours to kill and cook the chicken, or on special occasions the sheep, and while we waited, drinking bitter Arab coffee, we would talk about local councils, taxes, crops, schools, roads, clinics and all the day-to-day questions of administration which were close to the villagers life and interest. Tall stories were told, jests made about local personalities. And in exchange for the competitive hospitality of the villages we, on our side, were able to bring some talk of the outer world, a break in the monotony of village life, and also an anxiety to understand their wishes and needs. A new room for the school (if the villagers would find half the cost), an improvement to a road here, a new agricultural station there, a remission of tax in a bad year and a gradual encouragement of new forms of local government through Local Councils, minor municipalities and school committees—these were the subjects of our village conferences.

My teacher and closest friend in those early days was an Australian, L. Y. Andrews, who had come to Palestine in the war with the Australian Light Horse. He was a born administrator, patient, understanding, tireless, with inexhaustible good humour and a flair for political intelligence. His free and easy Australian manner made a welcome contrast to the aloofness of the average Englishman. Andy, as everyone called him, had friends in every village and knew more of what was going on below the surface in the political life of the country than any other official. When the Arab rebellion came his knowledge of Arab feeling and intentions was invaluable to the Government. He kept touch even with those close to the centre of the Arab rebel command.

But then those who directed the revolt in Damascus decided that he must be removed. He was placed on the rebel assassination list. He soon learnt of the intention to kill him and took careful precautions. But one day a close Arab friend came to tell him that the Arab command had withdrawn his name from the assassination list. Andy spoke to me cheerfully on the telephone to tell me what he had heard. It was his birthday and he decided to celebrate the good news by going to church in Nazareth. For once he and his guards were not ready. As he entered the narrow lane leading to the church he and the British policeman with him were shot dead.

It was Andy who had taught me my early lessons in administration. On the first day I went out with him visiting Arab villages he had pulled his car to the side of the rough track, switched off the engine and told me to note what he did. When we had finished our meeting with the villagers he again stopped the car on leaving the village and switched off the engine. "Let that be your first lesson in administration," he said. "Before you go to any conference or any meeting stop and ask yourself what you want to get from it. And when you leave, stop again, and ask yourself whether you have got it."

Perhaps the chief temptation of an administrator is to spread time and effort on a whole variety of purposes. There is so much to be done, there are so many good excuses for procrastination; it is easy to escape by hard work from hard thinking and making hard decisions. The man who gets important things done is the man who sets his priorities, limits and defines his objectives and then pursues the main aims he has set with relentless persistence. Specially in time of doubt and confusion one man who knows what he wants and is determined to get it can alter and often control the whole trend of events.

When I first arrived in the Samaria district I was told of one problem which had troubled the area for as long as anyone could remember. Indeed it probably had its origins a thousand years or more ago. This was the curse of tree cutting. Each village was divided into hamoulets, something between a large family and a small tribe. They were often in dispute and the traditional way to inflict injury on one's enemy in another hamoulet was to go out at night and cut down his trees, usually olive or fig trees. It was a heart-breaking sight to see great olive trees hundreds of years old cut down or burnt, but never would anyone give evidence against the culprit. Giving evidence would lead only to more tree cutting. Every week there were several cases of tree cutting. Tens of thousands of pounds of damage was done every year. But no one could suggest a solution.

Then we thought of a plan. It would need new legislation, new powers for the Assistant District Commissioners, and it would be difficult to persuade the Government to accept so drastic a measure. But we succeeded. The plan was that as soon as a case of tree cutting was reported the Assistant District Commissioner would go to the village and hold court amongst the destroyed trees. The Agricultural Officer would there and then estimate the damage, and the Assistant District Commissioner would then impose a collective fine on the whole village (amounting maybe to a few shillings a head) sufficient to cover the damage. The fine would be imposed on the spot and immediately collected—and the value of the trees would at once be paid over to the owner. Very soon this plan proved effective. It became pointless to cut down an enemy's tree if he was certain to receive their value in hard cash, and to receive it without any delay.

Within a year tree cutting had dropped. Within two years it had almost stopped. Our only misgiving was the suspicion that one or two villagers had cut down their own trees.

I was working away in my Nablus office one day when the messenger came in to tell me that there was an Englishman to see me. I went out to see who it was and found that it was Mr.

Winston Churchill on his way from Damascus to Jerusalem. He sat down in my office and asked about the big charts on my wall showing the reduction in tree cutting. He became much interested and sent for his wife to come to hear too. He questioned me closely, and went away muttering that it was all deplorable in principle—and admirable in practice.

Our administration was certainly rough and ready. It was, I suppose, paternalistic, though we were all the time encouraging elected municipalities and local councils. But it was good government. It was based on understanding and personal knowledge and genuine concern for the people's welfare—and every man knew that he would be given a ready hearing and a fair trial.

The training I received in Samaria was much the same as that of District Officers in all our overseas administrative Services—in India in the old days or in Malaya and Ceylon and the Sudan or East or West or Central Africa.

Take a young man with only a few years' experience in the territory to which he has been sent. Put him in charge of a District. Make him responsible for everything in that District. He may have a few technical officers, one or two doctors, engineers, policemen, agricultural officers, to help him, but he is responsible to higher authority for all the varied activities of the government in his District.

Leave him there for say five years; to get to know the people and work with and for them and learn their language and share their difficulties and disappointments and their aims and hopes. At the end of that time—there is no question of credit or merit in this, it is automatic and inevitable—he becomes wholly devoted to the people of his District. And he spends much of his effort fighting higher authority to get for his people what he thinks they need and deserve.

It is a good training for a Governor. When I was Governor of Jamaica I did not regard myself as the agent of London but rather as the advocate of Jamaica. And when I was asked whether I would go back to Cyprus as Governor when the island was rent by bloodshed and violence, I eagerly accepted the offer. I had been in Cyprus before, I knew and loved the people, and I thought that perhaps by putting their interests

46

first we might find the key to a problem which at one time looked beyond a hope of solution.

This seemed to me the obvious and natural attitude to take, and I can still recall the homicidal fury I felt when a visiting Minister arriving in a country of which I was Governor went out of his way to tell me—no doubt to annoy me—that he didn't care two hoots for the people of my territory, he was only concerned with strictly British interests.

While most of my time had at first been spent in the Arab villages it soon became necessary to turn more attention to the coastal plain. There were only a few Jewish settlements there when I first took over the District in 1932, but land purchase by the Jews was going ahead and soon there were urgent difficulties arising day by day. Land disputes, evictions of Arabs, burning of Jewish property, destruction of Jewish crops, new roads, town planning, all the problems arising from what amounted to a gradual transfer of the fertile plain from Arab to Jewish ownership.

I was specially interested in the problem of Nathanya. Early in the 1930s a group of energetic Jews led by my friend Oved Ben Ami had bought from the Arab Mukhtar of Um Khaled a great stretch of land, much of it sand dunes, along the coast about half way between Haifa and Jaffa. Ben Ami was a far-seeing planner, and he and the Mahnes brothers decided that they would found a model town on these sand dunes above the cliffs overlooking the Mediterranean. They were not content with any makeshift plan. They sought the advice of Abercrombie, the famous English town planner. They decided to create a statutory planning board under the Town Planning Ordinance. This meant accepting me as Chairman of the Board and other British officials as members. Few, if any, other Jewish settlements would contemplate such official interference, but Ben Ami saw the advantage of bringing in the Administration and making use of us and our legal powers. And so we sat down together and, with technical assistance from the Government, drew up together a town plan. We provided for wide streets, zoning areas, hotels, municipal offices, factories, all kinds of modern services, gardens, a stadium and a theatre. It all seemed rather unreal in the planning stage as we looked out on the bare sand dunes. But within five years we saw the town grow as we had planned it, and before we left Sylvia and I attended a performance by the magnificent Palestine Orchestra in the Nathanya theatre.

The centre of the town was given the admirable name of Foot Square—but I was sad to see when I went back years later that the sign had been taken down.

Meanwhile events were marching in Europe which were to shatter our peaceful existence. Hitler had begun his persecution of the Jews. While Jewish immigration had dropped to a trickle in the late 1920s it began to grow in the 1930s. Soon it was to become a flood. Land purchases by Jews were extended, boat loads of Jewish refugees arrived weekly at the ports, political activity was stepped up, the "absorbative capacity" of the country for new immigration became a burning issue. Arab alarm was expressed in strikes and demonstrations. Rumours of Arab armed resistance started to circulate. It was said that Arab rebel leaders from Syria and Iraq were on their way. The British Government was caught between the two forces of Jewish insistence on increased immigration of Jews fleeing from the German terror and the determination of the Arabs to defend their homeland.

We were slow to realise that rebellion was so near. But tension rose, rumours of armed revolt increased. One evening Michael Fitzgerald of the Police came into my office in Nablus to report that a gang battle in the hills between Nablus and Jenin had begun with several casualties already reported among the rebels and the Police. At first it was a matter of occasional skirmishes with Arab gangs in the hills. Never were there more than a few hundred armed Arabs engaged at one time. But the rebel leaders could rely on the Arab villages to contribute volunteers and rifles at any time, and to help them to escape.

By 1937 it was a full-scale rebellion. While at one time we had had only a platoon of troops in Nablus we soon had a whole battalion of Seaforth Highlanders. Sylvia was evacuated to Haifa. I moved from my house to the Nablus Fort. All ordinary administration ceased. Every morning I looked through a long list of disorders and destruction—telephones cut, bridges damaged, trains derailed, convoys ambushed, fighting in the hills. For two years I never moved without a gun in my hand—we soon learnt that it was useless to have a gun in a holster. Andrews had been assassinated in Nazareth. My friend, Festing of the Seaforths, was blown up and killed by a land-mine within sight of my Nablus house. Almost every day brought news of casualties on both sides.

When once it was clear that we had to fight a rebellion we entered into our task with a will. I was still in my twenties. It was exciting to ride through the hills in the early days with a Squadron of the Trans-Jordan Frontier Force with our mounted scouts on the hill tops ahead, or later to march all night silently and in single file with a company of British troops to surround a village at dawn.

At one time the leader of the rebels in our district was Sheikh Farhan. He was a fierce and fanatical old man, brave and ruthless. He never stayed for more than one night in one place, often living in caves, and all our efforts to catch him over a year or more failed. He became a legend amongst the Arabs, and our own troops were specially incensed against him for an ambush he had set at a bathing pool near Baisan in which several soldiers had been killed. We redoubled our efforts to capture him. Such intelligence as we had in those days was the responsibility of the Assistant District Commissioners, and I had the unpleasant task of keeping in touch with the informers. We had one informer from the area in which Sheikh Farhan usually operated. He promised to tell us as soon as he could be sure where Sheikh Farhan was. We bound over all the villagers from his village to report daily at Police Headquarters in Jenin, and every day each of the villagers including the informer would come for a minute or two into my office there. The time would come, we hoped, when the informer would make use of that minute or two to give us accurate information. But I went one day into Haifa to see Sylvia and our first son, who had been born a few days before, and I left the daily duty of seeing these Arab villagers to the Police Officer in Jenin. As soon as I got to Haifa I was summoned to the hospital telephone. It was the Police Officer from Jenin. He said that he had important information which he must communicate to me at once. We arranged to meet with the Army Commander of the District in an hour or two a long way off in the Tulkarm District. Here we heard that the informer had reported that Sheikh Farhan would be in Mazar village that night. Mazar was high on Mount Gilboa. It commanded a view of the whole countryside around from Jenin to Nazareth—impossible to surprise. We made our plan and at once it was put into effect. A small Army patrol under a Major left on the road to Beisan in a covered civilian truck. At dusk the soldiers would drop off the truck in a copse of trees. We knew that Sheikh Farhan, if he were in Mazar, would be watching all transport on the roads below. Then in the dark the soldiers would make their way up the mountain on a goat track, moving slowly and silently. The hope was that when they made their final dash to surround the village just before light the villagers would not have seen their approach. Soon after dawn we would come up to Mazar from the other direction with a battalion of troops to search the whole area. The Police Officer and I arrived in the village very early in the morning and met the Major. He told us that the dogs had barked as his party approached the village but he thought that there was a chance that his men had been quick enough. Then I saw the informer. He was greatly excited and said that he thought that the Sheikh was still in the village. I told him that he was mad to speak to me: he would be killed for certain if he were seen. And then we settled down to prepare for the search of the village. So often we had searched villages before without result, and we were not optimistic. We sent for a platoon to carry out the search and while we waited we went into the biggest house in the village. Here were three large corn bins built out of mud against the stone walls of the house. While we waited for the platoon the Police Officer and I occupied the time by starting the search. The corn bins could only be searched by breaking down the mud walls. We sent for a pick and as I swung it at the second bin there was a muffled shout from inside. We leapt back and covered the opening in the bin with our guns, and out climbed the Sheikh. He had two revolvers and a great amount of ammunition strung around him, but he realised that the village was surrounded and gave himself up.

He was a fine old man, dignified and calm, and he talked

gravely with us as we walked down the hill. He knew that he would be hanged.

I drove that afternoon to Jerusalem to see the High Commissioner to beg that the Sheikh's life should be spared, but I had little hope that my plea could be granted. He was tried and hanged in Acre Prison within a week.

Several months later I saw in a list of murdered villagers the name of the informer.

We were now caught up in a struggle to which there seemed no end. There were by then two Divisions of our troops in Palestine but still no indication that the resources of the elusive rebels were exhausted. The fight got rougher.

One day I was in the Jenin school when Gerald Templer came to report on a minor operation just completed. Major Templer was later to become Chief of the Imperial General Staff. When he was High Commissioner for Malaya carrying out operations against the communists he no doubt found his Palestine experience useful. Then as later he was restless, original, impatient. The operation which he had just carried out was typical of him. For months past the Army convoys entering Jenin from Nablus had been harassed by Arab snipers from high ground on both sides of the road. Elaborate and repeated military schemes to dislodge the snipers by enveloping movements had failed. Major Templer decided on a simpler plan. He trained a small force of soldiers in advance, and then on this day he had brought a convoy through the pass. As usual the snipers from their hill sangers opened fire. The convoy suddenly stopped. Out jumped the soldiers in gym shoes armed with fixed bayonets. They dashed straight up the hills on both sides. The snipers were taken completely by surprise. One or two were killed and the rest captured. Major Templer, chain-smoking as usual, told us the story in short matter-of-fact terms, and went quickly on his way to get on with the next job.

The struggle grew fiercer still, and I later heard that after I left Palestine in 1938 the methods used by some of our troops became more ruthless. For many years afterwards I heard stories of the patrols led by Wingate (afterwards to become famous in the war in Burma). He formed his own gang mainly composed of Jewish volunteers and went out to beat the Arab gangs at their own game. His methods were extreme and cruel. He had many successes, but he forfeited our general reputation for fair fighting.

Colonel Roy Spicer was Inspector General of Police. He had had his early experience in Ceylon, which had the reputation of having the best Police Force anywhere in the Colonies. The British Police he trained and inspired were a tough, highly skilled and most effective force, confident, dependable, resourceful. Nearly all of them spoke some Arabic, usually with strong British accents, and their rough knowledge of the people and the country made each one of them worth a platoon of newly-arrived troops.

The Inspector General used to teach his men that everything must of course be done to prevent, forestall or head off disorder. It was a policeman's basic and overriding and never-to-be-forgotten duty to prevent crime. But when everything possible had been done, every precaution taken and every warning given and still disorder came on, then was the time (so he used to urge us) to rejoice that we had a wonderful chance to show what we were worth. In the alarm and confusion of impending riot or gang battle in the hills each one of us should say to himself, "Now is the time when all my training and experience can be put to the top test. Every step I take today will be just right, deliberate, restrained, well-timed, and quick and sure and decisive as well. This is my big day."

Although the Army and the Police did fine work, many unnecessary and costly mistakes were made. Our intelligence was haphazard and patchy, and consequently much of our military effort against the rebels was clumsy and misdirected. It later seemed incredible that we could have been so stupid, but there was a time early on in the rebellion when a general order was made requiring the troops to return every day to barracks by dusk. The rebels soon saw what was happening and at that stage inflicted most of the casualties on the troops by sniping at the Army convoys as they returned to camp in the evening. Moreover there was sometimes a resort to tough methods which did much more harm than good. Searches for arms were sometimes made excuses for punitive destruction of private property. Arabs picked at random were made to ride at the head of military convoys to prevent ambush. After I left, my old friend the Mayor of Nablus, Suleiman Bey Toukan, was made to spend the night on the roof of the main hotel in a vain effort to stop sniping at the town from Mount Ebal and Mount Gerizim. Such methods defeated their purpose, turned the ordinary people increasingly against us and made it even more difficult to get the information about terrorist leaders and plans which was essential if military operations were to succeed.

There was disagreement sometimes amounting to open dispute between the Army commanders and the civil authorities. We heard rumours of coldness and anger at the top between the High Commissioner and his staff on the one hand and the central Army Command on the other. This disagreement was reflected lower down. In Nablus, for instance, I was in charge, and no operation or Army action could be taken unless and until I had made a request for military assistance. But I was younger than any Army Captain and I had to deal with Colonels commanding battalions. We usually agreed, but there were times of bickering and dispute. Certainly the civil administration and the Army were not acting as a single unified force. We learnt later in Cyprus that the first two essentials in combating a rebellion are good intelligence and complete understanding and co-ordination between all the authorities concerned, civil government, Police and Army. Palestine was a text book example of the waste and futility of operating without adequate intelligence and without fully concerted action.

Worst of all there was no political initiative. Repression alone is a slow and often hopeless task. There can be no solely military solution to any rebellion which is supported by the mass of the people. But throughout the Arab rebellion we had no political initiative to propose, no means of persuading the people to turn against violence, no alternative to submission to offer them, no assurance and no hope that their deep-seated fears might be removed.

Since those days we have had to deal with three major campaigns of violence in territories administered by the British Colonial Office—in Kenya, Malaya and Cyprus. It is some comfort to reflect that in those countries we showed that we had learnt the main lessons of the blunders and the blindness of the pre-war Palestine Emergency.

It was an evenly matched struggle. We had far superior forces and every advantage in arms, equipment and transport. The rebels had the advantage of surprise and mobility and the full support of the Arab population, and the additional advantage of terrain over which no Army transport could travel. Every now and then they would kill one of us by ambush or assassination. We inflicted about equal casualties on them.

We had no time to stop to think about the politics and the rights or wrongs of the complicated political issues involved. Our lives were in daily danger. Every day as we travelled on the roads we were liable to be blown up by road mines. The Arabs made them from old shells left from the first world war, using a simple mousetrap device for the detonator. There could be no hope of a settlement, so our masters said, until the rebellion was beaten. We had an obligation to protect the Jews whom we had allowed and encouraged to come to Palestine. A challenge had been made. We had to answer and defeat it.

I remember how uncertain and unhappy I was in the early months when I saw the gap between my Arab friends and the British Army widening into open enmity. But as the conflict became fiercer we put aside misgivings and doubts and entered into the struggle wholeheartedly. The danger was exhilarating; there was good comradeship with British Police and soldiers.

Strangely enough, although we were on opposite sides, good relations with my Arab friends in Nablus and in the villages remained. There was no hate between one side and the other. I respected the bravery of the rebels. The Arabs on their side knew that they could rely on most of us to play the game according to the rough rules; and they constantly came to me with complaints and requests. When I went back to Nablus years later I was received as an old friend.

By 1938 the whole country was in disorder and the fight was at its hottest. We heard that I had achieved the distinction of my name reaching the top of the assassination list issued from time to time by the rebel command in Damascus. I had replaced my old friend Andrews in that position. After a while the High Commissioner, Sir Arthur Wauchope, sent for me to tell me that in view of the new information received he must require me to leave. So, after nearly three years of continuous operations, I went with my armed Police bodyguard to Port Said, passing on the way the derailed trains, and my Police guard kept close with me up the gangway and into the ship.

It was not long afterwards that I heard that Moffatt, one of my successors in the Samaria District, had been shot dead in his office in Jenin. The assassin had waited for weeks for his chance and had then miraculously got clean away through the crowded approaches to the District Office.

By the time I left Palestine, still not thirty years of age, I had had a first taste of adventure and I had learnt to hate violence. A fair fight in the hills was one thing. What I hated was cruelty. When I had been only a few months in the country and had already seen the bloody riots of the summer of 1929, I was told one day that since the regular Magistrate was ill I should go the following morning to witness the hanging of a murderer in Acre Prison. I held a Magistrate's warrant and a Magistrate must sign the death certificate. I went, and what I saw that morning made me sick. I have seen many men killed in hot blood, but the cold killing of the wretched murderer in Acre remains to me far more terrible than any killing I have seen since. I have been haunted by the picture of the young Arab with a sack over his head being half carried to his execution. I cannot imagine how anyone who has seen a hanging can fail to be utterly opposed to capital punishment. As a Governor I have had to sign many death warrants. It was my duty to do so but I have never forgotten the horrible sight I saw that morning in Acre, and I hope the day will soon come when hanging is remembered as a barbarous and inhuman practice which lasted far too long.

Another picture of early days in Palestine has stayed in my mind. I went one day into the District Offices at Jenin and there saw a young woman huddled in a heap in her long black clothes. She was crazy with terror, and crouched like a wounded bird in the corner of the room. I was told that she was suspected of adultery. She realised that she would be killed — but how and when she did not know. Normally she would have been killed already by her fellow villagers, for amongst the Moslems even the suspicion of adultery meant that the suspected person must be killed at once. It would be an unbearable disgrace to her family and tribe if she remained alive. But on this occasion a Police patrol had happened to enter the village before the execution could take place and had brought the terrified woman in to the District Offices.

We made elaborate plans to save her life. We found a Christian family far away in another country who would care for her and keep her secret. We moved her first to Haifa and then sent her on her way, taking the utmost care to prevent her village from knowing where she had gone. We bound over her relatives in large amounts which would be forfeited if she were killed. I wondered when I left Palestine several years later whether she would survive. I doubt if she did.

These pictures remained clear, the blindfolded Arab being hustled to his execution in Acre, the young woman cowering in the corner of the Jenin Office—and once later I looked into the eyes of an Arab in Jerusalem Prison whom I believed had been subjected to torture under Police interrogation.

When I was appointed to be Governor of Cyprus I was in Jamaica. On the day of the announcement of my new appointment I had to speak to the Jamaica Branch of the United Nations Association. I said then:

"Violence is evil but one of the main lessons I have learned is that a worse evil is fear of violence. If there is fear of violence then the effect of violence is multiplied. It is a positive duty to us all to do what we think is right and not to allow violence—so often mean and cruel—to dictate to us what we should do."

How to defeat violence without becoming oneself cruel. How to fight a rebellion and to retain the respect of the rebels. How to keep the object of settlement and understanding uppermost in one's mind at times when malice and hate threaten to take over. These were some of the questions in my mind as I sailed home in 1938.

And why had we failed in Palestine? By 1938 the country had gone so far down the slope that it was difficult to see how the slide could be stopped. We, the British, had been caught in the cross-fire of Arab and Jewish nationalism. But had there not been a time perhaps in the middle 1930s when we could have taken hold of the situation and declared our policy and stuck to it? The two forces which we had unleashed in Palestine had been too strong for us. But we had been in charge. We had been entrusted with the Mandate. We could not rid ourselves of the responsibility.

Many years later in Cyprus I saw again a conflict between two national claims. I could not forget Palestine, and throughout my time in Cyprus I was obsessed with the need to take and keep the political initiative, to avoid at all costs the bloody partition which Palestine endured.

CHAPTER IV

A Beachcomber in Buckingham Gate

"We are grateful to the British officers whom we have known, first as masters and then as leaders and finally as partners, but always as friends."

Sir Abubakr Balewa, Prime Minister of Nigeria, on Nigerian Independence Night, 1960.

WHEN I arrived back in England from Palestine I was assigned as a beachcomber to the Colonial Office and put to work in the Appointments Department. I stayed there for a year and a half until I was posted to Trans-Jordan just after the outbreak of war.

A beachcomber was a member of the Colonial Service temporarily working in the Colonial Office. The staff of the Colonial Office was composed of members of the Home Civil Service, a race above and apart from us. They were skilled in drafting, minuting, preparing answers to parliamentary questions, advising Ministers. We were rough administrators pulled in from the bush to be given a veneer of Whitehall polish. Most of us beachcombers worked in the main Colonial Office, at that time in Downing Street, but I was allocated to the Appointments Department which lived a separate existence in a small office in Buckingham Gate and was engaged on the specialised task of selecting candidates for appointment to the Colonial Service.

Here I became the bottom man in a strangely assorted team under an extraordinary chief, Major Sir Ralph Furse, the Colonial Office Director of Recruitment. After Eton and Balliol he had commanded King Edward's Horse in the first world war and he looked and behaved more like a cavalry officer or a country gentleman than a civil servant. As he strode over St. James's Park to meet the black-coated civil servants of the main office he looked as if he had hurried in from a Devonshire hunting field.

He had dealt with appointments under the Colonial Office way back before the first world war. He never lost his zest and dash, and all of us who worked under him were carried along by his enthusiasm and energy. I also came from the West-country where we are more divided than most other parts of England between Tories and Church people on the one hand and Liberals and non-conformists on the other. At first I was apt to be suspicious of someone who looked so like a Tory squire—and had so many Bishops in his family. And I think he was inclined to look on Labour leaders as interesting but possibly dangerous oddities of the modern world. Perhaps too he was apt to put good administration of colonial territories before political advance. But he was a man who knew and did his job so well and with so much imagination that he won the respect of us all, including even someone like myself of radical upbringing.

He had built up over the years his own system of selection for the Colonial Service. Selection was by interview and not by examination—though the candidate's examination record was of course one of the main tests. I remember having to go to Sir Roderick Meiklejohn, the stern Chairman of the Civil Service Commission, with the annual list of "unsuitable firsts" to explain why a few candidates who had First Class Honours Degrees were not thought well suited for selection for overseas administration. Since Sir Roderick was the High Priest of the Home Civil Service, which was selected by examination, this was rather like explaining to the Pope the fallibility of the apostolic succession.

Selection by Board is a rotten system. On two successive years I had to attend the meetings of the Colonial Service Appointments Board and sit silent at the end of the table in the huge room in Burlington Gardens where the candidates short-listed for selection appeared before the Board. I knew the candidates. I had had long conversations with them before-hand. I had closely studied their records. I had corresponded about them with Housemasters and University tutors. It was often agony to see them do much less than justice to themselves through nervousness before the Board, or through not having understood what was expected of them. My experience is that members of selection Boards are often more intent on impressing the other members of the Board than on anything else. And anyhow ten minutes before a Board is a poor test; it puts a premium on the slick answer and the easy manner.

Sir Ralph Furse made use of the Board. It was a useful second check—and a shield against any accusation of favouritism. But he put his main faith in other methods. He had developed an amazingly thorough system of espionage throughout the universities and schools. He knew the tutors and masters who could be relied upon to give an honest assessment. Before any candidate appeared in the Appointments Department we had a file about his record which would have done credit to a Criminal Investigation Department. Moreover Sir Ralph Furse recognised that at an interview with a senior official a candidate is seldom at ease. So he brought to do the initial interviewing a few young men like myself who were within ten years or less of the age of the candidates and who had already had some experience of colonial administration overseas. Arthur Benson, later Governor of Northern Rhodesia, and Patrick Renison, later Governor of Kenya, at one time were in the same kind of job I had.

We told the candidates what it was like to be a District Officer. We explained the disadvantages—separation from family, difficulties about education of children, isolation from friends and books, bad climates and the rest. These individual interviews would often last for an hour or more. The candidates began to feel that we were being interviewed rather than they. They were talking to young men near their own age who had not long before had to make the same decisions as they had. They talked freely. They spoke of their reasons for thinking of overseas service. They asked our advice. And in doubtful or difficult cases they would be asked to come back once, twice or three times to be interviewed by different members of our Department, including Sir Ralph Furse himself.

By the time the confidential reports from schools and universities had all been collected, and reference back often made to check or seek explanation, and the series of personal interviews with junior and senior members of our Department had been completed, as thorough a review as possible of each case had been made. We left to the Board the final choice from the limited number recommended for selection. I remember that when I myself went to the Appointments Department as a candidate I thought the system surprisingly casual. But I have no doubt that before I went up to London for interview most of my misdeeds at school and at Cambridge were duly recorded in my file and had been carefully considered. And I realised later that at my interview I had probably been closely watched for indications of insolence or being over-pleased with myself.

Sir Ralph Furse was not content with organising an elaborate system of selection in London. He travelled throughout the colonial territories. He visited remote stations and distant islands. He worked out a new system of training both before and after a candidate took on his first appointment. He advocated a system of a Unified Colonial Service, and saw his proposals put into effect. He introduced a new method of recruitment for the Colonial Service in other Commonwealth countries. He gave special attention to agricultural and technical services and became intensely interested in Colonial Forestry in particular.

He was the founder, the creator of the Colonial Service. He earned the gratitude and devotion and admiration of everyone who worked under him. The results of his work have been decisive in every branch of the Service and in every corner of the Commonwealth.

*   *   *

While we were at home Sylvia and I with our small son Paul lived in a tiny flat near Battersea Park. My brother Michael was at that time starting out as a leader-writer on the *Evening Standard*, and he came to live with us. Michael and I would often set out in the morning on the same bus, I getting off at Victoria and he going on to Fleet Street. His lodging with us was a good arrangement for both of us. Our finances were greatly helped by having a lodger. He was glad to have a landlord who would not be unreasonably punctual in demanding the rent of his room.

It was good for us beachcombers to be pulled out of our

remote overseas Districts and to see something of a wider world, but the world in 1938 and 1939 was menacing and growing darker with the prospect of war. In the mounting crisis of the summer of 1939 I was told that I might at any time be sent overseas again. I was anxious to get back to the Middle East, and late in August I was told to await my transfer instructions which might come at any time. Then the order came for expectant mothers to leave London. Sylvia was expecting our second child at any time, and we set out for my family home in Cornwall. We had already sent Paul ahead to my mother. We were doubtful if we would ourselves get to Cornwall in time. When we reached Bath Sylvia thought it best to go no farther, and we managed to book her a bed in a Bath hospital. But then started a long wait. The baby was expected any day. I was expecting the telegram telling me to set out for the Middle East. As day after day went by we feared that the telegram would beat the baby. Three weeks we waited. Sarah then condescended to arrive, and on the same day I received my telegram telling me to report at once in London ready to proceed overland by Orient Express to Istanbul and then by the Taurus Express on my way to become Assistant British Resident in Amman.

CHAPTER V

A Back Seat in the Middle East

"Hang yourself, brave Crillon; we fought at Arques and you were not there."

HENRI IV

WHEN the carve-up of Arabia took place after the first world war, Trans-Jordan emerged as the poorest, the most artificial and apparently the most unstable of all the new States then created. It had a population of only about three quarters of a million, mainly Moslem villagers, with Christian and Circassian minorities. Most of its people lived in the narrow triangle of hills from the Syrian frontier on the Yarmuk Valley in the north down to Kerak, east of the Dead Sea; and beyond that the desert stretching away to the east was sparsely inhabited by bedouin tribes. The country had no oil, no industry and not even an outlet to the sea, except at the little fishing village of Aqaba which was separated from the capital at Amman by a long day's drive over open desert. Amman itself, on the site of the ancient Philadelphia, was no more than a small Circassian village in a stony valley. Geographically and politically and economically this, the smallest in population of the new Arabian States, looked like a minor monstrosity, likely to be buffeted and swept away by the powerful forces of change and revolt in the five countries which surrounded it.

Yet in the period of nearly half a century since Feisal's army swept through the desert to take Damascus, and Feisal's brother, Abdulla, pitched his camp outside Amman, this small territory has been the most stable and most peaceful and the best-administered territory in all Arabia. Storms of violence and revolution have ravaged its neighbours but the Hashemite Kingdom of Jordan has survived. In the early days it survived attack from the East when King Ibn Saud, the traditional enemy of the Hashemite House, sent his raiding forces over the desert. It survived the war with Israel and absorbed within its frontiers the poorest parts of Palestine, with the added burden of hundreds of thousands of Palestine refugees. Revolutions in Syria, in Egypt and in Iraq and in Palestine left Jordan still unscathed, precarious but persistent.

For the survival and peace of this island in a turbulent sea of Arabian trouble a small band of leaders have been mainly responsible—two Arab Kings, King Abdulla and his grandson King Hussein, and a few English officials, Sir Henry Cox, Peake Pasha, Sir Alec Kirkbride and Glubb Pasha outstanding amongst them, and a succession of able Arab Chief Ministers, amongst the first being Ibrahim Hashem and Tewfiq Abul Huda.

The Emir Abdulla, later King Abdulla, the son of the old King Hussein of the Hejaz and the brother of King Feisal of Iraq, presided over the first two decades of the mandated territory of Trans-Jordan. His shrewd acceptance of the limitations and realities of his small Kingdom enabled him to establish and maintain his uneasy position. He had not the fire of King Feisal but he was a skilled negotiator, and a poet too. He was a politician and a chess player rather than a soldier or administrator, and in the early years of the British Mandate over Trans-Jordan he was content to interfere only sporadically, leaving the administration of the country mainly to the British Resident, Sir Henry Cox, and to Peake Pasha, the first Commander of the Arab Legion. They ruled Trans-Jordan for a decade and gave the country an efficient, just administration. They created the traditions of good government which have survived to this day.

When I arrived in Amman in 1939 to become Assistant British Resident a new team had just taken over. Sir Alec Kirkbride, who had been Assistant British Resident under Sir Henry Cox, had succeeded as British Resident, and Glubb Pasha, who had come several years before from Iraq to command the Desert Patrol of the Arab Legion, had come to Amman from the desert to take over command of the whole Arab Legion from Peake.

It would be difficult to imagine more different men than

Kirkbride and Glubb, or two men better suited for the roles they had to play.

The first stage of direct British administration was over. Now it was a matter of transferring authority to Arab Ministers and officials. There is no more difficult art than that of devolving executive authority on others but Kirkbride had just the gifts to perform this task. He knew the whole of Trans-Jordan as well as any other man, Arab or non-Arab. While still in his teens he had fought with Lawrence in Feisal's army in the desert. In *The Seven Pillars of Wisdom* Lawrence speaks of him as "Kirkbride the summary". Lawrence described him as "a taciturn, enduring fellow, only a boy in years, but ruthless in action". Kirkbride was not an outstanding Arabic scholar like his younger brother but he had spoken Arabic since he spoke English. He was a huge, strong man with a keen political sense and a gift for saying what he had to say incisively. He also had an alarming capacity for being silent. When day-to-day responsibility had been handed over to Arab Ministers his old friends from the villages and the tribes would come to see him, bringing their troubles and requests to him as they had been used to do when he had been Assistant British Resident. He would listen quietly and politely, usually say nothing in reply, and then do nothing. He told me that the surprising thing when he first adopted this gambit, which incidentally enabled him to keep closely in touch with what was going on, was the number of occasions on which the petitioners came back later to thank him for what had been done. But gradually the people came to discover that while the new British Resident would always give them a welcome and a hearing they must in future take their requests to the Arab Ministers.

I myself often went to my chief with new ideas and enthusiasms. He would listen half-amused and occasionally tell me to go ahead with my proposal, but more often he would shortly tell me some very good reason why my plan should not be pursued. To be thwarted and corrected so often by any other chief would have been galling. But Kirkbride's robust cynicism made me all the more determined to learn more and do better.

Glubb Pasha, or Abu Huneik, "the father of the little chin"

as he was known by the Arabs because a face wound had left him with only half a chin, was about as different from Kirkbride as it was possible to be. Kirkbride was tall and heavy but Glubb was almost insignificant in stature. While Kirkbride was cynical Glubb was enthusiastic. Kirkbride never said or wrote anything unless absolutely necessary; Glubb wrote enormous memoranda in English and a stream of orders and notes and messages in Arabic. Outside Glubb's office at Arab Legion Headquarters was always a crowd of petitioners, most of them sitting on the wall. Many had come long distances to see him. They would sometimes wait patiently for days. They knew that in the end their turn would come and that however petty their request Abu Huneik would listen and give them a decision, usually a note in Arabic to some outlying Arab Legion post. Glubb was an organiser as well as a leader. No detail was too small for him. The Arab Legion was part Police Force and part Army. The Police with their spiked helmets and the Desert Armoured Brigade—"Glubb's girls" as they were called by the British Army—with their long hair, bedouin head-dresses and cloaks, and sleeves reaching to the ground, were both equipped and trained with the utmost efficiency. Some of the Arab Legion were mounted on horses, some on camels and some in armoured cars.

I went back in 1959 to see the Army Day parade of the Arab Legion in the desert near Zerqa—two divisions with horses, camels, armoured cars, tanks and guns—the finest military parade I have ever seen. Glubb had left by then, dismissed overnight by the young King Hussein, but we all knew that the Army we saw that day was the result of Glubb's planning and Glubb's training.

By the time he left he had perhaps outlived his time. The method of his dismissal was deplorable, but so great was his own personal hold that it was probably well that he should not continue for longer in the position of centralised and complete authority which he had built up. He had become too powerful not because he sought power but because his personal qualities made him unavoidably a dominating influence in the country.

Glubb did not have the opportunities for personal glorification that Lawrence had had. Nor did he seek personal publicity.

But his knowledge of Arabic and the Arabs was far superior to Lawrence's and the traditions which he built up on the earlier work done by his predecessor, Peake Pasha, have made and will continue to make a vital contribution in the future of Jordan and indeed of Arabia.

Kirkbride was mainly occupied in his dealings with the Emir Abdulla and the Chief Minister, and he sent me out to the villages and the desert. He said he didn't wish to see me often, but he wanted to feel that I was constantly moving amongst the villages and the Arab officials in the Districts and the Arabs of the desert to keep him aware of the feeling and the talk of the people. I had little or no executive authority. It was the Arab officials, the Mutasarifs and the District Commanders of the Arab Legion, who now administered the country. They were always glad to see me, to hear news of the war and of the capital, and to discuss with me their problems and difficulties.

Once I exceeded my authority. I had spoken to the Arab officials in the Irbid district about a new plan to build anti-tank defences along the northern frontier without first explaining the whole project to the Ministers in Amman. The Chief Minister, Tewfiq Abul Huda, might have complained about my action to the British Resident. Instead he sent for me and rebuked me. He did it very gravely and firmly, but he smiled as he got up to finish the interview. He knew not only that I would never again offend in this way; he knew that I respected him the more for giving me my medicine direct.

There was one executive function which remained to me even at this stage of Arab control. Since Trans-Jordan could exist only on British grant-in-aid, any reduction in the public revenues meant an increase in the British annual grant. No remission in the tithe or crop tax, which was the main source of revenue, could therefore be made without British approval; and it was my duty to assess crop failure year by year and to decide what reduction in tax could be approved. In theory this meant inspecting each hod or large field in the whole country. And since most of the cultivable land in Trans-Jordan had a full crop only once in about six years, it was necessary to visit every village and tribal area to make the assessment. Time made it impossible to do more than take sample hods in each area, but the work of assessment gave me cause to travel throughout the country every year. I used to start in the early spring by riding up the Jordan Valley from the Dead Sea to the Sea of Galilee and then work my way down through the hills from Irbid to Kerak and then go further afield into the edges of the desert. And at the end of the summer I started out again, this time to ride through the vineyards in the hills round the ruined city of Jerrash, and the Saracen castle of Ajlun. Everywhere I was made more than welcome by the cultivators, who hoped to see their tax reduced, and the work gave me the best opportunity to get to know the country and the people.

Such peaceful occupation was interrupted in 1940. Syria and the Lebanon were held by the French under the High Commissioner, General Dentz, who had declared support for Vichy, and preparations were put in hand by Middle East Headquarters to attack Syria and the Lebanon. I was sent to live at Irbid not far south of the Syrian frontier, there to make contact with the Arab leaders of the Hauran in the south of Syria and prepare the way with the Arabs for a military drive into Syria. Meanwhile secret negotiations were undertaken with Colonel Collet, who commanded the Vichy French Forces in southern Syria and hoped to bring his whole force over to the Free French. General Catroux came to a meeting with Collet under a railway bridge in the desert south-east of Deraa, and soon afterwards I got a message that Colonel Collet planned to bring his troops over to us at dawn in three days' time. I dashed to Amman to tell Kirkbride, and was sent post haste to report to General Jumbo Wilson in Jerusalem. Colonel Collet's last words to me were that the Free French should not be told, since he did not rely on some of the Free French officers at Jerusalem Headquarters to keep the secret. I was in Irbid on the night before Collet and his men were to come over. Just before midnight I was woken to be told that Colonel Collet and his wife had just arrived alone at Mafrak, about fifteen miles to the east on our side of the frontier. What could have gone wrong? I raced to Irbid to find a furious Collet. Had he not instructed me that the Free French were not to be told? Just as he was making his final orders on the previous evening he had been listening to the Free French

Radio from Brazzaville and to his consternation heard a report of his intended move given openly in the evening news bulletin. He jumped into a car with his wife and drove over the frontier cursing those who had thrown the game away.

At dawn all was confusion. Some of his officers had received Collet's orders, some had not. All were in doubt, but many of his officers arrived at Irbid and Mafrak. A few of them said they wanted to join the Free French; some said that they had come under orders from their superior officers, but wished to return to the Vichy French in Syria. We gave them all breakfast in the Trans-Jordan Frontier Force camp at Irbid and told them that they could decide whether to stay or go back. I don't understand French but as we gave them breakfast I could pick up some of the sense of the arguments which broke out. Most of them said that they wished to join the Free French but had families back in France and could not abandon them. Some said that as soldiers they must obey Colonel Collet. A few said that Collet was a traitor and that they were still under the command of General Dentz. They were all under great stress and as the time came for them to make a final decision they were loud in fierce argument; others were almost in tears. After breakfast the majority of them got in their trucks and drove sullenly back over the frontier into Syria.

In 1941 our forces in Palestine and Trans-Jordan were very weak. We had no armour of any kind and practically no aircraft. The urgent needs of the Western Desert came first. But it was decided that the Vichy French forces in Syria and the Lebanon must be dislodged. Unless we took over control of Syria and Lebanon they might soon be used as bases for Axis activity and attack. Already there were reports of German planes landing at Damascus airport. And so in 1941 a very mixed force of British commandos and cavalry, Australians, Indians and Trans-Jordan Frontier Force and Free French was built up along the Palestine and Trans-Jordan frontiers. I had been assigned as a political officer to the Indian Brigade based on Irbid and Mafrak. The forces against us were about equal to ours but the Vichy French had the great advantage of some armoured vehicles and aircraft. It was decided that before we attacked, a formal demand to surrender should be made to the French Commander in Deraa (the Syrian frontier town where Lawrence was captured and maltreated by the Turks). The Brigadier commanding the Indian Brigade decided that this demand to surrender should be presented by a British Gunner Major, a Free French officer and myself. I was selected to join the two officers because I knew Arabic and could tell the Arabs to get clear of the town before the attack started.

At midnight we heard the rumble as all our transport dispersed over the Irbid plain started up, and by dawn our troops were drawn up on the Trans-Jordan side of the valley which marked the frontier facing the Vichy French on the other side of the valley. Like two biblical armies, it seemed to me, facing each other across the narrow ravine.

The Gunner officer, the Free French officer and I put up a Union Jack and a white flag of parley on our staff car driven by an Indian driver, and we set out down the winding road into the steep valley. We were half way down when there was a shattering bang. Our staff car was hit by a French ·75. The shell had, very fortunately for us, hit the bottom of the engine of the car. The car was wrecked and our driver was wounded but the rest of us were unhurt. We tumbled out of the car and took cover and made the driver comfortable. He didn't appear to be badly hurt, but he couldn't walk. We were now well within rifle range of Deraa and it would have been as dangerous to go back as to go on. So we took our two flags and advanced on foot down into the valley and up the other side to the outskirts of the town. Here we were disarmed and taken to an officer. We saw by the way that, contrary to the plan, firing had already broken out between the two forces. The French fort to the west of Deraa was in flames; presumably our troops had lobbed some anti-tank shells onto its wooden roof. This didn't improve our welcome. We said that we had a letter for the Commanding Officer. But he could not be found. We were moved about while demolitions of ammunition dumps were carried out. Our Free French officer was abused and spat upon, and I thought at one time that they would shoot him. But still the Commanding Officer could not be found. We could get no one to read our pompous letter, and we began to feel foolish. It was now 6.30 a.m. and we knew that the time for our twenty-five pounders to open the attack was 7 a.m.

We started an odd argument amongst ourselves. The Free French officer, with commendable Gallic realism, claimed that we had done all we could, that it was quite clear that the garrison was not going to surrender and that obviously the best thing we could do was to take cover or get out if we could before our own troops attacked. The Gunner officer and I, with a proper public school obstinacy, argued that we had been sent to demand a surrender and that although no one would listen to us we must stay where we were until and unless we had done what we were told. The debate was academic anyhow, for we had no means of transport.

Our conference was cut short by a Vichy officer who said that he was second in command, that our demand for surrender was an insult and that he hoped we would be blown to bits by our own guns.

On this we agreed with the Free French officer that we were no longer serving any useful purpose, as they say in the despatches, but we could not see what we could do. Our car was wrecked and the valley separated us from our own troops. But then the Arab Police Officer with whom I had been talking earlier came up with a suggestion. Why not take his car? But, we said, we are on opposite sides and anyhow if we attempted to drive back to our lines the same French ·75 would no doubt have another go at us. The Police Officer said that he would take the risk to his car, if we would take the risk of the drive back. Anything seemed better than to be written-off by our own guns, so we got into the civilian car, put up our two flags again and gingerly drove down into the valley. Still no firing at us. We reached our own wrecked staff car, saw that the wounded Indian driver had gone—no doubt he had crawled back up the hill. All the time we were expecting to be hit in the back. But no shot came. We put on a final burst of speed and were over the crest of the hill; and had a good breakfast in the Brigadier's tent.

By this time the Vichy French were reported to be withdrawing under our attack and in an hour or two we were back in Deraa. My first very pleasant task was to return the Police

Officer's car, together with a hundred new pound notes for its hire. In the town there was utter confusion. The prisoners had broken out of the jail. Unexplained firing was taking place throughout the town and already in only an hour or two the town was looted clean. For a while there was no authority and no law. I saw one Arab dash down the main street and shake a wooden window frame from its masonry and rush away with it—to be shot dead by our troops, whose orders were to shoot looters. Several times later that day as we went about our task of restoring some sort of order I passed the dead body lying on its face in the gutter.

Later on and farther to the north the Vichy French fought back fiercely and our troops suffered many casualties nearer to Damascus. Almost a whole battalion of ours was taken prisoner when French armour counter-attacked. The officers were flown out as prisoners of war to Greece and then taken by train through the Balkans and Germany to France. Then when General Dentz finally capitulated they were brought back under exchange of prisoners in the ships which came from Marseilles to evacuate the Vichy French. In the cafés of Damascus they told us stories of their short captivity and their strange journey through enemy lands.

For a few days I was made responsible for the administration of the whole of southern Syria, but then British Political Officers were brought in to take over, and I went back to my Trans-Jordan backwater.

I remember particularly two pictures from the few days I spent in charge of Deraa.

It had been decided that for political reasons the Free French and not our troops should take Damascus. So when our troops had done the hard fighting and suffered the casualties we stood in the main street of Deraa and glumly watched the Free French Division, mainly Senegalese, drive through in civilian buses to have the honour of taking the Syrian capital.

A day later, to our astonishment, we saw driving through the main street a convoy of staff cars containing a bevy of beautiful young women. We gaped in astonishment. We had almost forgotten that such creatures existed and to see them in Deraa seemed a miracle. They were the drivers and nurses of the

Spears Ambulance Unit which did such fine work with the Free French first in Syria and later in North Africa.

Not long after I returned to Amman I was sent on another assignment, this time in the southern deserts of Trans-Jordan. I had occupied part of my time earlier on in exploring these deserts and I prided myself as an expert on the Wadi Araba, the desolate and beautiful valley which runs from the Dead Sea to the Red Sea. I had often ridden by camel from Aqaba to explore that area and I had made what we called a "going map" of the bottom of the valley and of the approaches to the gorge from Sinai and Palestine on the one side and from the Trans-Jordan side on the other. The valley for almost its whole length is below sea level and on both sides there are magnificent towering cliffs in blue, red and purple sandstone. The question I was investigating was whether a modern army could cross the valley by the few precipitous passes which descended into it from the high desert on either side. I scarcely imagined that my travels in this area remote from the fighting of the Middle East would ever become of strategic importance, but we had visions of guerilla resistance in Arabia if the Axis forces should capture Egypt, and anyhow it was good to feel that there was one area of the world which I knew as well or better than anyone else. Once I rode up the valley with Nelson Glueck, the Director of the American School of Archaeology in Jerusalem, and he taught me how to judge from the shards in the ruined cities of the valley whether these ancient sites were Greek or Roman or Nabatean. Glueck, who is probably the greatest authority on the history of these parts, is a Jew, and it is odd to think now that he and I could ride unarmed through that wild Arab area accompanied only by a few bedouin.

By 1942 it had been decided to carry out a military project in this area. It was thought that one day we might have to fight in Syria and Turkey to the North, and the plan was to build a second line of communication, parallel with the main supply line through Palestine, to serve an army operating north of Damascus. This meant constructing a lighter port at Aqaba and a road from Aqaba up through the Wadi Itm to the top of the escarpment west of Ma'an, and then building a railway from that point to connect with the Hejaz railway at Ma'an, thus providing a railway link to Damascus. British sappers were sent to Aqaba to build the port and the road, and a company of Australian railway construction engineers was sent to Ma'an to build the new railway. I lived with the Australians at Ma'an for six months while the work went forward. I had not known Australians before, but in that six months I spent all my time with them, read their newspapers, grasped the fierceness of Australian politics, learnt Australian slang and understood something of Australian character.

I was told that even by Australian standards Australian railwaymen are known to be tough. They gave us some trouble before the work started and again when the work was finished, but while the job was on they worked with an almost fanatical enthusiasm. The English sappers working on the port and the road beyond the escarpment who plodded on stolidly with their task were amazed at the feverish activity which prevailed along the new railway as the Australians threw themselves day and night into the final few weeks of their effort. The English could not understand what all the excitement was about.

The Australians' task was to rip up the rails from the disused railway line south of Ma'an—from the sections of line which had been so much damaged by Lawrence and his Arab raiders in the first war—and to lay these rails along the new line. The rails had the date 1901 on them but were still in excellent condition. We could not have wanted better skilled direction for the project and the material and equipment were adequate. What we lacked was labour, and it was my duty to try to persuade the bedouin of that area, of the Howeitat tribe, to provide it. The Howeitat under their famous old chief, Audeh Abu Tayeh, had fought with Lawrence. They were equally renowned for their bravery and for their avarice. They looked on the new railway as a wonderful opportunity to make money but they had no intention of doing more than a minimum, and they had no desire at all to see the work completed. They came with their black tents and we had more than ten thousand Arabs along the twenty miles of the new line. Each day I would go along the line to take coffee with the sheikhs and sub-sheikhs and to discuss the progress of the work. They obviously enjoyed these conferences which suited their taste for a mixture of diplomacy and blackmail. Gravely we would discuss questions of daily tasks and rates, they would assure me of their devotion and their fervent desire for Allied victory and I would appeal to their sense of honour. But manual work was contemptible to them, and they made it clear that their tribesmen were working only as a personal favour.

One day we had finished the earth work and the next task was to prepare the stone ballast. This meant raking up the loose flint from the desert with a primitive rake—the flint was plentiful on all sides—and carrying it in a four-gallon petrol tin to the line. I asked the Australian sappers how many feet of ballast at the right height and width a man could prepare in a day. They said fifteen feet was easy—they would think nothing of doing that in Australia. So we told the Arabs that the daily task would be ten feet. Immediate protests. Ten feet was quite ridiculous. The whole work came to a stop. For days I travelled along the long line of black tents arguing, cajoling, urging, threatening. No result whatever. The Australians were furious. They attacked me each night in the Ma'an mess. I called a conference of all the sheikhs. They stuck to their obstinate refusal, offering to do say five feet a day. "Very well," I said in the end in desperation, "tomorrow morning I will do the ten feet myself." They thought that I was jesting. But having made my declaration I couldn't go back. So on the next morning taking my petrol tin and rake I went out to do the task. I was followed by a line of protesting sheikhs. They begged me to stop. They said that I and they too would be disgraced. But still they made no offer to accept the task we had set. So I settled down to the work. The rake had a narrow iron handle; and a four-gallon tin filled with flint is unpleasantly heavy. When I had been at it for four or five hours my hands were blistered and I began to doubt if I could last. But in just under seven hours to my infinite relief I finished. The sheikhs would not speak to me. I had been guilty of an unpardonable indiscretion. But next morning ten thousand Arabs advanced with their tins and rakes, and there were no more strikes.

Then just as the work was nearing its end and the Australians

75

were working in a frenzy of urgency, we had really bad luck. In the high desert between Ma'an and the escarpment snow falls once in every four or five years, and that winter was one of the worst for very many years. One morning we woke to find all our transport and equipment frozen, and for a few days we had to turn our efforts from the railway to saving isolated Arab encampments caught in the snow. I remember one terrible sight we saw. We were searching in the desert north of Ma'an for single bedouin tents. We came upon one with a ring of dead animals round it—a camel or two and a few goats. The animals had been unable to find grazing through the snow. And inside the tent was the Arab father sitting with a small child between his knees and near by his wife with two other children, all dead and stiff.

In spite of diversions and delays the Australians finished the railway well ahead of the time allotted. I am sure they are still remembered by the Howeitat, and a number of very odd Australian words have entered into the language of that proud tribe. We, the English and the Arabs too, recognised in these Australian sappers qualities we did not possess—the drive and energy and the inspiration of a pioneer people. Some twenty years later I had cause to admire the same qualities when I saw in New Guinea evidence of the same pioneering Australian enthusiasm.

All my time in the first few years of the war in Trans-Jordan I had been agitating to be allowed to join the Army and go to the Western Desert. There I thought that my Arabic and my knowledge of Arab countries could be put to good use. To stay in Amman while the fate and future of the world were being settled in the battles of North Africa was intolerable. But all my pleas were rejected. I should stay where I was. There were only a few British officials in Trans-Jordan anyhow. No one could see how or where the war would develop. And there was no one to replace me. Sylvia, with Paul and Sarah, had long ago been evacuated to South Africa with all the other British families in the Middle East. My house in Amman had been turned into a mess. Gawain Bell, of the Arab Legion— later to be Governor of Northern Nigeria—shared the house with me and one or two other Arab Legion officers. From time to time other officers came to stay with us. Wilfred Thesiger, a romantic figure, with a D.S.O. from the Abyssinian campaign, was one. Lord Apsley stayed with us before being so tragically killed in a plane crash in Malta.

We became Arab enthusiasts. We didn't drink or smoke. We carried the string of Arab beads which we would run through our fingers as we talked of an evening. I gave more and more of my time to Arabic. I have no ear for languages but I went at it the hard way often working for four or five hours at night at the grammar. With much preparation and anxiety I gave a lecture in Arabic to the Arab Club in Amman. I became obsessed with the regularity and richness of the language.

Meanwhile the war news grew worse, and the humiliation of living a life in such a backwater became harder to bear. Each evening I would walk down the hill and along the main street of Amman to the Post Office to collect my letters from the evening mail delivered from Jerusalem. I knew every shopkeeper in the street and would stop and gossip with them as I went. But as the war news grew worse and we lost Tobruk and fell back to Alamein, and it seemed that our whole position in the Middle East would be lost, I sometimes hesitated before setting out for the Post Office. It was difficult to make conversation with my shopkeeper friends when the news was so bad and when at any time some other and bigger disaster might occur. But I thought that if I didn't go my failure to take my evening walk might be noted, so I made the effort and as I talked to people along the street I put a much more confident face on events than I felt.

Years later I saw an account by Glubb Pasha of a conversation he had had with the Arab leaders of Jordan. Why was it that when the news was so bad and when by all ordinary tests we had lost the war, the Arabs stood by us? Well, they said, they had of course listened to the news. They had heard the Axis broadcasts, too. True, there seemed no hope for the British when they stood alone in the world and their whole effort in the Middle East seemed to be collapsing. So they watched very carefully they said. They saw the British Resident drive to his office every morning just after eight, and they saw

Glubb Pasha as usual receiving a stream of petitioners and listening patiently to all of them, however petty the requests seemed. They watched the Assistant British Resident every evening as he walked down the street and spoke to his friends in the book shop and the garage and the café and the chemist's store. "Yes, we heard the news all right," they said, "and we came to the conclusion as we watched you that you must know something that we didn't."

By the end of 1942 our military fortunes suddenly changed for the better. Alamein had been won. General Montgomery's forces swept past Benghazi on the road to Tripoli. My repeated requests to be allowed to go to North Africa were at last reluctantly approved and at the end of the year I was appointed to the Military Administration of Cyrenaica. I gave away or sold up what was left of my belongings, reduced my worldly possessions to one small suitcase, took the train from Haifa to Cairo and managed to get a room in one of the crowded Cairo hotels with two South African sergeants. They were suspicious of a civilian in their room and more suspicious still when I emerged the next day as a Lieutenant-Colonel.

I set out for Alexandria and the long drive up through the desert to Tobruk and Derna. My instructions were to report to Brigadier Cumming of the Sudan Political Service, who was in charge of the Military Administration of Cyrenaica, now for the third time freed by British troops. Freed was right, for the Arabs of Cyrenaica, the Senussi, had for many years maintained their brave struggle against Fascist oppression.

Soon after my arrival at Brigadier Cumming's headquarters at Beda Littoria near Cirene, I went to represent him at the celebration of liberation to take place in Derna. The celebration took an odd form. It was to be a play, performed by a troupe of players who had once, we were told, performed before the King of Italy. But when Cyrenaica had been ruled by the Italians the Senussi players were permitted to perform only censored plays of no political significance. Now they were free to make up a play of their own, and the programme told us that the play was to be in three acts. The first represented the old days of comparative Arab freedom under the loose control of the Ottoman Empire. The scene was one of pastoral happiness with the Senussi tribesmen tending their flocks, living in their black tents and developing their own puritan form of Moslem religious organisation and discipline. The next act showed the long agony of the Senussi under Italian domination. They were driven from their fertile lands in the Jebel el Akhdar—Arabic for the Green Hill. Their leaders were, so the legend ran, thrown from aeroplanes; wells on which the people and their flocks depended were blocked with cement; the people were crowded into concentration camps and their flocks left to die on the other side of the barbed wire. The play was vividly acted, the parts of the Italians being played by Arabs in Italian uniforms and carrying Italian rifles, both being easily obtainable in the days after the Axis retreat; and the Arabs who played the parts of Italians spoke fluent Italian.

Then came the final scene which was described in the programme under the one word "Defeat". I wondered how they would portray their final subjection after the last rebels had been driven from the desert oasis of Kufra and their few remaining leaders had fled to Cairo. The curtain went up to show a school. The schoolboys were clean and tidy and neatly dressed, but they spoke in Italian and, when they were inspected by Marshal Graziani, resplendent in uniform and medals, they gave the Fascist salute. This to the Senussi was their ultimate humiliation. Now at long last, for reasons of world politics they could only partly understand, their enemies had been driven away and they were free again to speak their own beautiful language and bring up their children in their own way in accordance with their own religion.

They received their country back with interest. All the best land had been taken for Italian settlers. But on the last time the armies swept backwards and forward through Cyrenaica all the Italian settlers had been removed and taken back to Tripoli or to Italy. The order for removal of the settlers must have been a sudden one, for all over the fertile Jebel there were peasant farms obviously hurriedly abandoned. In those days in early 1943 one could walk into any farm and see the pathetic evidence of sudden departure—food on the tables, toys on the floor and all the possessions of the Italian settlers, except those already looted, still there. And outside in the stables and fields there were cattle, the magnificent long-horned cattle of Tuscany, and flocks and fruit trees and vineyards. The Arabs well knew the boundaries of the lands from which they had been evicted, and they returned to take over not merely grazing lands as they had been before but farmhouses and cultivation and cattle.

Soon after the liberation play in Derna I saw another strange play, this time in the Greek theatre at Cirene. This is one of the finest Greek theatres. It is cut out of the higher escarpment facing the Mediterranean, and as you sit in the theatre you have a feeling of being perched between earth and heaven. In the Cirene Museum the Royal Air Force had established one of its main tracking communication centres and there must have been some thousand R.A.F. men stationed there. They announced that they would give a play in the Greek theatre, and the play was to be *A Midsummer Night's Dream*. The theatre, which seats several thousand spectators, was crammed about equally by troops in their dusty desert uniforms and by Arabs who had come from miles around, and before each scene a summary of what was to follow was given in Arabic. It was an hilarious success. The troops on their way up to the fighting were astonished to see such a performance—and the Arabs roared with laughter and applause.

Many of the troops who passed through Cyrenaica knew little of the Senussi. They saw pathetic Arab figures on the roadsides wrapped in their blankets holding up eggs for sale, but not many of the recent arrivals knew of the brave support given to so many of our soldiers and airmen in the previous desert campaigns. A Senussi encampment had always been a safe haven for a British soldier or airman lost behind the Axis lines, and a number of Senussi had been shot under suspicion of harbouring our men. I had the pleasant task of paying out rewards to Arabs who brought in the scribbled notes of thanks from our men whom they had saved.

Once in Derna a British Gunner sergeant came in to tell me that he had been given a few days' leave to look for an Arab friend. On one of the retreats he had been seriously wounded in the thigh in the hills above Derna and left on the roadside because the jolting of the Army truck had been too much for him to bear. He expected to die or possibly to be captured by the Germans, but a ragged Arab found him. The sergeant feared at first that the Arab would rob or kill him, but instead he pulled him to a cave and later brought him food. Every day the Arab came with simple foodstuffs and over a period of several months the soldier's leg slowly got better. They worked out an elementary language between themselves. Then the Arab brought some Arab clothes and later a camel. The sergeant gathered that the plan was to ride together on the camel back to the British lines, but neither of them knew how far the British had retreated. They set off to follow the line of the desert road in the direction of the Egyptian frontier, travelling just out of sight of the road, usually by night, and lying up by day. As day after day of travel passed they begged food from Arabs they passed. The British lines were in fact at that time 500 miles away at Alamein. Eventually they came to the rear of the German lines. The sergeant said goodbye to his Arab friend and, using the rocky coast, managed to get through to the British lines. Now he had come back to find the Arab, but he knew only his name. We sent him with a guide to the tribes above Derna and two days later the British soldier brought his friend into Derna. Of the many rewards I paid there was none which pleased me more than that.

There was another happy reunion soon afterwards. When for the third and last time the Axis forces retreated from Cyrenaica they took with them the tiny Jewish communities from Benghazi, Derna and Barce and put them in two concentration camps south of Tripoli. Why they went to this trouble in the preoccupations of their withdrawal no one knew. It seemed a senseless act of spite and cruelty. But having taken the Jews away they forgot about them in their further retreat to the Tunisian frontier, and the Jews remained abandoned and neglected. I was sent up from Benghazi to Tripoli early in 1943 to discuss various matters with the Military Administration of Tripolitania and I was told to look out for the Jews and, if possible, make plans to bring them back to their homes in Cyrenaica. So when I had had my conference in Tripoli I set out for Gharian where I heard that the main body of Jewish refugees could be found.

It was night when I arrived there. I found the Jewish families in a state of despair and bewilderment and utter destitution. Our troops had given them what they could spare from their rations, but the Jews had no news of the war and no hope of ever getting home again. I spoke to them in Arabic. At first they didn't seem to take in what I said. They were too depressed and bewildered to react or care. But then as I spoke one old woman suddenly gave a shout. "He has come to take us back, back to Benghazi," she cried. Then there was pandemonium. Men, women, and children cheered and wept and hugged each other. When eventually the hubbub subsided I sat down with a committee of the men to talk about plans for their return. They said that they were prepared to face any hardships to get back—and in the meantime they begged for two things, milk and soap. It was not easy to see how they could return. All military transport was required for the Eighth Army and its operations in Tunisia. It was in any event many days' journey back across the Sirte desert to Benghazi. Moreover anyone travelling back would be going against all the military traffic coming up to supply our armies. But eventually we managed to find a number of Italian diesel trucks with huge, open trailers. We made a double row of big water barrels on the trailers and against these some thirty or forty of the Jews huddled on each trailer covering themselves from the sun with rough tents. It was an extraordinary convoy which set out for Benghazi, but the Jews sang as they set out. Some five days later they sang again as they approached Benghazi. The Arab leaders of Benghazi came out several miles along the road to welcome them home again.

Brigadier Cumming had his headquarters in a house in the village of Beda Littoria. There he and I and a London lawyer and an Irish amateur steeplechaser and an Oxford anthropologist lived in a mess where I think the food was the worst I have ever eaten—army rations cooked by Sudanese houseboys on a smoky Italian stove. This was the house which Rommel had for some time made his headquarters, and it was here that Colonel Keyes had made his celebrated commando raid in an attempt to kill Rommel. Having landed by submarine on the coast to the north, Keyes and his small party had made their way over the rough hills to this house in Beda Littoria, overcome the guards, and forced their way into the house firing and throwing grenades as they advanced. They killed four Germans in the house but Rommel was not there that night, and before the raiding party could withdraw Colonel Keyes was fatally wounded on the threshold of the house.

The Arabs told us that his grave was in the little cemetery a mile or so from the village. We went to see it. There was Keyes' grave alongside the graves of the four Germans he had killed. The graves were the same and the crosses put up by the Germans were the same for all five. Going closer we saw that after the name of Colonel Keyes someone had later carefully added the V.C. which had been awarded to Colonel Keyes posthumously.

Years later in Jamaica I spoke to Colonel Keyes' sister about this. She and her husband Brigadier Jimmie Johnson were amongst our closest friends first in Jamaica and later when he was Military Attaché in Athens. I said to Mrs. Johnson how much we admired the action of the Germans in giving her brother an honourable grave, and even adding the V.C. when they learnt of the award. She told me that she and her family were also grateful to the Germans for the respect they had shown for her brother, but the V.C. was added on the cross not by the Germans as I had imagined but by her other brother. On the second advance of our troops through Cyrenaica her brother had sought out the grave and himself added the V.C. And now, she told me, the cross had been brought back to be kept in their village church in England.

The task we and the others who formed the British Military Administration had to tackle was a fascinating one, and we were a particularly happy team.

After subduing and evicting the Senussi the Italians had developed Cyrenaica for their own settlers. Everything had been done by Italians. We had no clerks, no technicians, not even telephone operators. The Arabs were incapable of cultivating the Italian farms and our efforts to teach them to care for the cattle and prune the vines and prevent the goats from eating the fruit trees were only very slowly effective.

Usually they would pitch their tents alongside an Italian farm and use the farmhouse as a store or a stable. The large Barce plain was covered with little white farmhouses but since there was no one to run the farms we organised a vast and motley line of tractors and damaged tanks and ploughed the whole plain for wheat in one operation, the tractors and tanks making detours to avoid the houses and then proceeding in line abreast across the twenty mile plain.

Not only were we without trained staff of any kind but the towns had been damaged and stripped. No house in Benghazi had been spared by the bombing and the looting. Except in the scattered hill farms there was scarcely a table or a chair undamaged in the whole country. The desert and the road-sides were still full of land mines. The shops were empty. The normal currency was in eggs.

One thing the Italians had left us. When they developed an area for agriculture they would first build a village centre—a church, a school, a municipal office and a coffee shop round an attractive village square. These model village centres were better than anything I have seen in any British-administered country. They provided centres of administration which well suited the Senussi system of Zawias where the Arabs had for centuries based their tribal organisation on centres with mosques and schools.

Slowly life returned to the towns and to these new villages. We made the beginnings of Arab municipalities, local councils, and police force, courts and agricultural services. The Arabs began to occupy the abandoned shell of Italian colonisation. When we went back to Cairo to report to the Senussi chief Said Idris es Senussi (now the King of Libya) we were able to tell him that his people had made a good start in laying the foundations of a new administration.

When I had left Trans-Jordan I had been told that I was released for six months to start with. But once having made my escape to the Army I never imagined that I should be recalled. Sir John Macpherson, the Chief Secretary in Jeru-salem, had told me that they didn't expect to see me again. So when I had become wholly immersed in the fascinating work of establishing the administration of Cyrenaica I was amazed and appalled to get an order from Cairo to come back since the six month period was up and Trans-Jordan had demanded my return.

I found another officer bound for Jerusalem and, boiling with indignation, I drove with him first to Cairo and then to Jerusalem over the Sinai desert. As I went I rehearsed what I would say to the authorities in Jerusalem. When I saw Sir John Macpherson I spoke in fury as no subordinate should speak to his superior. I was sent on to see Sir Harold Mac-Michael, the High Commissioner, but he too was quite unmoved by my protests. Before returning to Amman I went to Damascus for the week-end to brood on the injustice of the world, and there late at night I went to the famous old fortune-teller, Victoria. She told me in broken Arabic and French not to worry. Within a month, she said, I would move to another post more to my liking.

I took little notice of what she said and applied for ten days' leave to visit Sylvia and the children in South Africa. A month after my meeting with Victoria I set out in a flying boat from the Dead Sea to Cairo on the first stage of my journey. When I got to my hotel in Cairo I was called to the telephone and told to return to Jerusalem. This meant abandoning all my hard-won priorities on the flight to South Africa, but back I went—to be told in Jerusalem that I was to be sent to Cyprus as Colonial Secretary.

CHAPTER VI

Working with Arabs

"He is crazed with the spell of far Arabia,
They have stolen his wits away."
WALTER DE LA MARE

THE Arabs are children of the desert. Deserts have taught
them their distinctive qualities, and the purest Arab characteristics are the result of the influences of the remotest desert.
It was the battle for existence against the austere conditions in
the deserts of Arabia and North Africa which gave them their
endurance and their generosity and their courage and their
dignity.

The humblest bedu who has never seen a school, who has no
possessions beyond a few animals, and no prospect of ever
acquiring any worldly goods, will live on less than any other
human being—and will kill his last goat to provide a meal for
an unknown guest. He will gladly die for his religion or his
tribe and will carry himself in adversity or danger with a
dignity which I have seen in no other race.

He will speak to a king as an equal, respect learning and old
age, observe to the letter the exacting rules of desert hospitality
and hold the honour of himself and his family above all else.
His religion is his life. He is, moreover, a poet; I have seen
illiterate tribesmen weep to hear the beauty of the Koran even
when they could not hope to fathom the obscurities of the text.
Their beautiful language is an essential part of their religion
and their lives.

These qualities have been blurred and half-forgotten in the
towns, but the springs of Islam remain pure in the desert.

Have they no weaknesses? Certainly they have. They are
quick and sensitive to take offence. They are individualists,
and dislike discipline. They quarrel easily and cherish enmities.
Their newspapers and their radio propaganda are full of mean

86

abuse and shrill with hate. For long past they have been lacking in an urge either to co-operate with others or to construct, to create. There was, of course, a time centuries ago when the Arabs made an outstanding contribution to the science and literature and architecture of the world. For centuries past they have, however, been destroyers and not creators. The chant which I can still hear from Palestine riots in the Moslem town of Nablus in times of disorder is the rhythmic reiteration of the defiant cry "The religion of Mohamed was founded on the sword."

At their best, their manners are superb, their endurance almost superhuman, their hospitality spectacular, their courage romantic and their dignity unequalled. One day, if God wills, they will again combine these qualities with an ability to work together and a determination to make a new, positive, creative contribution to the world.

I have never ceased to rejoice that I had the privilege of spending my early years in overseas service with the Arabs. I was never in any doubt that, however politely they received me and whatever trouble they took to put me at my ease, they regarded me as an inferior, as an infidel.

Sometimes when I have watched officials in Africa dealing with Africans I have been embarrassed and ashamed. There has occasionally been in the official manner an arrogance, a superiority, which made me intensely uncomfortable. Even my friends from the Sudan Political Service, who regarded their Service with a good deal of justification as the élite of the overseas Services, used to speak to their subjects with a certain aristocratic condescension. With my Arabs I knew that I had a temporary official authority, and I hoped that they would learn to like me, but I never imagined that they received me as an equal. It certainly never occurred to me that I was a superior. I came to identify myself with the people I worked with elsewhere, Jamaicans, Nigerians or Cypriots, but from the Arabs at the very beginning of my overseas service I learnt, without realising at the time what I was learning, or understanding its fundamental importance, that a governor should be a servant and not a master.

When I went back to Cyprus as Governor in 1957 I said on

the day of my arrival in a short speech to the people of Cyprus:

"Let me at once assure you that my training and my experience and my strong inclination combine to make me put first and foremost the best interests of all the people of Cyprus. That is my principal and over-riding object. More than anything else I should like to serve you well and to help you to overcome the difficulties which confront you. I most earnestly desire to associate myself and identify myself with you in sympathy and understanding. I come back as your friend and your servant."

I remember as we went along the corridor of Government House to the swearing-in ceremony an official who had scanned through the text of the speech as it was being copied for the Press said, "Couldn't you leave out the bit about the servant?"

The King Abdulla was assassinated as he entered the great Mosque in Jerusalem in July 1951. I never knew him closely. I was too junior when I was in Amman to see him alone except on the rare occasions when Sir Alec Kirkbride was away. But I felt a deep loyalty and affection towards him. I remember him most clearly when he was entertaining important visitors, Kings and Field Marshals and Foreign Ministers, for then I would be able to watch from my place near the end of the table.

Once when Commander-in-Chief Auchinleck was dining with the Emir at the Palace in Amman, the conversation had dragged a little early in the meal. The Field Marshal didn't initiate conversation and the Emir seemed to be taking the measure of his guest. Then Abdulla turned to Auchinleck and asked him to speak of the qualities of the Indian soldier. Auchinleck's face lit up. This was the subject closest to his heart. For half an hour, with Glubb translating, he described with almost passionate pride the magnificent characteristics of the different kinds and categories of Indian soldier to whom he was so greatly devoted. Abdulla, and the rest of us, listened and watched, enthralled.

It was in his winter camp at Shuna in the Jordan Valley that Abdulla liked to entertain rather than in the formality of the Palace in Amman. At this simple camp, with his Circassian and Bedouin retainers round him, and with Arab mares grazing near his tents, he was at his ease and his best. His mischievous wit, his skill as a mimic, his keen and sensitive understanding, his brilliant gift for poetic description and his concern for his guests, however unimportant they might be, made him the finest host I have ever seen.

His grandson King Hussein was plunged into anxieties too early to acquire his grandfather's scholarship and subtlety. He loved fast cars and jet aircraft. Danger became his daily companion. He thrived on it. It gave him a steadiness and seriousness and a firmness of purpose almost alarming in so young a man. Once when I went to call on him with Air Marshal Patch in his summer cottage near Amman, he remained quite quiet for the first few minutes of our meeting. Ordinarily such a silence would have been embarrassing. With King Hussein it seemed natural and somehow admirable, rather like a Quaker grace. After a while he looked up and smiled and then embarked on a most lively and penetrating discussion on new kinds of aircraft, and then turned to questions of Arab politics. All the time he was thoughtful, well within himself, as if what was going on in his mind was more important than what we were saying.

I remember waiting for him on Nicosia airport when he was due to make a stop there on his way to Europe in 1958. He didn't arrive at the appointed time and after half an hour's waiting, we dispersed to find out what had prevented him from coming. We heard that he had set out from Amman piloting his own aircraft as usual, but that when he was over Syria his plane had been intercepted and attacked by Egyptian aircraft. The young King had dived to escape, and hedge-hopped home to Amman. A year later he did arrive in Cyprus on his way to Europe. Again he was piloting his own small aircraft. When I greeted him I said that it was almost a year since we had expected him at Nicosia. "A year to the day," he said. "I thought I would celebrate the anniversary by showing that no one could stop me." And when I asked him if he were well— "Yes," he grinned, "except for a slight crick in my neck from watching to see if the fighters would come again."

King Hussein has cheerfully survived bitter and persistent personal attacks from Egypt and elsewhere, and repeated and violent attempts to destroy himself and his country. Beset by all kinds of difficulties and dangers his short erect figure is an example of courage and an inspiration in his steadiness and dignity.

These qualities of generosity and dignity are not only royal prerogatives in Arabia. They are the common currency of the desert, the heritage and pride of every Arab worthy of the name.

Early in the war, before the fall of France, when the French were still in control of the Lebanon and Syria, I had a week's leave and decided to walk from Tyre on the Mediterranean coast to Damascus. When I arrived at Damascus I wrote a matter-of-fact account of my uneventful expedition to my mother. What I wrote reminds me of the natural friendship and kindness of Arab villagers:

A WALK TO DAMASCUS

I walked in a bush shirt and khaki slacks with an Arab hattar and agal. I could not of course have been mistaken for an Arab villager, but I might possibly have been taken for a reasonably well-dressed Arab road foreman. Most educated Arabs would, of course, have known from my accent, if not from the redness of my face, that I was an Englishman, but in remote villages one or two villagers paid me the compliment of asking whether I was a Christian or a Moslem.

Just beyond Tyre on the main Sidon road I got out of the Beirut post car with my pack and stick and said goodbye to the occupants who regarded me with mixed feelings of pity and astonishment. Some Arabs who were working by the roadside also made it clear when I told them that I was off to Damascus a hundred miles away that they considered me quite mad.

It was just short of nine in the morning when I set off in high spirits on the rough track running due east into the hills, not stopping until I had done well over ten miles. The country was brown and scorched at that time of the year but there were pleasant patches of green round most villages, many valleys to be crossed, a range of hills to the south and the indistinct mass of Hermon ahead. I carried no water and I was lucky to come across a Christian shepherd who fetched me a drink of water in my mug. Being the Moslem Ramadan, when Moslems neither drink nor eat between sunrise and sunset, one can hardly ask them for water or food in the daytime, and it is not polite to consume either in front of them. Children and the sick and travellers are specifically excluded from the fast by Moslem law but even when one is travelling it is better manners to appear to fast in Moslem company.

After four hours' walking I came up the green valley—very much like the valley west of Nablus—leading to the large Shia village of Nabatiya (the Shias are a branch of the Moslem faith mainly found in Persia and Iraq but with some followers in Syria and elsewhere). It was a fair-sized village with a market and some prosperous red-tiled houses. First of all I went to a small cobbler and got him to repair my rucksack which had broken a strap. As I sat in his shop an interested crowd of youngsters collected and speculated on my origin, nationality, destination and secret intentions. They were all very friendly and cheerful. I then strolled up to the Police Station where two Gendarmes were having a quiet game of trick-track. To disarm the suspicion which the French authorities were likely to feel when they heard of my trip, I told them who I was and where I was going, and after half an hour's conversation I pushed on eastwards with a boy to guide me to Arnoun.

In the afternoon we arrived at Arnoun, a small village at the foot of the hill on which is perched the Crusader castle of Beaufort. I made myself known to the Mukhtar, and it was of course at once assumed that I would be his guest. I slept for an hour in the watchman's look-out raised on stilts above the threshing floor where the men were working a new simple hand-worked threshing machine. Up to this year like the Arabs elsewhere they had employed the ancient threshing methods of the Bible with the cattle or horses treading out the grain on the ground—but they were now much pleased with the hand-worked innovation.

In the cool of the evening I walked up to the ruined castle. It is not one of the biggest Crusader castles in these parts but it is in goodish repair (the French have started to do some restoration) and the site is tremendous. The approach from the west is steep and on the east there is an almost sheer drop of over 1,500 feet to the bed of the River Litani below. The

Crusaders carved steps down this enormous precipice to enable them to fetch water but they are not now passable. The view from the top of the castle's battlements is magnificent. Away to the south is Galilee, Hermon to the east, and the Mediterranean to the west; to the north are the vast valleys and mountains of the Lebanon and anti-Lebanon.

I watched the sun set and scrambled down the hill to Arnoun to a good light supper. As a rule when we visit villages in Trans-Jordan a sheep is killed (or at least a few chickens) in honour of the official guest. It was good to have no such formality and to take part in the normal evening meal— lebban (the sour milk), cheese, olives, an omelette, a lot of thin white bread and later some local honey. They were glad to have someone to talk to who brought news of the outside world and the war and of neighbouring territories and would gladly have gone on talking all night (Moslems do most of their sleeping by day in Ramadan) if I had been able to keep awake. But about eleven I couldn't keep my eyes open so I quietly withdrew and went to bed. At seven the next morning they prepared a special breakfast for me in spite of Ramadan (much the same menu as the previous night's dinner) and I was away early, led to the top of the Litani gorge by the small son, Rafiq, who had taken an amused interest in me throughout and made my entertainment his special concern.

It took over half an hour to scramble down to the bottom of the Litani gorge, and it was already hot between the steep cliffs. Luckily I found a man driving a donkey who showed me the quickest path up the eastern face and carried my pack for me on his donkey. It was a long hot climb to the top, but short of the crest a small Christian girl gave me some fresh figs, and when we eventually reached the little village of Qubeia I was glad to accept the invitation of the donkey driver (another Christian) to sleep for half an hour under a fig tree in his small garden while he prepared a simple meal of millet bread (he had no wheat flour) and some honey from the hive in the back yard. He had an enormous and dirty family, one girl rejoicing in the name of Juliet. They were very poor but they had their own store house and a small garden and just now there was plenty of work in the fields. Two of the sons were away serving in the Gendarmerie. Big families like these without land of their own will suffer later when agricultural prices and wages drop and military and police employment are reduced after the war.

It was an easy stage along the high ground into the town of Judeida which is the administrative centre of the southern Lebanon. I had a quick lunch of bread and coffee in a big bare café before setting out again with an Arab who was going part of the way with me. After an hour's walk in the direction of Hermon, I left him and crossed a river and started on the long pull up into the Hermon foothills. It was still the hottest part of the day and about four in the afternoon I lay down tired under a tree by the roadside without much hope of reaching Shubaa, the village at the top of the valley which was to be the base for the final climb up Hermon. Half an hour's sleep made a difference and then two villagers from Shubaa arrived on donkeys and took my pack. After a long drink of cold water at the next village I set off at a good pace ahead of the donkeys to cover the last two hour lap to Shubaa. It was a little cooler as the sun went behind the southern wall of the steep wadi up which the road wound but it was still hot. Round a corner I suddenly came upon a posse of horses led by a mounted French officer, who represented French interests in the southern Lebanon, on his way back to Judeida. He couldn't speak English and I can't manage French so we conversed for five minutes using his Arab officer as an interpreter. I explained who I was in Arabic and that I was going to Damascus by way of the top of Hermon. This statement, together with my solitary and dusty figure and my Arab-headdress, astonished the fat French officer, and as he rode on down the valley and I continued my walk I could hear the amazed and amused comment of his party.

I made good time to Shubaa and when I arrived a small boy showed me a spring where I drank cold water while waiting for the donkeys to catch up. A great river gushes out of the side of Hermon just above Shubaa and waters the terraced gardens which run up both sides of the steep valley. This was the first place, by the way, where I had seen Arab water mills working. There are ruined water mills all over Palestine and

Trans-Jordan but nearly everywhere petrol engines rather than water power are used for milling in these days.

The village of Shubaa is built tier upon tier on the precipitous northern slope of the valley. Only the day before my visit a horse which had missed its footing at the top of the village had fallen a hundred feet to be killed in the valley bed below and its carcase still lay near the steep path. I arrived at the Mukhtar's house to find that he was away attending a court case in a village fifteen miles away but his son Suleiman hospitably invited me in and I was surprised to find the Mukhtar's wife at the top of the steps to receive me. Normally in a Moslem household the women would keep very much to their own quarters but I found that in these southern Lebanese villages they are much freer, sitting with the men at the end of the day and taking an equal part in the talk of the household. Soon after I had sat down the Mukhtar himself returned. He had been told by the French officer that he could expect an odd guest for the night—an Englishman who walked by himself without guide or kit, speaking only bedawi Arabic. I was immediately made at home and the small daughter, Buran, who joked with everyone and was greatly amused by me, soon brought our simple supper, much the same as the night before with some fine apples grown in Shubaa to finish off with.

The Mukhtar has had an odd history. As a very young man he, like many thousand other Lebanese, emigrated to America, where he made a small fortune in a grocery shop near Montreal and then lost it in a slump. He came back soon after the last war and has been in his village ever since. His English he had almost forgotten but he enjoyed an opportunity for airing a few of the words he remembered. He was a talkative fellow occasionally flying into quick tempers but kind and simple. His wife, with her patient and humorous face, was the strong character of the household, and the small mischievous daughter was a special friend of mine. They had quite a big rambling house set into the valley side, with floors of slab slate which reminded me of Cornwall (the whole atmosphere with the talk of farmers and village gossip and local jests was rather like the farm of Lynher). Although the house was big everyone congregated for talk in the guest room with a lovely view over the gardens up the valley. We talked a bit about Canada and Trans-Jordan and marketing difficulties and local politics and as we were tired after our travels we went to bed, the Mukthar on the outer balcony and I on a bed specially made up in the guest room. The family sat on talking.

I had walked about eighty kilometres in two days and before going to bed, I accepted the Mukhtar's pressing invitation to stay the following day in Shubaa leaving the climb up Hermon to the following night.

After breakfast the next morning I walked down with the Mukhtar to attend a funeral in the village. Everyone turned out while the funeral procession was led by with flags and drums and then the relatives of the dead man lined up on one side of the path and the rest of the villagers filed by murmuring their condolences. Quite a number of the villagers came up later for a chat about the war and affairs in Trans-Jordan, Palestine and North Africa. I then strolled along under the giant walnut trees to the Mukhtar's gardens further up the valley where his three smaller sons lived during the summer. These youngsters between seven and fourteen had a tremendous time. They slept under a great tree, and fed on fruit and the bread which their mother brought up to them from the house every few days. They control the irrigation canals, gather the fruit and direct the few extra labourers who come in at harvest time. They dreaded the day when they would have to go back to the village school. One of them, Walid, took me up to the spring head where a cold spurt of water comes out of the hillside straight from the ice and snow of Hermon. We went back for an early lunch and then I tried to get an hour or two's sleep, but as I was put in the bed in the best bedroom I got little peace from bugs. The state beds in village households are almost always to be avoided!

In my honour meat was cooked that evening in a glorious stew and after dinner the little guest room was crowded with visitors who had come to gossip with a stranger. Again it was good to feel away from official responsibility. Often the talk drifted into questions of village disputes and the elections for the Lebanese Cabinet and difficulties of marketing fruit with existing trade restrictions. I noticed that they several times

95

referred to the coming salib (which means the Cross) and I
enquired from a Christian who was sitting by me what the salib
meant. He told me it was the festival which marked the end
of the summer and beginning of autumn and that the Moslems
all know of the feast of salib without realising its meaning. The
story is, so he said, that when Queen Helen having searched
for the Cross eventually found it she ordered a holiday which is
observed to this day and told her followers to light bonfires on
all the hills. He himself still climbed to the hill south of the
village and lit his fire on the appointed day, and he said he
could see other fires far away on the hills of Palestine and
southern Syria.

There were only a few Christian families in Shubaa but my
guide to the top of Hermon was to be a Christian. He was a
huge fellow with a hook nose and a fierce dark face—what I
imagine an Albanian brigand looks like. As a youth he was a
shepherd on Hermon (he now cultivated some land near Dan
at the source of the Jordan) and he knew every track on the
mountain.

After supper we set out. It was a moonless night and we
carried a lantern. He went ahead and all I could see was the
circle of light on the ground ahead as we scrambled and
stumbled up the steep path covered with loose stones. We
stopped after an hour at the last well and filled his water
bottle. It was very hard walking and my pack was an awkward load. It got colder as we went higher and I was exhausted
long before we reached the top. We did the last hour along the
back of the mountain in short stretches of a quarter of an hour
at a time, stopping for short rests. At last just as the waning
moon came up we reached the top after five and a quarter
hours' hard climb. We lit a fire of brushwood but couldn't keep
warm so we sought refuge in a cave and lit another fire. We
tried to sleep but the smoke from the fire drove us out again
just before dawn. The sunrise seen from Hermon on a perfectly
clear day was beyond every expectation. The sun came up a
great red ball out of the eastern Syrian desert and soon the
whole of the great Hauran with its scattered villages and small
patches of gardens was set out below in the morning light. To
the west the hills and valleys of southern Lebanon stretched

General Sir Arthur Wauchope in Nathanya. On his right is Oved Ben Ami; behind him to the left, wearing a topi, is District Commissioner Andrews, assassinated in Nazareth.

Orient Press Photo, Tel Aviv

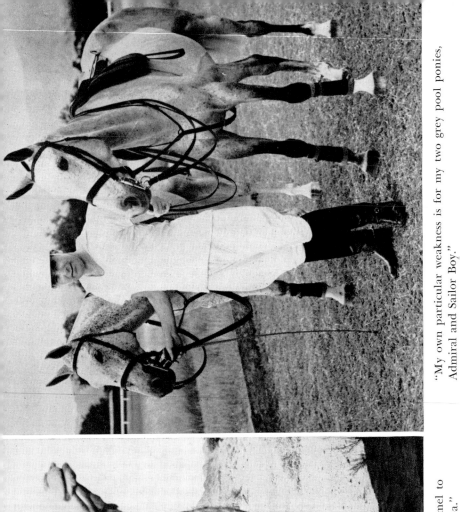

"I would set out from time to time on a camel to continue my explorations of the Wadi Araba."

"My own particular weakness is for my two grey pool ponies, Admiral and Sailor Boy."

A parade in Kingston, Jamaica, with an effigy of the Governor. Mr. Norman Manley, then Chief Minister of Jamaica, and Mrs. Manley are at the right of the saluting base.

Her Majesty the Queen and the Duke of Edinburgh at Kings House, Jamaica, 1953.
At the right of the picture is Sir Alexander Bustamante, Prime Minister of Jamaica.

Sir Winston Churchill in Jamaica, 1953. "What would Michael say about all this?"

Independence day, Nigeria, 1960. "Nigeria has shown the way."

"I went out to meet the people in the villages."

With Sylvia and Cypriot workers at the Salamis excavations, 1960.

With Archbishop Makarios at Government House, Cyprus,
on Independence Day.

"A Colonial Governor who ran out of Colonies."

Joshua Nkomo talking to Sir Patrick Dean and Sir Hugh Foot at the United Nations, 1962

The family at Government House, Nicosia.

away to the sea. The great gardens of Damascus were a dark green smudge against the brown and black of the Hauran plain. Trans-Jordan and Palestine could just be seen to the south. We were thankful when it grew a little warmer in the sun. Hermon is over nine thousand feet and has some snow on it all the year round. Having eaten an apple or two and some Arab bread my guide and I parted—he returning to Shubaa and I seeking a descent to the east in the direction of Damascus. This was by no means easy but I missed my way only once in the rough valleys, and after three and a half hours reached a small Druze village where I slept for half an hour in the Mukhtar's house. I gratefully accepted some water and grapes, answered questions of some suspicious gendarmes who found it difficult to believe that people spent the night on Hermon for pleasure, and pushed on along the road to Damascus. After two and a half hours in the heat of the day I arrived very dusty and footsore at Qatana, sat for a while in an open air Arab café eating bananas, and then gratefully accepted a lift from a Syrian army lorry for the last few kilometres into Damascus.

I had a hot bath, changed and set out for a monster dinner in the Damascus suq. The restaurants of Damascus are famous throughout Arabia, and to do justice to a Damascus dinner in Ramadan, which goes on all night, it is well to have prepared by a walk over Hermon.

*   *   *

The Arab villagers of Palestine and Trans-Jordan lived much the same life as the villagers of southern Lebanon and Syria. They were predominantly Moslem, with a strong Christian minority. They were in fact essentially one people whose country had been split into four by the international intrigues and rivalries following the First World War.

Beyond these settled villages stretched the desert to the east and south. I never knew the desert so well, but I recognised that from the desert came the strength and inspiration of the Arabs, and I was able to spend a year or two in the war years learning something of the bedouin.

I had a car equipped for the desert with a specially high clearance and extra tanks for petrol and water, camp beds, food for a week and two short French cavalry rifles which I had stolen from a French armoury in Syria in 1941. My Arab driver and I didn't carry the guns for protection. The desert was indeed the safest place, much safer than the towns of the Middle East. But many of the bedouin would carry rifles much as an Englishman carries a rolled umbrella in London. It was traditional. One felt a little lost without one. So we went armed too—and sometimes, I am ashamed to say now, we would shoot gazelle from the car as we and they sped over the desert flats. This later became a pursuit for parties of so-called sportsmen from the towns and many herds of the beautiful, bounding gazelle have been decimated. If we were not staying with the Arabs my driver and I would stop wherever we liked at dusk, brew our tea, warm up some army rations, pitch our camp beds beside the car and sleep under the stars. And from Ma'an or Aqaba I would set out from time to time on a camel to continue my exploration of the Wadi Araba. I would usually have two or three mounted Arabs with me. Sometimes I would ride with only one Arab Legion jundi (soldier) of the Desert Patrol.

An Arab Legion jundi and I set out one evening from the Police Post near the site of the ancient city of Petra. We rode through the narrow entrance gorge and passed the red Petra cliffs with the sunset light on the ancient rock-hewn temples, and slept under our sheepskins on the lip of the great Rift Valley. At dawn we led our camels down the steep pass into the valley below, along a path worn deep by countless caravans from the days of Nabatean rule two thousand years ago. Then we rode north that day up the Wadi Araba.

At dusk we saw ahead of us a cloud of dust, and, making some pace to catch up with it, we met three merchants of Medina who were driving their herd of camels to sell them in the Beersheba market.

We stopped for the night and ate our evening meal together. The merchants would reach Beersheba, they hoped, in two weeks' time. They had already taken three or four months in the journey from Saudi-Arabia. They carried no arms and no passports. Their money was in Maria Theresa dollars. They knew more of the progress of the war than I had expected, and their comments on world affairs were original and shrewd. As we talked and drank coffee that night I thought how much the Arabs have to teach us in civilised custom, in a way of life in which courtesy and endurance and courage are the qualities most prized and most admired.

Two days later my Arab Legion jundi and I arrived at the south end of the Dead Sea where the Jews had established a working colony for the extraction of potash from the waters of the sea. We made our camels kneel outside the barbed wire that surrounded the settlement, and I walked through the guarded gate into a different world.

The south end of the Dead Sea is one of the most desolate and one of the hottest places in the world, but the Jews had made it tolerable. I had a cold beer from the refrigerator, read the weekly *Manchester Guardian*, listened to talk of the war, discussed questions of local security, slept a little in the air-conditioned guest house, and then walked back through the barbed wire. My escort and I mounted our protesting camels and, turning our backs on the twentieth century, set off to ride south to the Red Sea.

CHAPTER VII

Nigeria

"Freedom provokes diversity; diversity preserves freedom."
LORD ACTON

MOST of the first fifteen years of my overseas service had been spent with Arabs. My work for the next twelve years was to be with people of mainly African descent in the West Indies and with the Africans of West Africa.

I was unhappy to leave the Arab world. No one lives with Arabs without becoming devoted to them and, although my years in Arab countries had been years of disorder and violence and war, I had understood something of the Arabs' language and religion, and increasingly admired them. I was uneasy about the prospect of starting out in new work amongst entirely different people.

When I speak of Africans, I mean Africans south of the Sahara. The Arabs of North Africa are of course Africans too, and in these days there is sometimes talk of association or alliance between all the States of Africa. But that is a political association. It is, I think, an artificial one; for in fact the Arabs have little in common with the Africans south of the Sahara. Islam long ago extended down the coast of East Africa and crossed the Sahara in the Sudan and into the northern areas of the West African countries. In Nigeria most of the great Northern Region is ruled by Moslem Sultans and Emirs. Nevertheless the gulf is great between the Arabs in their countries bordering the Mediterranean and the Africans of the rest of Africa. The Sahara is a more formidable barrier than any ocean, and when I entered the gates of the walled city of Kano it was like penetrating a new world.

In variety, in complexity and in size the obstacles which faced the huge country of Nigeria at the end of the last war seemed overwhelming. No one knew the true population. It was said to be about thirty-five million; some thought that it was nearer forty million—certainly it was much the largest population of any country in Africa. It had been administered as one only since the beginning of this century and was the size of France and Italy put together.

Its people, Moslems, Christians of every denomination, and pagans, had no common language, religion or national consciousness. The Christian missionaries had shown devotion and courage in bringing rudimentary education and health services to the South, but had never been admitted to the great Moslem North. When I was posted to Nigeria as Chief Secretary in 1947 there was no university and no technical school in the whole country, and in the North, with a population then estimated at about seventeen million, not one secondary school.

There were over two hundred separate languages. Nigeria was a great artificial section of Africa desperately poor, apparently hopelessly divided, gravely handicapped by disease—there were, for instance, three quarters of a million lepers—and bedevilled by superstition and ignorance. There was no central parliament and no Nigerian participation in the making of central policy. In 1945 many people thought that the most Nigeria could hope for was a continuation of paternal administration, a few decades of marking time, at most a slow and steady development of the policy of indirect rule.

But fifteen years later a miraculous advance had been achieved. At midnight on the 1st of October 1960 the green and white flag of the Federation of Nigeria was raised and Nigeria became a self-governing, independent State. The next morning we saw assembled the first Parliament representing a united and free Nigeria.

The opening of Parliament was a glorious scene, witnessed by representatives of nearly every country in the world. Princess Alexandra, representing Her Majesty the Queen and performing her first main State duty with beautiful poise and dignity, read the Queen's speech from the throne. The Prime Minister, Sir Akubakr Balewa, with grave eloquence made a graceful speech in reply. Dr. Azikiwe, now President of Nigeria and then President of the Senate, brought the proceedings to an end in due parliamentary form. The Princess, the

Ministers, the Judges in their scarlet robes and long Queen's Counsel wigs, withdrew, followed by all the members of the great parliamentary assembly—the dignified Northerners in their turbans and long flowing clothes, the sophisticated Yorubas in their splendid robes, and the Easterners in their gay caps and capes which in variety of colours and designs did justice to the freedom of their fertile imaginations.

The Nigerians had won a victory for freedom and friendship. The obstacles had been enormous, but every time during the previous fifteen years when a new crisis in difficult negotiations had been reached the leaders of Nigeria met together determined not to be defeated, resolved to go forward in conciliation and agreement. At conference after conference they had cleared the hurdles with gathering speed and increasing ease. Each advance gave them more confidence. They went from strength to strength in an accelerating momentum of success.

Let no one misjudge or minimise the magnitude of their achievement. To form a free federation is surely the most difficult of all political operations. And never before, except perhaps in India, has a federation been formed by transition from a central bureaucracy to a federal democracy. When federations have been created in the past, in the United States or Canada or Australia for instance, they have usually built on the basis of separate states surrendering to a federal centre some of their powers for the benefit of all. In Nigeria we were engaged on a reverse process—that of the creation of a federal system of government by devolution from the centre. There were no precedents. It was a new venture, a new experiment in political endeavour.

How were the interests of the Regions to be reconciled with the need to achieve a strong central government? What powers must be reserved to the Regions? How was the reluctance of the North to be associated with the South to be overcome? On the other hand, how were fears to be met that the Northern Region, with a population greater than that of the rest of the country put together, would dominate the whole? Most difficult of all, how was the allocation of revenue between the three Regions to be decided? How were the central parliament and the central cabinet to be composed? What was to be the system of election both to the Regional legislatures and to the central Senate and House of Representatives?

On any of these issues the negotiations between the leaders of the three Regions could easily have come to grief. The Nigerian leaders were determined to succeed and at three main conferences between 1951 and 1959 they triumphantly solved every constitutional conundrum and every complicated financial puzzle; they resisted and overcame every selfish, sectional pressure.

What part did the British Government and the British officials take in all this? The Secretaries of State for the Colonies descended from their Whitehall pedestals to lend a hand. First the present Lord Chandos and then the present Lord Boyd presided most successfully over Nigerian constitutional conferences. The Governors played their full part. The present Lord Milverton, who often allowed his intelligence to overcome his delight in pretending to be a cynical reactionary, set things off in the 1946 constitution. Sir John Macpherson was sensitive and quick to see the need to make the main move forward at a critical time; and finally Sir James Robertson, by the warmth and sympathy and joviality of his personality, took all Nigeria into his big, bear-like hug.

British politicians and British officials could not have created a free Nigeria. That was the proud achievement of the Nigerians themselves. What then was the British contribution? It was first in the progressive realisation that it was right that Nigerians should govern themselves—and that it was possible. It was also in the methods and means of attaining the goal. At every stage experts, legal and financial, were readily made available to suggest and advise. But the vital, the essential British contribution was in the timing.

I arrived in Nigeria as Chief Secretary late in 1947. Sir John Macpherson came to take up his post as Governor in 1948. Not long after his arrival we had a vital conference in Government House. The Richards constitution had then been in full effect for little more than a year, and it had been stipulated that it must remain in force unchanged for nine years. We reviewed the whole political situation; we took into account the disorders and the changes which had recently taken place in what was then the Gold Coast. We came to the conclusion that we must at once take a new initiative. The Legislative Council was to meet in August. That seemed the best time to make an announcement. A recommendation was made by telegram to the Colonial Office. There was a quick reply.

On the 17th of August 1948 Sir John Macpherson, addressing the Legislative Council, said:

"The progress already made has been, in my considered view, so rapid and so sound that . . . I propose that, if it is the wish of the Council and of the Country, constitutional changes should be made not at the end of nine years but in the second three-year period which will start at the beginning of 1950."

We were off. It was two and a half years before a new constitution was complete and ready to be put into effect. But now we had the initiative. Nigerian effort was devoted not to dispute and abuse but to the constructive task of deciding what the new constitution should be. We had the people with us.

Early in 1949 the Legislative Council met at Ibadan—in those days the Council met in the Regional capitals in rotation. I set out the list of complicated constitutional questions which had to be decided, and we worked out with the Council the method of consultation with the people by which these questions would be considered. This is what I said about the method to be employed for preparing a new constitution:

". . . We must certainly try to form the best body or bodies for this purpose which can be devised but it would be wrong, in my view, to imagine that everything will depend on the composition of whatever body is established. We must not put our faith in one body alone to the exclusion of other opinion. The solution to be found will and should depend not solely on some specially formed body but on the views and opinions of the people, expressed in many different ways. There is some inclination to believe that all that is necessary is to send a committee like Moses into the mountain and that all the people need to do is to watch and pray—pray that the committee will in due course return from the clouds with the perfect constitution to last for ever, written on tablets of stone. No one can hand over his responsibility in this matter to others. Every Nigerian has a stake in his own country and it is for him by means of village meetings and Divisional meetings and Provincial meetings throughout the country and through the organisation of which he is a member to make his views known. Your Excellency has insisted that there should be the fullest opportunity for public consultation at every level. The Regional Houses in separate resolutions have already made it clear that they are of the same opinion. It is not only the Government and Government officials and members of the Legislative Council and the Regional Houses and the Native Authorities and leaders of public opinion who have a responsibility in this matter. Everyone in Nigeria has a responsibility. It is for us on our part to see that the people are consulted and it is for the people to see that their views are made known."

It was, I believe, the most ambitious plan for public consultation ever undertaken in any colonial territory. And its purpose was of course not only consultation but also the awakening of political awareness in every corner of the country.

Most of the rest of that year the process of consultation continued and in October 1949 a Committee was established to draft the new constitution. There were two Nigerian representatives of each of the Regions on this Committee and I was the Chairman. We completed our work before the end of 1949 and in January 1950 our draft was considered and substantially approved by a General Conference composed of fifty-three members of whom all but three were Nigerians. The proposals recommended by the General Conference were approved by the Colonial Office. The Secretary of State's despatch to the Governor said:

". . . In the view of His Majesty's Government the recommendations which have emerged are of the utmost value. I have been particularly impressed by the wide measure of agreement reached. All who have taken part in the constitutional review are to be congratulated on their contributions and Nigeria is to be congratulated on the results; these have amply justified the initiative which you took in 1948 in proposing that such a review should be undertaken and the decision of the Legislative Council to accept your proposal."

The new constitution introduced in 1951 did not long survive. It was twice amended and greatly improved before the constitution for an independent Nigeria was adopted in 1960. In 1948 we certainly did not hope or expect to go all the way in one jump, but the initiative taken in that year, not in response to public pressure but in advance of it, set the course and set the pace.

I tell the story to illustrate one principle only—and it is the essence of my experience whether in Asia or Africa or the West Indies or anywhere else. The most important thing is to take and to hold the initiative. That is another way of saying that timing is all important. Not to allow frustration to set in. Not to allow opposition to bank up. The people must be given a lead, a hope, an assurance that orderly and constructive effort will be worth while. Once the purpose and the course have been set, and once it has been shown by urgent, practical, fearless effort that there will be no going back and no wavering, target dates and time tables become irrelevant. The direction and the pace are what matter. Everything depends on a clear lead and a sense of urgency in pursuing it.

Nigeria succeeded in this most difficult political operation, in the creation of a federation. And it is in the formation of federations, the bringing together of small states in co-operation, that hope lies in Africa as in other parts of the world. I trust that we may see a federation in East Africa, and a new federation in Central Africa, and one day, after all, a federation in the West Indies. Nigeria has shown the way.

Nigeria's strength and her weakness are in her diversity. The young Englishmen who came out to join the Nigerian Administrative Service were posted to one of the three Regions, the North or the West or the East. They usually stayed in the Region to which they were first sent, for, having learnt Hausa or Yoruba or Ibo, it was obviously wasteful to transfer them to another Region where the main language was different. They consequently became absorbed in one Region and devoted to the people of that Region with a fierce loyalty to them, and they pretended a contempt for the others. An American who came back from touring Nigeria years ago said that if the Africans were to leave Nigeria fighting would break out amongst the British.

To go from Lagos, the capital, to the Northern Region was to enter a very different world. To make a state call on the Sultan of Sokoto or the Emir of Kano or the Shehu of Bornu was to see Moslem courtesy and dignity in a spectacular African setting. I was acting as Governor of Nigeria when I went first to Maiduguri, the capital of the Kingdom of Bornu. There in the great maidan were drawn up hundreds of horsemen, the leaders of the cavalcade dressed, astonishing to see, in medieval chain mail armour with the horses dressed like an illustration from a book on the Crusades (these suits of chain mail armour had been brought, I was told, across the desert from Ethiopia years ago and were much prized in the Northern Emirates). And then I was received with courtly courtesy by the old Shehu of Bornu in his mud palace.

Polo is the national game of the North where the people are natural horsemen. The Emir of Katsina was the best polo player in Nigeria, and when he came to take his place in the Legislative Council at Lagos he would bring a polo team in his car—the team made up of himself, his brother, his secretary and his driver. I remember particularly one polo game we played on the hard fast ground at Katsina. It was during Ramadan, when the Moslems neither eat nor drink from dawn to dusk, and I was surprised that the Emir would play. It was a hard game in the burning heat of the dry wind from the Sahara. The Emir rode as hard as ever and when we had finished, and the strings of ponies were being led back to the walled town kicking up little clouds of dust in the evening light, the Emir could not speak through the red dust on his parched mouth. He wrote down a note inviting us to visit him for coffee later that evening when he had broken his fast. He was a fine polo player, and an enlightened ruler and very modern and progressive in his ideas, a man of restless energy devoted to his million subjects. With them he had the same easy, straightforward, frank relationship which I remembered from watching King Abdulla in Arabia, and none of his subjects, however humble, would hesitate to speak to him straight in the spirit of the brotherhood of Islam.

Very different were the state occasions in the West amongst the Obas and Chief of the Yorubas. I found the Yorubas much the most difficult to understand amongst the peoples of Nigeria. The Northerners have the predominant characteristics of Moslem dignity, courtesy and courage. The Ibos in the East are quick to learn, volatile, uninhibited, gay. The Yorubas are much more complex. They have a long-established system of administration, a complicated set of rules governing the conduct of their government and their lives—a strange combination of what seems to us barbaric custom and personal dignity and political finesse.

It is said that when an Oba has forfeited the confidence of his people the processes of disapproval are put in train in a well understood series of consultations working upwards from village gatherings to the Obas Council. And if by this process of consultation the general weight of public opinion is shown to be dissatisfied with the Oba, all that then takes place is that the appointed member of the council approaches the Oba in full council displaying in his out-stretched hand a parrot's egg. No word is spoken. The Oba and everyone else knows immediately what it means. There is no doubt or argument. When he sees the parrot's egg the Oba must at once go out and commit suicide.

The Yorubas think of everything. Their system includes this simple provision for dealing with tyrants—a system which many peoples in other parts of the world might well envy.

I called one day on the Alafin of Oyo. I was acting as Governor and I was wearing the white uniform suitable for a visit to one of the leading Obas of the country. As I advanced through the lines of councillors and courtiers the Alafin rose to greet me from his stool behind which there was a pair of magnificent elephant tusks. I could not see his face, for over it was a screen of beads. He made a speech of welcome and directed his attendants to present the gifts set aside for me. One of them was a large, live turkey. I have sometimes had to make speeches in difficult circumstances, but high on the list I put the speech of reply I made that morning holding the turkey under one arm. The turkey obviously thought the proceedings odd. As I spoke he turned his head to look me in the eye. His gaze was embarrassingly close and I thought as I continued my formal speech—and feared for my white uniform—that I could see in the turkey's eye a look of contempt. I also thought as I turned from the turkey to the Alafin that I caught, through the strings of beads, a wink of delight at my predicament.

When the Legislative Council met in 1949 in Enugu, the capital of the Eastern Region, Dr. Azikiwe, the leader of the first Nigerian political party, the N.C.N.C., made one of his most violent speeches. He spoke of the tree of freedom being watered by the blood of martyrs. This was altogether too much, and I went for him in reply. What was the point of using such extravagant language? Where was the blood? And where the martyrs? Was he merely indulging in the doubtful luxury of meaningless rhetoric, or had he perhaps some more sinister intent? I warmed to the attack and I thought when I sat down that, although we had often had lively exchanges in the Council before, my strong language on this occasion in his own Eastern capital might have angered him. So after the fierce debate I went out onto the steps of the Enugu House of Assembly. There was Dr. Azikiwe amongst all his supporters with a crowd below him. I went up to him, fearful that perhaps he might openly snub me. I held out my hand, and said that I hoped he bore me no personal ill-will. Everyone round us stopped and watched. He laughed and warmly shook my hand and said he would deal with me in the Council at the first opportunity. Dr. Azikiwe's generous gesture that day made a lasting impression on his followers. Many times in different parts of the world Nigerians have told me how much good the Enugu debate did in setting the standard of public controversy in Nigeria.

One morning as I was going into my office at Lagos I heard a rush and a scuffle behind me and felt a blow in my back. A young man had sprung from behind a pillar and attempted to stab me in the back. The Nigerian messenger with me struck his arm and the blow did me no serious damage, merely grazing my back. Half an hour later I went into the Governor's

Executive Council. The meeting was long, and before it was over I felt a little shaky in reaction. I did not know till the meeting was over that our Nigerian driver had caused so much alarm by picking up the bloody knife and carrying it back to Sylvia at our house, telling her that I had been attacked.

A few days later the Commissioner of Police reported to me on the telephone that my assailant had been caught. I asked him what the man had to say, why had he attacked me. "Well," said the Commissioner, "he says that he really intended to attack the Governor but, having hung about Government House for several days and finding that the Governor left and returned to Government House by car, he decided to make do with the Chief Secretary."

I called the Governor and said that I wanted to make a brief report and then to tell him a short story. The report was that the man who had attacked me really intended to go for the Governor. And then I told him the story. When the historian Macaulay was at Cambridge he got involved in an election riot and a man threw a dead cat which hit Macaulay full in the face. The man who had thrown it shouted, "I am sorry, Mr. Macaulay, I meant it for the candidate." Macaulay replied: "I wish you had meant it for me, and hit him."

After the preliminary enquiry the man who had attacked me stood his trial. The case had naturally attracted public interest. It obviously had racial and political implications. And when I went down to give my evidence there was a large crowd outside the Court in the centre of Lagos. The Court itself was packed. I went to the witness box. As I stood to give my evidence I looked round and noted that I was the only person in that crowded Court who was not an African. The Judge in his wig was a Nigerian. The prosecuting Counsel came from what was then the Gold Coast. We had English as well as African Crown Counsel but on this occasion it happened to be an African who conducted the prosecution. The defending Counsel was a Nigerian and all the Court officials and the police on Court duty that day were Africans. The evidence was heard. The case was clear. The verdict was "guilty". The Judge imposed the maximum sentence for attempted murder, fifteen years' imprisonment. Subsequently the case went to appeal where it was reviewed by three English Judges. They reduced the sentence to one of seven years' imprisonment.

I like to tell that story in England and America to show that Africans were perfectly capable of administering justice without fear or favour or without regard to race or politics or anything else except the requirements of equal justice.

Many years afterwards my brother Dingle was excluded from Nigeria by administrative decision of the Nigerian Government, and the ban prevented him from defending Chief Enaharo. I believe that the Nigerian Government did itself nothing but harm by this decision, but I have no more reason to doubt the integrity and the impartiality of the Nigerian Courts now than I had fifteen years ago.

Amongst Nigeria's main assets are an understanding of the principles of the rules of law and just administration and representative government. Its strength in maintaining those principles will depend on the calibre of its leaders. In Africa generally, one of the most striking developments of modern times is the emergence of leaders of such high quality. Once released from the impediments of poverty and given opportunities of education, faced with the enormous responsibilities of leadership often in circumstances of appalling difficulty, so many Africans come at one bound into the first rank of ability by any standards in the world. Men like President Nyerere of Tanganyika and Prime Minister Obote of Uganda and Tom Mboya of Kenya and Kenneth Kaunda of Northern Rhodesia have already made their mark. They have stepped with youthful confidence and dignity onto the stage of world events, and in producing leaders of the highest capacity Nigeria is in the forefront of African advance.

Sir Abubakr Balewa, the Prime Minister of Nigeria, has risen from being a village schoolmaster to become a statesman of the finest accomplishments. Frail in build, almost ascetic in appearance, charming and at ease in manner, a magnificent orator by any standards, he is a man of clear brain and absolute integrity, a born leader—tough in negotiation, patient in council and courageous in action.

I think, too, of Kenneth Dike, the Vice-Chancellor of Ibadan University. I knew him first when he was fresh from academic distinctions as a young historian in London. I visited him in Ibadan in 1960 when he had recently become head of the University, facing calmly and confidently his huge task of doubling and redoubling the first university of Nigeria on which the future of Nigeria so much depends. Still in his forties, he brings to his exacting task a freshness and an originality and a combination of humility and courage which have won him high respect amongst all sections of the Nigerian nation and in the wider academic world beyond.

What a great happiness it was to meet my old friend Chief Simeon Adebo when he came to the United Nations as the Head of the Nigerian Delegation in 1962. I had known and worked closely with him during my years in Nigeria. Steady and thoughtful in judgment, quick in humour, generous and fair, he is one of the finest Christians I have ever met. I trust him much more than I trust myself. A man I should be very proud to serve and to follow.

The independence of Nigeria has given men like these their chance; and it is men like these who are making the name of Nigeria respected in Africa and in the world.

Nigeria faces all kinds of trouble and difficulties. There are stresses and strains all the time, and they will continue. Government action in Nigeria will always necessarily be a matter of compromise, of accommodation between its different peoples and interests and between the old and the new. The misgivings and the suspicions and the tribal and religious rivalries will persist. But the stresses and strains can be turned to use as checks and balances. The hope lies in Nigerian leadership; and the start made by Nigeria in independence gives reason to believe that leadership of a very high order will not be lacking.

CHAPTER VIII

Jamaica

"Thou shalt laugh at all disaster,
And with wave and whirlwind wrestle."

Longfellow

I

THE worst thing about a hurricane is that you have to wait for it. Everyone knows days before that it is a danger. Every hour the radio reports on its course. The all-too-familiar precautions are taken. The hospitals and the Red Cross workers and the welfare organisations get ready. Food supplies are laid in. Appeals go out for everyone to go home and take cover. Doors and windows are barricaded. And when everything has been done you just have to wait, and then at long last when the time approaches, to listen.

Hurricane Charlie (each hurricane of the year is given a name by the meteorologists) was first observed on the morning of Wednesday, the 15th of August 1951, a thousand miles away near Martinique in the Eastern Caribbean. All that day and all the next we followed its course. It prowled slowly westwards, gathering force and savagery as it came. Unpredictably, its direction shifted. At one time it looked as if it was destined to hit Puerto Rico and Cuba, but by the afternoon of the 17th of August it veered again and made straight for Jamaica.

We had had an emergency meeting of the Executive Council that morning. Everything we could do in advance had been done. When we dispersed we had an eerie feeling of being suspended in unreality. We counted the hours ahead. We looked up at the sky and out to sea. Everything was very still, overcast. It seemed impossible that within a few hours hell would break loose. As the long wait dragged on we felt a sense of foreboding, and helplessness.

Sylvia went to finish her work on the preparation of medical supplies at Red Cross Headquarters. We estimated that the storm couldn't hit the island till about seven o'clock. She promised to be back well before then. I went to the Radio Station to broadcast to the people of Jamaica.

I finished the broadcast and hurried to my car. We started back on the short journey to Kings House. The streets were deserted. Then suddenly at Half Way Tree, the wind started. Branches, refuse, wooden shingles from roofs, were blown across the road and dashed against the car. We got as far as Kings House gates. A great tree was down ahead of us across the drive. I told the driver to leave the car and run to his home. As I got out of the car I was blown over on my knees. The wind screamed. The rain, horizontal and blinding, drenched me to the skin in a second. If it had not been for great flashes of lightning I would not have been able to see my way at all. I had to climb over several felled trees. It must have taken ten minutes to crawl to the door of Kings House which I had left warm and dry in good order less than an hour before. The Kings House servants had been sent home to look after their families. The big house was deserted. I shouted to the children. Where was their mother? They didn't know. She hadn't come back. She was somewhere out in the storm—no means of knowing where.

The children, our four and two of their small friends staying with them, were frightened. Benjie, then not yet two years old, was crying. I put mattresses on the floor of one inner room and crowded the children all together. Water came in through the windows and through the roof. There was no light, no water in the taps, no hope of a telephone working. A river was running down the main staircase. I looked out of one window and in a flash of lightning as bright as daylight saw the great royal palms sixty feet tall banging their heads on the lawn and then suddenly, released for a second by the terrific force of the wind, whipping back like fishing rods. Nature had gone wild. Strange forces were let loose and sweeping the every-day world away. Half horrified and half fascinated I wanted to shout with a mad sense of elation.

I hadn't known it at the time but even as I spoke on the radio that night the hurricane had already hit the parish of St. Thomas in the south-east of the island, and dealt a crippling blow. Villages on the coast and hill settlements felt the full force. The shacks of the poor people were blown clean away. Crops and cultivations were obliterated. Sixty-two people died in St. Thomas alone in the fury of the night. A woman who had come from the Yallahs valley to Kingston to shop couldn't get back; when she did she found that five of her six children had been washed away and drowned in the torrent which had swept through their home. The people of the village of Llandewy rushed from their houses to the Methodist Church, but the church collapsed and killed the huddled throng inside. Nearly every village and valley of the parish had some tragedy to tell.

A little later the eye of the hurricane passed just south of the capital city of Kingston, the wind reaching velocities of more than 125 miles an hour. At the first impact of the storm the city was plunged into darkness as power lines were cut off. Raging torrents swept along the gully courses to the sea. In the huge harbour, wind and waves drove vessels from their moorings and sent them crashing against wharves and beaches. Four ships were sunk with sixteen seamen in them drowned, and three ships blown onto the land. In the city—and most of all in the slum areas—buildings collapsed, thousands of trees were blown down in a tangled network of high-tension cables and telephone poles and wires. Fifty-four people in the city died in that night's nightmare. The ancient pirate city of Port Royal at the entrance to Kingston Harbour was entirely destroyed except for the church and the seventeenth century Fort Charles and the shell of the old naval hospital where a thousand people sought shelter. Property damage in Kingston was estimated at well over twelve million pounds. More than 50,000 people were homeless, most of them without the means to maintain themselves. Food crops had been destroyed, coconut trees lay flat on the ground in even rows, scarcely a banana tree was left standing in the whole island.

Sylvia made her way back to Kings House early in the morning after the hurricane had gone. She and Sergeant Stevenson, one of the Kings House drivers, had taken refuge in a small house which had scarcely stood against the beating of the storm. When we surveyed the damage and the wreckage that morning and when reports of devastation started to come in from St. Thomas and St. Andrew and Spanish Town and from a hundred villages we felt that all hope of progress and prosperity in Jamaica had been shattered.

But a year later when we looked back on all the hard work and its results we could say that the hurricane had been turned from a curse into a blessing. Everyone had forgotten divisions and differences and had worked with a will first on relief and then on the huge task of reconstruction. Voluntary contributions to the Hurricane Relief Fund from all over the world brought in three-quarters of a million pounds, and nearly five million pounds were given by the British Government mainly in free grants and the rest in interest-free loans. New housing schemes were started and an ambitious Farm Recovery Scheme put in hand. A stimulus was given to new development, and the impetus carried Jamaica into a new era of economic expansion. A year after the hurricane, agricultural production in everything except coconuts approached the pre-hurricane level. By the end of 1952 the new planting encouraged by the Farm Recovery Scheme had led to a level of production far greater than before the storm. Within eighteen months of the hurricane the rate of banana exports was double that before the hurricane. And what was more, the Farm Recovery Scheme, based on subsidy to individual farmers in support of improvement of their holdings under expert direction, had set the pattern for the Farm Improvement Scheme which became one of the main methods of raising agricultural production and productivity in subsequent years.

A hurricane can be a shattering, a crippling blow. I am appalled to think of the terrible consequences of the damage done in October 1963 in Haiti and in Cuba by hurricane Flora. But Jamaica showed in 1951 how a national calamity can be turned to an opportunity, not merely for recovery but for advance not previously thought conceivable. Several things were necessary. Generous outside aid; that we received from so many sources but principally from the Government and people of Great Britain. Honest administration; that we had in the experienced Jamaica Civil Service. A rallying of voluntary effort; that we had in abundance and a strong national committee including representatives of both political parties and all the Churches administered the relief funds. But most important of all was the determination of the ordinary people of Jamaica of all classes and categories not to give up, to fight back, to help each other, to plant and build again, to plan and win. The 1951 hurricane was for the people of Jamaica something like Dunkirk was to England.

The politicians say that the beginning of modern Jamaican nationalism was in the labour disorders of 1938. That was the start of a revolt against poverty and social hopelessness and political subservience. But Jamaican patriotism also had part of its origin, as it showed its strength, in 1951 when the Jamaicans rose as one people to the challenge of the hurricane.

I returned to Jamaica as Governor in April 1951. It was five months later that the hurricane hit the island, and the next year was mainly devoted to the work of relief and recovery and reconstruction.

I had been in Jamaica before as Colonial Secretary from 1945 to 1947 and had learnt to love the island and its people then.

The charm and strength of Jamaica are in her variety. Although only a hundred and fifty miles long and, at its widest point, only about fifty miles across, it would not be possible in a lifetime to know the whole island thoroughly, and there are parts of the Cockpit country still uninhabited except for the coney and the wild pig, and still virtually unexplored. Every valley is different; every one of the island's fourteen Parishes has its own special character. There is little in common, for instance, between the wide plains of the south and west with their tens of thousands of acres of sugar cane and the stone walls and rolling pastures along the north coast or the steep coffee plantations of the Blue Mountains. Every bay and every valley has its own beauty. And while bathers bask on the beaches a roaring wood fire is welcome even on a midsummer evening in the Great Houses of the high mountains.

Fortunately for Jamaica its crops are equally diverse. When Columbus first discovered Jamaica in 1494, and the Spaniards then exterminated the peaceful Arawaks, there were, strangely enough, few crops and probably no food trees and no animals, and in the early days one of the most pressing problems was to find means of feeding the small population. It is difficult now to believe that this was so only three or four hundred years ago, for nearly every tropical and subtropical crop and fruit now flourishes, and one of the main sources of food is from the trees including the breadfruit (brought to Jamaica by Captain Bligh of H.M.S. *Bounty* fame), the banana, the mango, the ackee and the avocado pear, all of which were imported from overseas. Jamaica now depends on a wide variety of crops including sugar and bananas and coconuts and citrus and rice and cocoa and coffee and potatoes and yams, as well as fine herds of cattle which can supply the island's full needs in beef and milk.

This diversity is not limited to the countryside and the crops and the climate. Although most of the people are of African descent there are many other nationalities represented. There are English farmers, a few of them descendants of the early English settlers who came to Jamaica in the days of Cromwell or Charles II. There are Indians and Syrians and Chinese. The variety is not only in racial origin but also in character and temperament. Nowhere I know in the world is there such a variety of people in such a small compass or such a mixture, and nowhere does racial origin matter less.

The Jamaicans have a beautiful English dialect of their own, with a kind of Welsh lilt to it. Sylvia, with her quick, musical ear, could pick it up and imitate it; I had great difficulty in understanding the market women, for instance, as I passed them on mountain roads carrying their fruit and vegetables in great baskets on their heads, and I never trusted myself to try to speak like the Jamaican country people. But it was a great help to work in a country where the only language was English. When I was dealing with Arabs I was handicapped by having to communicate with them in a language which I laboriously studied for nearly fifteen years but which I knew I should never be able to master fully. And in Nigeria, where there are some two hundred separate languages, I was frustrated by not being able to stop in a village or by the roadside and speak to the people.

The fact that I could speak and be readily understood everywhere in Jamaica, from little gatherings in remote hill villages to big formal meetings in the towns, made it possible to enter public life in a way which had been impossible in Arabia or Africa. The Jamaicans are great orators, and they dearly like public speaking. A Governor was expected to make several speeches a week, and by means of radio talks he could be in close touch with Jamaicans throughout the island. There was no barrier between us.

I had one particular tie of understanding with Jamaicans which gave me a special sense of close association with them. With all their gaiety and warm-heartedness and the quickness of their reactions and affections, they are a deeply religious people. When I was in Cyprus in 1945 and first heard of my transfer to be Colonial Secretary in Jamaica I at once sent word to my father. I knew how happy he would be to learn of my promotion, and I hoped for some word of congratulation and commendation. The telegram came back—"Glad you are going to Jamaica. There is a strong Methodist community there." There was hope for me yet!

I must at once explain, as I always do to a Methodist audience, that I certainly cannot claim to be a good Methodist. My life at Cambridge and since then has been disreputable. But the Methodists of Jamaica took charge of me. I became anxious not to disappoint them. In my public as well as my private life I was concerned to live up to what they expected of me. Their leader, Hugh Sherlock, became my closest friend. The Methodists of Jamaica made a much better man, and a better Governor of me.

Most Sundays Sylvia and I and the children would go to the crowded Coke Church, the principal Methodist Church in Jamaica. Our second son, Oliver Isaac (called Oliver after Oliver Cromwell, in whose time Jamaica was captured from the Spaniards, and Isaac after my father), was born in Jamaica in 1946 and christened in Coke Church; and our daughter, Sarah Dingle (named after my Cornish grandmother) was confirmed there before we left in 1957. And when we were not in our beloved Coke Church on a Sunday we would visit the Churches of other denominations and we were most welcome

in all of them. The Nonconformists are strong in Jamaica—
it was Nonconformists who had led the campaign in the
island for emancipation from slavery early in the last century—
and our association with the Churches gave us a close fellowship with Jamaicans. It was a fellowship which united us and
uplifted us as a family.

I first arrived in Jamaica in 1945 to be Colonial Secretary,
and within a few months of my arrival, I acted for Sir John
Huggins, the Governor, when he went on several months'
leave. I was transferred to Nigeria in 1947, but I came back
early in 1951, this time to serve nearly seven years with the
proud title of Captain General and Governor-in-Chief in and
over Jamaica and her Dependencies.

So I have spent nearly a third of my working life in Jamaica.
I know the Jamaican people better, I often think, than any
other people—including the English. I am proud to think of
myself as a Jamaican by adoption. Of all the experiences of
my life none was more refreshing or absorbing or exacting
than that of being fully identified with the people of Jamaica
at the critical time when she was advancing at an accelerating
pace towards her coming of age in independence.

When I had served for five years as Governor my term of
office was extended for another two years. This is what I said
to the people of Jamaica when I heard that news:

"We think of the many things we can continue to enjoy. We
love to go to Coke Church on a Sunday morning where our
Jamaican son Oliver was christened eight years ago. The
family likes to go up to the cool quiet of Irish Town for a
few weeks every summer, and to cook our own evening meal
on a coal pot in the garden. We like, when we haven't got
too many visitors, to dine at night under the stars on the
little balcony which is our own private and favourite place.
My wife gets special pleasure from the Kings House gardens
and from her regular Monday morning tour of the gardens
with Mr. Downes. My own particular weakness is my
affection for my three grey horses—Admiral and Sailor
Boy which I bought four years ago in St. Elizabeth, and the
little mare I got from Sir Alfred D'Costa. She is apt to get

over-excited, but when I can hold her I still claim that she is the best polo pony in the island.

I go out every morning for a ride through the lovely Kings House pastures and see the sun come up over the Blue Mountains—a daily preview of paradise.

All this sounds like sheer joy, and so it is. Of course there is more to it than that. There is the stream of red boxes and piles of correspondence. There is always an anxiety to go faster and do better, and sometimes there is depression and disappointment, and occasionally set-backs and deadlocks. Speeches to be made and no time to prepare for them, guests to be entertained and no chance to talk to them, things going wrong, and urgent things forgotten, and mistakes made and disputes and differences to be resolved, and injustices, some of which one can't hope to put right, and irresponsibility and hardship and ignorance—and poverty enough to break your heart.

All these things make up our daily life and all the time there is the need to keep clear in one's mind the main purpose of it all.

My wife constantly tells me that what matters most is the purpose of creating good homes with children brought up with the affection of a mother and a father. No doubt she is right.

For myself there are two purposes which I set above all others. First that the people of the British West Indies should show that they can govern themselves well. It isn't just a matter of casting off an out-of-date Colonial system. It isn't negative. It isn't destructive. It is the positive aim of showing that West Indians in every sphere of national activity can govern themselves in a way which can be an envy to our neighbours and an example to all—with freedom and fairness and fearlessness and faith in themselves. I am convinced that we can do it.

The second purpose is even more exciting and important—and it is a purpose in which we in the West Indies can lead the world—the purpose of showing that people of different races can live and work together freely and equally, respecting each other, trusting each other, defending each other, helping each other.

A Start in Freedom

You know, in these days nearly everyone says that they believe in racial equality. They pay lip-service to it, but great numbers of people in many parts of the world don't really believe in it at all. They don't think it can work. There are many who secretly don't even want it to work. We here in the West Indies have a wonderful opportunity to prove that the brotherhood of man is not an empty phrase or an idealist's delusion but an exciting, immediate possibility —a practical adventure which can and will and must succeed.

I believe that it will succeed because we build on the sure foundations of individual freedom and equal justice and democratic practice. I as an Englishman know very well how many faults and failures there have been in England's long history. But some of the finest things that the world has ever known have come from England. We see them here in our religious life and our judicial processes and our education and our form of government—in our Churches and Courts and Schools and in our University and in our Parliamentary system. It is my conviction that these things will not only remain but will thrive and flourish in the fertile soil of the British West Indies.

I passionately believe in the course which has been set. I feel a confident faith in the capacity of the people of the British West Indies to succeed in the purposes on which we are agreed.

The fact that I and my family can continue to live and work with you and to share in the adventure on which we are engaged and to serve you humbly to the utmost of our ability is something for which with all our hearts we thank God."

Amongst the happiest of our experiences in Jamaica was the entertainment of a stream of visitors. Kings House was a hotel. I made this comment in speaking to the Jamaica Hotel Association:

"It is odd how long the popular delusion persists that in Jamaica the Governor is paid a salary. This, of course, is not so. The Governor receives only an inadequate contribution towards the maintenance of an official guest house. There are hotels in Jamaica which are more luxurious than Kings House. There are hotels where the society is more exotic and aristocratic. But I am glad to say that the bookings at Kings House nevertheless remain brisk—particularly in the tourist season. Though there are no doubt a few dissatisfied guests, I think that it can be claimed that the general view is that Kings House compares favourably with the average run of guest houses. It is, after all, quiet and respectable and it is cheap—and that claim cannot be made by all the hostelries of the island."

We had guests of all kinds, Heads of State, President Tubman of Liberia, President Magloire of Haiti, President Samoza of Nicaragua and Governor Munoz of Puerto Rico. Adlai Stevenson came to stay with us. Sir Anthony Eden came for three weeks to recover from his breakdown after Suez. The Earl of Athlone and Princess Alice came often, the Princess to visit the West Indies University of which she is Chancellor. Princess Margaret spent five days at Kings House in 1955. Winston Churchill came for three weeks when he was Prime Minister. I told this story afterwards:

"Permit me to tell you a personal story about something which happened only a few yards away at the top of King Street. When I knew that the Prime Minister of England was to visit Jamaica I wondered what reference, if any, he would make to other members of my family. I myself have followed the straight and narrow path of official life, but all my family are politicians and all of them have at one time or another been political opponents of Sir Winston Churchill. Some members of my family are respectable Liberals—but there is one goat amongst the sheep. There is one, Michael Foot, whose political beliefs are not dissimilar from those of our present Chief Minister.

Well, I wondered what the Prime Minister would have to say about him. You can imagine what a relief it was when the Prime Minister in the whole of his first week in Jamaica made no reference whatsoever to any of my political relatives. He didn't even refer to the fact that I had any.

Then came the great day when Sir Winston Churchill was received with such overwhelming delight by the people of Kingston. We drove through the streets to the deafening roar of the wildly enthusiastic crowds. The Prime Minister climbed onto the back of the car. He waved his hat and his cigar. He gave the "V" sign. The crowd went wild, and as we came up King Street, the climax of that great warmhearted unforgettable welcome by a hundred thousand people was reached. The Prime Minister leant down to speak to me. I wondered what he would say at that thrilling moment. Scarcely could I hear his words above the din of acclamation. He said, 'I wonder what Michael would say about all this.' "

The Queen and the Duke of Edinburgh came to Jamaica at the start of their round-the-world Commonwealth tour in 1953.

"And as we drove through on Wednesday on the hundred-mile drive from Montego Bay to Spanish Town and then, on Thursday, on the ten-mile drive through the streets of Kingston and St. Andrew there was a cry that came like a wave across the Island. At first I couldn't quite hear what it was the people were calling out more than anything else, and then having heard it once I heard it again and again—amongst the little groups of country people along the road and in the Parish capitals and in Spanish Town and then up and down the crowded streets of the capital—the cry that came like a wave across the Island breaking with the Royal progress was the cry of 'Sweet, Sweet.' I suppose that that word is more commonly used in Jamaica than I had realised. Certainly that was the word that came immediately to thousands of country and townspeople as they caught the unforgettable sight of the Queen and the Duke smiling their pleasure at the Jamaica welcome. Whenever I remember the Royal visit to Jamaica that cry will come back to me, 'Sweet Queen. Sweet Lady.' What a lovely Jamaican phrase!"

II

"To make a government requires no great prudence; settle
the seat of power, teach obedience, and the work is done. To
give freedom is still more easy. It is not necessary to guide, it
only requires to let go the reins. But to form a free government,
that is to temper together these opposite elements of liberty
and restraint in one consistent work, requires much thought,
deep reflection, a sagacious, powerful and refining mind."

EDMUND BURKE

The problems facing Jamaica at the end of the last war were
indeed formidable. How could the patriotism of all Jamaicans
be mobilised in such a way that the people could go forward
united into the uncertain future of self-government? How
could the economy of the country be strengthened and the
terrible poverty in the slums of the towns and on the steep and
eroded hill holdings be alleviated? How could the means be
found to replace the disgraceful conditions in many of the
hospitals, schools and poor houses? Above all, how could the
problem of rapidly growing population be tackled? And what
hope was there of fulfilling the dream that Jamaica would join
with Trinidad and Barbados and the Leeward and Windward
Islands to form a free federation?

In political advance, the first big step had been taken in 1944
when Jamaica was amongst the first of the British colonies to
achieve full adult suffrage.

A great deal is said these days about adult suffrage, about
"one man one vote". Let me state my own strong conviction on
that.

It may be expedient and it may often be justified to proceed
step by step. Restrictions on the franchise are sometimes de-
sirable as power is gradually transferred from a privileged
minority to the whole population. Temporary restrictions on
the franchise may well be the price to be paid for orderly
progress, for confidence in investment and for national unity.
But it is a delusion, I maintain, to believe that a man or
woman is incapable of exercising the vote because he or she is
poor or has had no schooling. And the delusion becomes an
intolerable deceit when it is put forward by those whose real

purpose is to enable a privileged class or a dominant race to hold on to power.

There were people in Jamaica who feared the consequence of a free franchise and prophesied dreadful disasters. But their gloomy prophecies proved groundless. In fact we can now clearly see that to have withheld the full suffrage would have invited a far greater danger—the danger of frustration and resistance and the still greater danger of splitting the people between the haves and the have-nots.

I am convinced by experience in the West Indies and in Africa that restrictions on the franchise, whether by property or income or literacy tests, except as a temporary measure, are fundamentally wrong. In Jamaica the people who would have been excluded from the vote by a restricted franchise were some of the best people in the island—the sturdy, independent, self-respecting people of the hills. Had restrictions in the franchise been maintained political power would have been withheld from the countryside and handed to the towns. But why should clerks be enfranchised and cultivators excluded? The illiterate hill cultivator of Jamaica is just as capable as anyone else in the world of exercising the basic function of democracy, the function of choosing whom he wishes to speak for him. The fact that a man or woman is poor and illiterate makes it more and not less necessary that he should have the right to choose. The vote is to him not a luxury but a necessity. It is well to remember Lord Acton's famous comment:

"Laws should be adapted to those who have the heaviest stake in the country, for whom mis-government means not mortified pride or stinted luxury, but want and pain and degradation and risk to their own lives and to their children's souls."

Some people imagine that there is somewhere a race of supermen capable of making up their minds on the whole range of the issues, now so various and complicated, which confront a modern state. I have not yet met such paragons of political and economic judgment. I don't believe they exist. I myself

am certainly not capable of forming sound decisions on all
the problems that face my country. But what I am capable of
doing is deciding on the man I want to represent me. That is
the essence of democracy. The illiterate hill farmer of Jamaica
is just as capable of making that essential decision as I am.

So in Jamaica in 1944 the first main hurdle in constitutional
advance had been surmounted, and every Jamaican man and
woman has since had the right to vote. But the 1944 constitution did not attempt to introduce a system of full self-government. Ultimate power was still concentrated in the hands of the
Governor, and the Government Service which was responsible
to him alone. The elected Legislature had the power to make
laws and authorise expenditure, but it could be overruled by
the Governor. The Governor was required to refer questions
of policy to his Executive Council in which there was an equal
balance between elected Ministers on the one hand (in fact,
although they were called Ministers, they had at that stage no
executive power at all) and the official and nominated members of the Council on the other. But in the Executive Council
the Governor's ultimate authority was also complete since he
had the casting vote.

This system of a combination of adult suffrage with a com-
posite Executive Council, and with the Governor still holding
final authority, had survived from 1944 until I returned to
Jamaica as Governor in 1951. It was a useful system of transition while elected representatives gained experience, but it
was dangerous. The so-called Ministers had participation in
government but no real responsibility. They could claim credit
for what went well, but blame the Governor for what went
wrong. To that extent and for a time it suited them well, but
the danger was that the transitional system would be retained
too long, and would create a habit of irresponsibility.

There was no strong public pressure to change it. Indeed,
many sections of opinion, particularly amongst the landed and
professional classes, were against any forward move. They knew
they couldn't go back, but they feared to go forward. It seemed
to me when I returned in 1951 that it was urgently necessary
to break out of this halfway house of timid compromise. I set
myself the first task of working out with the political leaders of

both parties the next constitutional move. We got down to work at once. Within two years in general agreement we had a new constitution in effect. Power had been shifted from the Governor to the elected Ministers.

There have been constitutional changes since 1953, the most important being the withdrawal of the Governor from Executive Council by the changes approved just before I left Jamaica in 1957, but it was the 1953 change which gave Ministers executive authority, and, most important of all, gave the elected Ministers a majority in the Council. Thus it was that the three main steps in Jamaican constitutional advance were taken in 1944, when adult suffrage was introduced; nine years later in 1953, when for the first time the elected Ministers took control of policy; and nine years after that, when, in August 1962 Jamaica attained full independence. About two decades in the processes of transition from colonial status to independence. Too long? It could have been faster. But in those two decades Jamaica has learnt and digested the main lessons—faith in parliamentary government and in an impartial Civil Service and Judiciary and recognition of the need for a nationalism which transcends both party and race.

The next principal problem of Jamaica was economic. The economic history of the island, like that of so many colonial territories, has been like a game of snakes and ladders. Over past years there had been an occasional ladder due to sudden and temporary increases in the prices paid for such crops as sugar, bananas or coffee, but there had been longer and more frequent snakes. Price slumps, hurricanes and agricultural disease have repeatedly knocked the whole economy of the island endways. How could the curse of instability of price of agricultural exports be overcome? How could provision be made against destruction by hurricane? How could the standards of cultivation, particularly in the small holdings on the hills, be raised? How could industry be encouraged? How could development capital be attracted to the island? Jamaica has since the last war performed wonders in tackling these problems; indeed within the past two decades there is probably no country in the world which has done more to improve its output, income and standard of living.

There was, however, one basic social problem which should dominate politics and economics and everything else in Jamaica. Unfortunately it does not. It is the population problem. It is the problem of how this small island can hope to survive, not against outside attack or political subversion within or hurricanes or market collapse, but against the single danger of too many Jamaicans being born. It is this which threatens to sweep away all political and economic achievements like sandcastles before an incoming tide.

In 1870 the population of Jamaica was only about half a million. In 1930 it was just over a million. Now it is well over a million and a half. At the present rate of increase it will be two million in 1970 and three million before the end of the century. Everyone who lives in Jamaica likes to forget, shelve or avoid this. And yet everyone who seriously considers it secretly knows that it is far the most important problem of all.

Early in the last century William Knibb, the Baptist Missionary, with other Nonconformist Ministers, had campaigned for freeing the slaves and had been persecuted for his efforts. At last the great day came when the labours of the emancipators were to be rewarded, and the slaves were to be free at midnight. That evening William Knibb preached in his church in Falmouth on the north coast of Jamaica. It was a packed congregation. The crowd outside the church spread as far as he could see through the open windows of the church. Opposite to the pulpit was a great clock, and as the service proceeded the congregation turned from the preacher to watch the clock. Excitement rose as midnight approached. Then as the hand of the great clock came round to midnight, William Knibb threw his arms in the air and cried: "The monster is dead." The cry was taken up by the congregation and by all the people gathered outside. Messengers ran through the hill villages of all the north of Jamaica carrying the cry, "The monster is dead."

But the influence of slavery persists to this day. Slavery wiped out whatever social system the African slaves originally possessed, and the slaves were forbidden to adopt European marriage. Slavery therefore created a society in which for the great mass of the people there was no alternative to promiscuity. Slavery was the direct cause of a situation which strongly persists more than a hundred years since slavery was abolished —a situation in which marriage is still regarded as a privilege of the well-to-do and beyond the reach of ordinary working people, in which a woman is looked upon with contempt and called a mule until she has given birth to her first illegitimate child. Jamaica has an illegitimacy rate of 70 per cent, possibly the highest illegitimacy rate in the world, and, as a result, thousands of Jamaican children scarcely know their parents and are left to the care of aunts and grandmothers. The monster of slavery created a problem which still makes all the other problems of the island seem insignificant.

When I left Jamaica in 1957 it was possible to look back on a decade of rising production and rapidly accelerating economic advance. The Commonwealth Sugar Agreement had given the principal industry of Jamaica a new security and confidence. Markets for other main exports such as bananas, coffee, citrus and coconuts had been steady at good prices. Land Authorities were created to tackle areas of special agricultural difficulty. An Agricultural Development Corporation did excellent work specially in encouraging and undertaking cultivation of rice. The Farm Development Plan was put into operation to help and guide the smaller cultivators. And while agricultural progress was healthy there was spectacular advance in industry. An Industrial Development Corporation was set up and new legislation granting tax incentives to attract capital for investment in industry was passed. The tourist industry boomed. Most striking of all was the development of the bauxite industry in which some two hundred million dollars of United States and Canadian capital were invested in less than ten years. The value of exports rose from £5 million in 1945 to £33 million ten years later. The value of imports in the same period rose from £10 million to £45 million. Government revenue much more than doubled.

The decade was one of astonishing economic progress. Everything conspired to increase the pace. We had a combination of circumstances of amazing good fortune. Our schemes of agricultural and industrial development all prospered. As for the danger of hurricanes, we introduced self-supporting statutory schemes under which by cesses on production every coconut tree and every banana tree in the island was insured to its full value. The main exporting industries built up large reserves. Many new light industries were established. The enormous investment in the bauxite industry and the heavy new revenue which that industry brought to the island were windfalls of astonishing proportions.

But in spite of all this good fortune—and a rate of economic progress possibly unsurpassed in a single decade in any country in the world—in spite of the great pace of prosperity, the dreadful spectre of over-population inexorably made ground. A thriving agriculture, a booming industry, a high rate of emigration to England, did not shake off that pursuing giant. Indeed the economic advance increased and emphasised the dangers. While the few enjoyed wages hitherto undreamt of, the many suffered from the high cost of living. The wage-earners were doing much better but the mass of peasant farmers were being left behind. There could surely be no more striking illustration of the lesson that if the population problem is not solved no amount of agricultural or industrial progress will provide an escape. Jamaica made great exertions. They brought great successes. But the monster of over-population with terrifying relentlessness was still overtaking.

There was one other main problem which had been in the forefront of Jamaican and West Indian public affairs for the past decade. It was the question whether Jamaica could join a free federation of all the British West Indian islands. It was an ambitious and imaginative enterprise—a project for bringing together the three million people of Jamaica, Trinidad, Barbados and the Leeward and Windward Islands to create a new independent nation. When I left Jamaica at the end of 1957 all the West Indian leaders were in full support. But five years later the enterprise had failed. Jamaica decided in 1962 by a narrow vote in a plebiscite not to participate in the proposed Federation and now Jamaica and Trinidad have come forward separately as independent countries. I was myself from the first a convinced advocate of West Indian Federation. I said in the Jamaican Legislature in 1957:

"I gather that there are some people in Jamaica who still entertain a lingering doubt whether Jamaica would have been better advised to abandon the movement towards Federation and seek Jamaican self-government alone. They admit that most of the other West Indian territories are too small to achieve self-government separately, but they still wonder if it would not have been best to follow a policy of every island for itself—and the devil take the hindmost.

They speak as if the West Indian convoy, which set sail from Montego Bay in 1947 and has sailed well together since then, should scatter in all directions at the first signs of danger or bad weather. They would leave the smaller ships to be destroyed or wrecked in the hope that one or two of the larger ones could thereby save themselves. I say nothing now of the advantages of a single convoy under the same flag with the same course making for the same port. We all know what those advantages are. But permit me to say that it would be a shameful thing if Jamaica, seeking her own advantage alone, broke the convoy and left the little ships in the lurch and thus destroyed the hope of bringing the whole convoy safely through."

The convoy broke up, the little ships are left in the lurch now. It was indeed a shameful failure.

When I went back to Jamaica for the Independence Celebrations in August 1962, I wandered out of the State Ball to watch the people dancing outside the big new hotel. They were dancing to a new calypso called "Jump up for Independence." I have forgotten exactly what the words were but they were a rejoicing to be free from association with the rest of the West Indies—a cheap scoffing at the small islands. I felt suddenly alone and utterly wretched. A fine idea was being ridiculed. A great conception had failed. The forces of isolation had won. I remembered the teaching of my Caribbean hero, Governor Munoz Marin of Puerto Rico, that true liberty is not a freedom of narrowness, not a freedom to cut yourself off, but a freedom to associate, a freedom to combine new friendships with old ones, a freedom of genuine brotherhood with free men everywhere. Jamaica had chosen a selfish second best. It was a victory for reaction. I called for my car, with its Independence number plate, and went home miserably to bed.

As I flew back to New York the next day I reflected on the factors which could be put on the credit side in independent Jamaica. I would put first the good tradition of public service in Jamaica. When I had been Colonial Secretary and later when I was Governor I had been proud to have a position of leadership in a first-rate Civil Service. Twice that Service has shown, when a change of government has taken place by the process of free elections, that it will serve with impartial integrity any government duly elected by the people. Corruption in the gross sense of financial dishonesty is practically unknown in the Jamaica Service. In the sense of political partiality it is also rare. Of course many officials have their own personal strong opinions, but that does not prevent them from carrying out loyally the policy of their political masters. They know and accept the principle that it is the duty of an official first to give honest advice fearlessly and secondly to carry out the final decisions of those in ultimate political authority, and carry them out with all his ability and enthusiasm, whether he personally agrees with them or not.

There is another national asset in Jamaica which is lacking in many other colonial territories. That is a class of strong, independent and public spirited Jamaicans who are prepared to give their time and effort unsparingly to public work. The Custodes (roughly equivalent to Lords Lieutenant in England) play a part in public life which is still important. The Development Corporations and the Marketing Boards and the Land Authorities, and a score of energetic charitable organisations too, are largely manned and run by people who have a big stake in the country, and gladly give their service free. It is people in this category, who are not by any means necessarily wealthy, together with the professional class coming from the long-established secondary schools, who give to Jamaica a steadiness and balance which counteract, and indeed by example influence and reduce the vagaries of the politicians.

Not that I am decrying the politicians. On the contrary, the politicians of Jamaica have risen to the challenge of the past decade and a half, and have served Jamaica well. It is the successful working of the parliamentary system and the two-party system which has been the outstanding contribution of Jamaica in recent years. In this particular achievement no other colonial territory or recently-independent country has excelled or equalled the Jamaican example. When the Queen spoke to the two Houses of the Jamaican Parliament in the crowded old Legislative Chamber in 1953, she said: "May you build on the principles of parliamentary government which have been tested and tried through the centuries and found to be sure and true." She referred to the first constitution of Jamaica under which the first parliament had been established in the reign of Charles II. "Your parliamentary tradition is nearly three hundred years old," she said; and then she paused and continued, "Indeed it is older than that, for it goes back to the earliest days of our Parliament at Westminster."

It was well to point to parliamentary tradition as the outstanding feature of Jamaican public life. It is not just a matter of the House of Representatives or the Senate as it is now called (it used to be the Legislative Council when I spoke for the Government in the Upper House), it is a matter of a deep understanding of democratic process, a capacity to organise and maintain political parties, a respect for the will of the majority, and the readiness to give and take hard knocks in debate without malice or rancour. These things are well understood and deeply respected in Jamaica.

A visiting member of the United Kingdom House of Commons was astonished to discover that in a branch of the Banana Growers' Association in a remote village in the hills of the parish of St. Mary the villagers had clubbed together to buy a second-hand copy of Erskine May's *Parliamentary Procedure*. They were determined to conduct the debates in their little branch meetings in proper parliamentary form.

While the parliamentary tradition has been long established and deep rooted the fact that the two-party system has flourished in recent times in Jamaica has been principally due to Jamaica's good fortune in having had such outstanding leaders of the two parties as Sir Alexander Bustamante, the leader of the Jamaica Labour Party, and Mr. Norman Manley, M.M., Q.C., the leader of the People's National Party.

These two great men have dominated the Jamaican political scene for as long as most people can remember. They are cousins, and after the riots of 1938, which set alight the political consciousness of the island, they joined forces to form a new political movement. But they soon parted company and at the first elections under adult suffrage in 1944 Bustamante's Labour Party almost swept the board, gaining 22 seats to only 5 seats won by Manley's People's National Party. Manley himself was defeated in that election, but he set himself to reorganise his party throughout the island. The result of the 1949 General Election was much closer (the Jamaica Labour Party won 17 seats to the People's National Party's 13 seats) but it was another six years before Manley's party came to power, and although he has since done great things in office I often think that his persistence and faith in keeping his party together in the long years in the wilderness of opposition was his finest political achievement.

Sir Alexander Bustamante, the present Prime Minister of Jamaica, is now in his late seventies. He is well over six feet tall, with a Lincoln-like gauntness of figure, and a shock of hair now turned white. His fine head and commanding nose and flashing eyes and pale complexion give the impression that he has more Spanish than Negro blood. In fact in spite of his name, which he adopted for himself (his name originally was Clarke) he probably has no Spanish blood. He claims that he has some Arawak ancestry—the Arawaks being the original Indian inhabitants of the island who were annihilated by the Spaniards before Oliver Cromwell's army captured the island in 1655. But I doubt if he expects his claims of ancestry to be literally accepted, any more than the astonishing and varying stories he tells about his early life. On occasion he will recount his adventures in the Riff war in Morocco, or in Cuban disorders or in strange occupations in New York. His physical strength and endurance are amazing. He has many odd theories about food (he persuaded me at one time to drink regular quantities of carrot juice) and in alcoholic drink he combines a prodigious capacity with a wide and varied choice—and a strong head.

He came to notice first as a wild leader of the waterfront workers in Kingston and the sugar workers of the plains, but his political support is spread throughout the island particularly amongst the poorer people. He was imprisoned for a while during the last war but as soon as he was released he set himself to organise the Bustamante Industrial Trade Union, of which he is life President, and the Jamaica Labour Party. Having been in office from 1944 to 1955, he won the General Election of 1962 and so became the first Prime Minister of independent Jamaica.

Politically he is an opportunist, unpredictable but brilliant. He sometimes appears reckless and irresponsible—or rather he used to in his earlier days—but always he shrewdly calculates the effect of his actions. While he draws his main support from the poorest people, he is a fanatical opponent of communism and he professes a contempt for socialism. He has, however, always had a deep concern for the cause of raising the standard of living of the poorest people and, with all his violence of speech and action, he has a deep natural gentleness and courtesy, specially towards women and the weak.

He seldom reads official papers, but we soon discovered when he became a Minister that he had an astonishingly quick and sure grasp of administrative problems, and a political sense which was almost uncanny.

I remember him first coming into the Executive Council with blood flowing from a wound in his head when he had just led a mob of waterfront workers against the rival trade union which had called a strike amongst the staff of the Mental Hospital. On another occasion, when there had been a minor riot outside Headquarters House, he came into my little office when I was Colonial Secretary, swinging two revolvers. Later when I was Governor and his faithful secretary, now Lady Bustamante, had been arrested by the police he stormed into Kings House, tore off his coat, threw it into a corner, and terrified all within hearing by his furious denunciations of the police.

The story which I always remember as best illustrating his

gift for surprise was told to me by a leading supporter of a political party which fought the 1944 General Election. It was the party of the respectable and the well-to-do, of those accustomed to authority and privilege. They could scarcely imagine that the electorate would prefer the wild Bustamante or the extreme Manley to their moderate and responsible appeal. This party was having its final rally in the Ward Theatre in Kingston, which is the traditional place for important political meetings in Jamaica. The theatre was full, the speaker was an eloquent leading lawyer, there was a growing and comforting general feeling of polite enthusiasm.

But then the speaker on the stage saw way up at the back of the dress circle an unmistakable figure. It was Bustamante, alone. Slowly he made his way down the aisle of the dress circle and then, to everyone's astonishment and consternation, he pushed past the knees of the socially prominent ladies who had the best seats in the front row of the dress circle and stood in the very centre of the circle, surveying the scene with his hands deep in his pockets in an attitude of contempt and defiance. By this time the people in the stalls were turning to see what was happening, the speaker on the stage stopped, an absolute hush of amazement, of outrage, descended on the crowded theatre. No one knew what to do. Nor could they imagine what Bustamante would do, or say. He said nothing, but stood his ground. The silence and the suspense were well-nigh intolerable. No one moved or spoke for what seemed an unbearable time. And then slowly Bustamante again pushed his way past the knees of the ladies in the front row, and very slowly walked up the steps of the dress circle—and out of the theatre. The meeting petered out. The restrained enthusiasm collapsed and could not be recaptured. Everyone was anxious to finish the meeting and discuss the strange incident, to ask their neighbours the cause, the explanation, of such an impudent intrusion, such preposterous behaviour.

The Democratic Party in fact never had any real chance of success but when news of the Ward Theatre incident spread, its hopes melted away. When the poll took place a few days later Bustamante's party had won by a landslide. The Democratic Party had not won a single seat.

Norman Manley, the leader of the People's National Party, was in every respect in striking contrast to Bustamante. He was a Rhodes scholar and a first-class athlete. For many years he held the Jamaican hundred yards record—no mean feat in a country which has produced some of the finest runners in the world, including the relay team which beat the whole world at the Helsinki Olympic Games. He fought in the first World War and won the Military Medal in France, and on his return to Jamaica he soon secured and long maintained a position of unrivalled pre-eminence at the Jamaican Bar.

For many years he dominated the Jamaican legal world like a giant, terrifying the judges and contemptuously defeating his opponents, and it was popularly believed that he never lost a case. But meanwhile, having broken with Bustamante soon after the 1938 riots, he set himself to create the People's National Party. He was a Socialist and an associate of Sir Stafford Cripps, who came to Jamaica when the party was founded, and caused offence to old-fashioned opinion in Jamaica by a violent attack on imperialism. Building the new party was an uphill task. Manley himself was defeated in the 1944 election and it was eleven years before at last in 1955 the People's National Party won a General Election, even then only by the narrow margin of eighteen to fourteen seats. And now, following the defeat of his party in the 1962 General Election, he is leader of the Opposition again.

The two chief influences in Manley's public life have been first his brilliant career and outstanding position at the Jamaican Bar and second the fact that for more than a decade he was engaged in the thankless struggle to keep his party together in the unrewarding days of opposition. He likes to deal with one major subject at a time like a lawyer concentrating on one case after another, and he is apt to regard each political issue as a case to be won against obviously inferior counsel on the other side. When he finds himself with a bad case—usually as a result of being put in a false position by someone from his party or the trade union affiliated with his party—he is particularly offensive and he turns on his opponents the full force of his blistering invective.

It would be difficult to single out any particular example of his service to Jamaica during his seven years as Chief Minister (the title was subsequently changed to Premier and now to Prime Minister) but I shall always specially remember his negotiations with the bauxite companies—the Renolds Company, the Kaiser Company and Alumina Jamaica Limited (the Canadian Company).

The discovery of what is claimed to be the largest single deposit of bauxite in the world had been made almost by accident only a few years before and the three big North American companies had already invested over a hundred million dollars in plant and purchase of land. The royalty had been deliberately fixed at a low rate—a shilling a ton—for the first five-year period and I, as Governor, began negotiations with the Companies for a higher rate of royalty in future. The Government was in a strong position. It was certain that a big increase in royalty could be achieved. We began to realise that bauxite might contribute several million pounds a year to Jamaican revenue. Then Manley took over the negotiations with the three companies. It was a task for which he was superbly fitted. His main difficulty was that the Jamaican Government had previously agreed to tie the rate of Jamaican income tax to a stipulated rate of profit on the exported bauxite, and the problem became as complicated as it could be by questions of United States and Canadian and Jamaican tax requirements. Some of the best lawyers in America came to do battle with Manley in the negotiations. He relished the struggle, he widened the extent of the negotiations, he always kept in mind the long-term purposes. Step by step he won ground against the companies and in the end he achieved a comprehensive agreement which brought to Jamaica, and will continue to bring, a major increase in revenue which makes all the difference between Jamaican stagnation and progress. And what is more, in spite of pressing the negotiations with the utmost skill and relentless determination, he achieved an agreement which the companies recognised was fair, and which enabled them to justify greatly increased capital investment in the island. Manley was at his brilliant best in negotiation and in exposition. It was a joy to hear him take a complicated question and make it beautifully clear. He also had a quickness in cross-examination and debate which was a delight to see. Once when he was in England he had a television interview with a number of newspaper men, one of whom was being very hostile and unpleasant. The journalist raised two awkward questions. He asked whether the story was true that Manley suffered from a sense of inferiority and injustice because he had been refused an Officer's commission in the first World War on account of his colour. A more difficult or offensive question could scarcely be imagined. Manley kept his temper. He said that he was glad that this old story had been raised because it enabled him to deny it publicly. "You see," he said, "I was offered a commission, but I was a sergeant in the Gunners and I preferred to remain a sergeant in the Gunners." A marvellous reply for an English audience. But the awkward questioner was not content. Earlier on he had attacked Manley for being a Socialist and his last question was why Manley had done nothing to deal with the disastrous increase in Jamaican population. This was a very difficult and indeed damaging question. Manley smiled and finished the interview by saying that it had always seemed to him that relations between the sexes were "peculiarly matters for private enterprise".

It is natural to look for faults in such an outstanding man. But whatever failings he has are far outweighed by his positive qualities—a commanding and constructive mind and a courageous determination to stand by his beliefs and an unquestioned personal integrity of the highest order.

What had been the function and duty of a Governor in relation to these two outstanding political figures, Bustamante and Manley? It must be remembered that when I returned to the island as Governor at the beginning of 1951 the Governor still exercised full ultimate authority. Self-government was a remote aim; independence had scarcely been imagined. The initiative lay with the Governor, and there was a reluctance on the part of the propertied classes and the poorest people alike to escape from the old colonial attitudes which looked to the Governor to solve the island's problems. How to give a lead and also to prepare for the transfer of authority to the elected representatives of the people? And how to carry everyone along under a two-party parliamentary system in full national patriotism? How to overcome both the fears of the old brigade, of the privileged class, and at the same time how to shake the ordinary people from their habitual subservience? One mistake would have been to avoid taking an initiative, to drift and to leave everything to take its course. The other would have been to strengthen and perpetuate the Governor's overriding authority. Either course would have led to reaction, to frustration, to the banking up of extreme feelings, to a deep split and antagonism amongst the people of Jamaica. To lead and take the initiative and lose no time in stimulating a new sense of readiness to accept political advance and responsibility; to encourage a new sense of confident patriotism; a Governor's initiative in order to limit and finally to eliminate the Governor's authority—that was the main task before me, as I saw it, when I sailed into Kingston Harbour to be Governor in the spring of 1951.

At the speech I made that day after I had been sworn in at Kings House as Governor, I said:

"God willing we shall show that we can work a system of free government, and we in this small island will help to show the world that free institutions and representative government are not the preserve and privilege of a few great nations. We shall help to show the world that democracy knows no frontiers of race or creed or colour."

My last official act before leaving Jamaica was to go down to the main square of Kingston and in front of Queen Victoria's statue to read the Royal Proclamation which in effect gave full internal self-government to Jamaica.

In my farewell message to Jamaica as I left in 1957 on my way to attempt to deal with a rebellion in Cyprus, I said:

"As to the future, many people have wished us success, but you will agree with me that success is not the most important thing. You will wish, I am sure, that I should not deceive anyone. You will wish that I should not betray what I

believe in. You will wish that I should not be afraid of anyone or anything, and you will hope that, on those tests,
whether I face success or failure, I should not disappoint
or disgrace you."

CHAPTER IX

Cyprus

"The use of force alone is but temporary. It may subdue for the moment, but it does not remove the necessity of subduing again; and a nation is not governed which is perpetually to be conquered."

EDMUND BURKE

I

WHEN I went back to Cyprus as Governor in 1957 I had one great advantage. I had been there before as Colonial Secretary of Cyprus in the last two years of the war.

After my first arrival in 1943 I had been in the island for only a few weeks when I had to take over. I went with the Governor, Sir Charles Woolley, to the temporary airport near Nicosia. He was going on leave and I was to act as Governor in his place for four or five months. He inspected the Guard of Honour, said his farewells and entered the plane. The engines roared, the plane rose, circled, and disappeared. I turned on my heel to face my first command. The flag flew from the Governor's car which took me back to Nicosia. The Government House Guard saluted. Mustapha, the Turkish Kavass, in his ceremonial dress, his tarboosh, his embroidered coat and his huge baggy trousers, hurried down the Government House steps to greet me. I went into the Governor's office and sent the usual telegram to London in the standard wording: "I have today assumed the administration of Cyprus." I grinned to myself as I did so. I was thirty-five years of age.

There had been a time a year or more before when Cyprus was threatened by invasion. Greece, Rhodes and Crete had fallen to the enemy. It looked at one time as if Cyprus would suffer the same fate as Crete, and that the German paratroops would descend on the Cyprus plains. When I arrived in Cyprus in 1943, however, although the Germans were still in Greece

143

and the Greek Islands, the victories of the Eighth Army in North Africa had lifted the threat that the German thrust into the Middle East would be renewed. We had a Divisional Command in Cyprus and kept up the pretence of a busy garrison, but, in fact, we had very few troops. We knew that by the skin of our teeth we had been saved from invasion. As we read the reports of steadily more distant battles in Europe we turned with a will to our local tasks of practical administration.

The history of Cyprus was rich in variety. Aphrodite had risen from the Cyprus waves. Paul of Tarsus had set sail from Paphos. Richard Coeur de Lion had come to Cyprus to marry Berengaria. The Knights of the Order of St. John had built their castle at Kolossi. Othello had arrived as Governor at Famagusta. Greeks, Romans, Crusaders, Venetians, Turks had been the rulers. And finally the English had taken over the island in 1878 under Disraeli's famous deal with the Turks. The previous rulers had left their monuments, Greek temples and theatres, Byzantine churches and monasteries and Turkish mosques. The ancient battlements of Famagusta and Kyrenia, the fairyland Lusignan mountain castle of St. Hilarion and the broad walls of Nicosia stood as evidence that through two thousand years Cyprus had been a stronghold, a fortified outpost, a prize to be fought over, a point of conflict between West and East, between Christendom and Islam.

In all this long history the Cypriots had never governed themselves. They had always been a subject people. Their loyalties were not to Cyprus but outside the island. They thought of themselves not as Cypriots but as Greeks or Turks. They had looked for their inspiration and support to Istanbul or Athens or Ankara. And so even in the strange lull at the end of the war, when local animosities and fears were in abeyance, there always just below the surface lay the explosive emotional nationalism of the Greek majority and slow awakening suspicion and distrust amongst the Turkish minority.

These feelings, temporarily submerged, were to erupt into violence ten years later. But in 1943 and 1944 and 1945, while Greece was still under German domination and Turkey neutral in the war, the Greeks and Turks in Cyprus were glad to have a breathing space. They were content to work with us, and together, in overcoming the difficulties of war shortages and giving attention to every-day tasks of practical advance.

The Government of Cyprus was a bureaucracy under the personal rule of the Governor. His authority was, of course, subject to directions from the Colonial Office in London, and in the war years Cyprus could not have survived without a substantial annual grant in aid from British funds. But, in fact, the Governor and his small band of British officials exercised wide authority on their own. There was no legislature to persuade, no elected representatives of the people to convince or cajole. The Governor's Executive Council was composed of his own officials with only two unofficial members, one being a Greek Cypriot and one a Turkish Cypriot. Control of legislation and finance was wholly in the Governor's hands.

But though the administration of the island was authoritarian and bureaucratic, it was efficient and fair. And we were able to tackle the day-to-day problems with speed and confidence. Supply was our immediate problem. We took over the markets, encouraged maximum production of food by ensuring stable prices to the farmers, and met the needs of the consumers by transporting produce from one part of the island to another and rationing supplies of all imported goods.

Looking further ahead we established land authorities covering whole valleys or watersheds in which the development of agriculture, forestry and water supply was pushed forward in accordance with overall regional plans. A fifth of the area of Cyprus is under mountain forest and the control and administration of the forest areas were much the most efficient of any Middle East country.

We tackled the age-old problem of the devastation caused by the wandering herds of goats. These herds were owned and led by tough, ruthless mountain goat-herds, who terrorised the people of the settled villages and drove their goats through the cultivation of the plains, destroying trees and crops as they went and adding to the wide-spread damage caused by soil erosion. We hit on the plan of appealing to the Greek love of politics. We introduced a new law under which the people of any village area could hold a local plebiscite. If the popular vote was in favour of the tethered goat, then the wandering herds of goats from the mountains would be outlawed. For some time no village dared to vote for the tethered goat. They feared the wrath of their traditional enemies, the mountain goat-herds. But then one village at last voted for the tethered goat. Immediately the full force of the police went into the area to enforce the decision. Within a month or two the result of the elimination of the damage done by the herds of goats began to be seen. One village after another applied for a goat plebiscite. Overwhelming popular opinion backed by the authority of the Government triumphed. A scourge which had held back agricultural development for centuries past was brought under control, and in wide areas eliminated altogether.

Another pressing problem in which I became personally interested was the problem of housing. Cyprus prospered in the war owing to stable prices of agricultural produce and heavy military expenditure, but all building materials were in short supply and the building of houses in the towns, in spite of intense demand, had come to a stop. I worked out a new housing scheme. Government architects prepared standard plans of good working-class houses. Under my scheme building supplies would be provided from Government controlled stocks. Local builders would put up the money for the building and construct the houses on condition that they followed the approved plans and conformed to town planning lay-out. They must also undertake for three years to lease the houses at controlled rents to working-class tenants selected by a team of welfare workers. The scheme seemed to me to have every advantage. The cost would be found by the builders and there would be no charge to public funds. The short supplies of materials would be put to the best use, private enterprise would be given a major part to play, the builders would eventually own the houses and be free to lease them as they wished, employment would be created, and the people most in need of houses in the war years would get them.

I went into the press conference to announce and explain the scheme. I confidently expected an enthusiastic response. I came out an hour and a half later sadder and wiser. The correspondents raised every possible objection; they were loud in their criticisms. The Communists, always strong in Cyprus, were contemptuous of a scheme making use of private enterprise. The right wing objected for opposite reasons; they called the scheme a wild socialist exercise. Everyone seemed against it. I learnt that day that whatever you do when you are dealing with Greeks you must expect fierce division of opinion, violent abuse, high-powered criticism. Very salutary, no doubt for a bureaucrat—and discouraging to an enthusiast.

The project went forward, the houses were built, the benefits were obvious. At the same time the Greeks had shown me that their merit and their strength are in opposition. They are quick to draw a knife, fast to sense a slight or an insult, contemptuous of authority, suspicious of every official motive. And their gift for destructive opposition is directed as readily at their own leaders as at any foreign official. The heat and hatred of their politics is terrifying. Charm and gaiety and generosity and patience and long suffering they have in abundance in their private lives. But they bring to the world of politics the fury of the blood feud and the fanaticism of the assassin.

To read the newspapers of Cyprus is to appreciate the extreme of vitriolic vituperation; to hear the venom of personal comment at a Greek dinner table is to be startled by what seems like a caricature of spite. I do not envy anyone who has to govern a people so agile in opposition, so eager to destroy, so expert in denigration.

Perhaps it is something to do with having been always a subject people. All Greeks are individualists: I almost said anarchists. And yet they are the most sophisticated, the most articulate and the most fascinating of all the different peoples I have known. No wonder they have taught the world the art of politics. They love freedom passionately—particularly the freedom to attack anything and anyone.

* * *

While I had been in Jordan and North Africa, Sylvia and Paul and Sarah had been in South Africa, evacuated with all British families under the general Middle East order made when it looked as if the Middle East would be overrun by the enemy. While I was in Cyprus they came back to me. I went down to Famagusta to meet the little ship, the *Foua-dieh* which brought them from Alexandria on the last leg of their uncomfortable journey. They had been away for three years. I doubted if Paul, then aged six, and Sarah, aged four, would know me.

I went very early in the morning into the ship and up to the little upper cabin where they were. The two children were quiet and strained. They looked at me non-committedly, as if they had a lot to forgive me. For a few minutes they were silent and stiff. Then suddenly they let go. They pushed me over on the bunk and jumped on me. It was at first hysterical and then hilarious. We were a family again.

One of the penalties of overseas service is the family separa-tions. Sylvia was evacuated under rifle fire from Nablus before Paul was born. She was left behind in England just after Sarah was born at the beginning of the war. She and Paul and Sarah then spent three of the war years in South Africa. Subsequently, I went ahead alone first to Jamaica and then to Nigeria and the children have been shunted about the world in their school holidays to Africa and the West Indies and Cyprus and New York. Until very recently we have not had a house of our own in all the years we have been married.

At any rate we now had a peaceful year together in Cyprus before my transfer to Jamaica. It was a year in which we lived part of the time in Government House and part of the time in the Colonial Secretary's big house near the Secretariat. In those days the Governor would spend the summer on the Troodos mountains, and in the years before the war the whole Secretariat had moved up to the cool hill station for the full summer. Now with so much to do I preferred to stay below in spite of the fierce heat of the Nicosia plain. But I could escape for a weekend occasionally to join the family in their Troodos cottage amongst the pine trees—and Troodos always remained our favourite place in Cyprus.

The time came in 1945 to go to Jamaica, to my second post of Colonial Secretary. We went to Port Said on V.E. Day and that night barricaded ourselves in at our hotel as the Egyptians noisily celebrated a victory they had done so little to win. We sailed the next day in the last of the war convoys through the Mediterranean. I had not been home at all during the war years, and for most of the past fifteen years I had been in the Middle East. In that time I had learnt the rudiments of administration. The Arabs and the Jews and the Greeks and the Turks had taught me many lessons, the most important being that you can achieve success only by working with the people. It was twelve years before I returned to Cyprus. I left a peaceful and friendly island. I returned to Cyprus in 1957 to face a rebellion and imminent civil war which threatened to set aflame the whole of the Eastern Mediterranean.

*   *   *

A colonial official necessarily concentrated his whole attention and interest on the people of the colony where he served. He saw and knew little of the outside world. A Government House, particularly Kings House in Jamaica, was constantly full of visitors but they came for a meal or at most a night or two. The Governor was almost wholly pre-occupied with the people and the personalities in his own territory. Usually the only outside political leader with whom he had close contact was the Secretary of State for the Colonies. Even the Secretary of State he would only see very occasionally. But now when I came back to Cyprus as Governor in 1957 and became absorbed in the problem of an island in revolt, I found myself in a situation very unfamiliar to me. So strained were political relations for almost the whole of the fateful year of 1958 that no Greek leader would willingly be seen entering Government House. I went out to meet the people in the villages. One or two brave Greek leaders, like fine old John Clerides, would come to lecture me. My friend, Stelios Pavlides, who had been Attorney-General when I was in Cyprus before, came in sorrow and in anger to point out the frightful errors of the British Government and myself. The Communist leaders, including Partisides, the brilliant Mayor of Limassol, would occasionally give me a broadside of political precept. But Archbishop Makarios was still in Athens following his exile in the Seychelles. He was the sole spokesman of the Greek community, so all the Greeks maintained. No one could speak in his stead;

and consequently for my first year after I came back to Cyprus I had to live in unfamiliar isolation.

Instead the main characters in the drama at that time were international statesmen. I worked closely with our own Prime Minister and with our Foreign Minister, Selwyn Lloyd, and my own chief, Alan Lennox-Boyd, and repeatedly went back to London for consultation with them. Sir Pierson Dixon, the United Kingdom Ambassador at the United Nations, was another figure who played a vital part, as I shall presently describe. And on two visits to Athens and Ankara I got to know the Greek and Turkish Ministers—Karamanlis, the Prime Minister of Greece, and his Foreign Secretary Averoff, and the ill-fated Prime Minister of Turkey, Menderes, and his Foreign Minister Zorlu (later both hanged in their own country). These were the men, with Makarios, on whom the fate of Cyprus depended at that time far more than anyone in the island itself. For all of them I learnt to have a respectful gratitude.

Zorlu, the Foreign Minister of Turkey, was the most ruthless of them and was, I think, the rudest man I ever met. Once in Ankara when we had sat up most of the night drafting a statement of the British position and when we had gone back to the final conference with our Foreign Minister, Selwyn Lloyd, and our Ambassador in Turkey, Sir James Bowker, Zorlu flicked through the pages of the document and threw it contemptuously on one side without even reading it. On another visit to Ankara we were on the point of agreement when Prime Minister Macmillan, infuriated by Zorlu's intolerably insulting behaviour, got up and left the conference room followed by a stream of officials begging him to come back. We in Cyprus had no reason to love Zorlu. He had, I have no doubt, known of and perhaps himself given the orders for the Turkish riots and the attempt to burn Nicosia. But we never had any doubt about his ability or his patriotism, and, now that he has gone to such a terrible end, all of us concerned with Cyprus should pay tribute to his courage in finding with Foreign Secretary Averoff of Greece a settlement which saved Cyprus from civil war.

Menderes I didn't know so well. But I remember him affectionately. Throughout 1958 I was an unpopular figure in

Turkey, to say the least. At first the Turks wouldn't even let me visit Ankara and when they did I was not allowed outside the British Embassy and the Turkish Foreign Office. But when I met Prime Minister Menderes he went out of his way to be kind to me, asked me to sit by him at official receptions, said that he realised what a difficult time I was having, asked me to give him my own assessment of the situation. He was short, shrewd, gay and charming. I remember how greatly shocked I was when a year after I first met him I was in a conference at the Foreign Office in London and the news came that his plane had crashed on arrival at London Airport. At first we thought he had been killed in the crash, and although I had only met him a few times I felt that I had lost an old friend. He survived that crash only to suffer the more ghastly fate of being hanged by his own people. I grieve when I think of him.

How different were the Greek Ministers. We could agree with the Turkish leaders and find their methods unbearable. We were in blank disagreement with the Greek leaders right up to the end, but their courtesy and charm made our disputes seem like quarrels between friends. There is a natural affinity between Greeks and English—stronger, I often think, than between any other two peoples. Karamanlis, the Prime Minister, was good looking with an easy dignity of carriage and manner. He spoke at our conferences through Bitsios (now the Greek Ambassador to the United Nations) and it was not easy to get on personal terms with him, but in his presence one always had a sense of his fairness and steadiness. The Foreign Minister Averoff, on the other hand, was equally and brilliantly articulate in English, French and Greek. He was well-groomed, dark, elegant, eloquent, with a mind like qiuck-silver and a generous enthusiasm. When I think of the qualities we have always admired in the Greeks, including the gift of political courage, I think of him.

My own masters were very patient and long-suffering with me. Sometimes at the conferences at London and Chequers the Prime Minister would turn to me saying, "Now wheel on the idealist." Selwyn Lloyd was an old friend from Cambridge days. It was a great help through so many anxious times to be able to speak to him without reservation—and without undue respect. I was impressed by his thoroughness and his mastery of detail. I was dealing with Cyprus alone. He, as Foreign Secretary, was being closely informed of all the crises of the world. But I believe that he knew all the complicated Cyprus documents better than I did. He brought a barrister's grasp to the Cyprus case. I remember chiding him once with taking too much of the detailed work on himself; he replied that in a negotiation you must never allow the other side the advantage of knowing more than you do yourself.

Lennox-Boyd too I had known since undergraduate days. My first recollection of him was when he was President of the Oxford Union and he came with Giles Isham to speak at the Cambridge Union. They were both tall and strikingly handsome. They wore large red carnations in their button-holes. They infuriated us by speaking in the tradition of the Oxford Union, superior, trivial, supercilious, as if they would not stoop to dirty their delicate hands by using an honest argument. But we had grudgingly to admit that even as representatives of a tradition which we so much disliked they were magnificent specimens.

I have served under Lord Boyd (as he now is) for many years both in Jamaica and Cyprus. In politics I probably disagree with him on almost every issue, but his good nature and his good humour and his generous fairness repeatedly rescue him from the consequences of his reactionary policies. When I used to come back to London from Cyprus to report and we would drive together to the Colonial Office or to Downing Street or to Chequers in his huge blue open car I used to feel that I had come up through a trap door into a sort of Ian Fleming world of high politics and international intrigue. Every scene and every character seemed rather larger than life, part of a most improbable adventure.

The worst time in Cyprus was in the spring of 1958. As I shall presently describe we were at that time without a policy. My first initiative had failed. We had not yet prepared the second. Meanwhile EOKA violence steadily increased. I feared that at any time some EOKA outrage would set off Turkish resistance and that the civil war between Greeks and Turks which we most dreaded would result. I looked around for some diversion. I thought that possibly I might be able to make a direct contact with Grivas the leader of the Greek rebels. I decided to invite him to a secret meeting. I wrote him a letter accordingly, and found a private means to send it. I didn't tell anyone, not even my closest military and civil advisers, for the simple reason that if I had consulted them they would have prevented me from doing what I proposed. I knew the danger of what I did. I knew moreover that Lennox-Boyd would be furious if he ever got to know. Nothing annoys him more than not being told what his subordinates are up to. I knew too that what I had done might well be made public by Grivas. But I thought that Grivas might possibly be flattered by the idea of a secret meeting with the Governor. His vanity and sense of melodrama might do the trick—and although he would stick at nothing, I believed that if I did go alone and unarmed to meet him his honour as a soldier would not allow him to doublecross me. So on the 12th of April I wrote to Grivas. No reply came, though soon afterwards the campaign of EOKA sabotage temporarily stopped. As the days passed I became increasingly nervous that Grivas, having apparently decided not to meet me, would publish my letter. Accordingly on the 1st of May I wrote a statement which I would publish immediately if there were any leak.

This is the statement:

"During the first ten days of April there were over fifty bomb explosions as the EOKA campaign of sabotage increased. It seemed to me that if the campaign continued it would inevitably lead to more bloodshed and suffering, and I was particularly concerned lest it might cause strife between the two communities. From every point of view it seemed to me important that it should be stopped as quickly as possible.

With the object of doing everything I could to stop it at once I wrote a letter on the 12th of April in the following words:

' Colonel Grivas,
I am convinced that if the present campaign of sabotage

153

continues disaster will result for all the people of Cyprus. In their name and interest I call on you to save them from that disaster by ordering the campaign of sabotage and violence to cease.

If it would help I am prepared to go to any place at any time you nominate to meet you and urge you to act on this call. I would come alone and unarmed and would give you my word that for that day you would be in no danger of arrest.

I make this call and this proposal to you because I believe it to be my duty to do everything I can to save the people of Cyprus from the disaster which is so near.

Hugh Foot,
Governor.'

(Addressed from Government House, Cyprus.)

My first attempt to get this letter delivered failed, but on the 17th of April it was despatched again and a week later I learnt that it had been delivered on the 20th of April. I have received no written reply but I have been told that Grivas gave orders to stop the sabotage as soon as he received the letter.

In fact the campaign of sabotage came to an end on the 20th of April. There had been over forty acts of sabotage in the previous four days. There were three on the 20th of April and there was none on the following days.

I have two things I want to do more than anything else. The first is to assist in finding a just settlement. The second is to prevent violence. We cannot hope to succeed in the first unless the second is achieved. That is why I took the action I did.

I shall make this statement public if there is any disclosure of the letter I wrote.

(Signed) Hugh Foot,
Governor."

Still nothing happened. I began to think that my indiscretion, if such it was, would never be known.

Nearly two months later, on the 24th of June, I was due to

fly to London for discussions on the new policy, the Macmillan Plan, which had just been announced. I had to go that morning to visit an Army Camp and I had left myself just time to rush back to Government House to pack and dash to the airport to get my plane to London. When I hurried into Government House at the end of that morning I was told that a newspaper correspondent whom I knew well wanted to see me. I said I had not time, but he waylaid me in the hall of Government House as I left. He stopped me in my tracks by saying "What have you got to say about the secret meeting with Grivas?" I was appalled. What a time to bring out that skeleton. He told me that several correspondents had just obtained some knowledge of my letter and that wild rumours about a secret meeting would be published at once. I dashed to my personal safe and took out the statement I had written on the 1st of May, gave a copy to the correspondent, told the Private Secretary to give other copies of it to the Press generally, dived into my car and made for the airport.

I had a number of anxious air journeys during the Cyprus Emergency. This was one. I pictured Lennox-Boyd's anger. A new policy had just been announced—the most important act of the British Government since the Cyprus trouble started. Had I prejudiced it all? Would I be dismissed as an irresponsible adventurer? When I got to London Airport I had as usual to face a Press conference. I managed to get through it somehow and made for a telephone. I spoke to the Secretary of State. He was curt. He said he had to see the Prime Minister. He would see me in the Colonial Office first thing in the morning. Ominous. Next morning I made my way into Lennox-Boyd's office like a schoolboy going to see the Headmaster. I didn't like the look on the faces of the Private Secretaries in the outer office. It was the only time I saw Lennox-Boyd really angry. He said that he had seen the Prime Minister the night before, that he had said that when I was appointed to Cyprus I had been told to exercise my initiative, that Ministers couldn't complain when I did so in a way they didn't approve of, that in fact no great harm had been done and there might even have been some advantage in this unorthodox endeavour to end violence. The Prime Minister had agreed. So that was that.

I promised not to do it again. That struck Lennox-Boyd as funny, and he took me home later to a very good lunch.

When things were at their worst in Cyprus the Prime Minister decided to tackle the problem himself. Many people advised him that things would get worse, that feeling between Greece and Turkey was irreconcilable, that violence in the island must soon lead to civil war between the Greek and Turkish communities, that all efforts to find a settlement had failed, that Archbishop Makarios was impossible to deal with, that Grivas, the leader of the rebellion, was a maniac, and that whatever the Prime Minister did he should not get personally involved in such a hopeless mess. Mr. Macmillan said that if things were as bad as that he had better see what he could do himself.

In February of 1958 Mr. Macmillan had been returning from a Commonwealth tour and his plane put down to refuel at Nicosia. I had an hour's discussion with him at the airport. He asked me what I thought could be done now that my first initiative had failed. We went over all the possibilities and from that conversation gradually there evolved what was called the Macmillan Plan, announced on the 19th of June. He followed this up by visiting Athens and Ankara in August and then made a brief visit to Cyprus itself. Eight months later on the 19th of February 1959 I sat under the gallery in the House of Commons to hear the Prime Minister announce the settlement signed that morning by the Prime Ministers of Great Britain, Greece and Turkey. Mr. Macmillan said that day:

"I regard this agreement as a victory for reason and co-operation. No party to it has suffered defeat—it is a victory for all. By removing a source of bitterness and division it will enable us and our allies and the people of Cyprus to concentrate on working together for peace and freedom."

That was on the Thursday afternoon. On the Saturday morning I was to fly back to Cyprus with the task of putting the agreement into effect and making all the complicated preparations for the new Republic of Cyprus in one year. Mr. Macmillan was also to fly from London early on the Saturday morning. He was going to Moscow on a mission of world importance. As I put my mind to the practical problems ahead of us in Cyprus I thought of the Prime Minister turning his mind to far greater problems. But on the Friday evening to my surprise he sent for me. He was reading papers in bed. He had no business to discuss with me except to wish me luck in the year ahead. But he talked for a while about the experiences of the Cyprus Emergency, and as I left he said, "I wonder if you ever felt in all these strange events that there was sometimes the intervention of divine providence?" I went out into Downing Street that night repeating to myself that unexpected question.

Providence? I didn't know about that, but I did feel that amongst the evil—and all the sordidness of hate and cruelty—there had been a great deal of bravery and devotion and compassion and sometimes strange flashes like lightning on a dark night which suddenly saved us. I said when I first heard of the agreement between the Foreign Ministers of Greece and Turkey that it seemed "something like a miracle". Throughout, evil had held nearly all the cards but good seemed to have had some of the luck. Or so it seemed as I looked back on that happy evening on all the hazards and horrors of the past year and turned with an overflowing thankfulness to the constructive work of reconciliation ahead.

I had first met the Prime Minister in 1957 when Field Marshal Lord Harding was about to retire from the Governorship of Cyprus and I was under consideration to succeed him. I had been on leave in England and had arranged a short speaking tour in Canada and the United States on my way back to Jamaica. In Ottawa I received word that there was an urgent message for me in the British High Commissioner's Office. I had only an hour before I had to speak that night but I hurried to the office and was shown a telegram from London. It said that my name was being considered in connection with the post of Governor of Cyprus. But before a decision was taken would I give an assurance that, if appointed, I would not resign on grounds of policy? An immediate reply was essential. I had not long to think, but it seemed to me at once that it was quite impossible to give any such assurance. I had been a Government official for nearly thirty years and I well knew the obligations of an official, but I didn't know what the policy in Cyprus was. Indeed I didn't know there was one! How could I possibly agree in advance to accept and carry out a policy which, even if it existed, I didn't know? Sadly I sent the reply that I would have very much liked to go to Cyprus but that I couldn't give the assurance. I went on to my meeting in Ottawa and set out the next morning for Quebec. I was very depressed. Nothing would have pleased me more than to go back to Cyprus. I had watched what had gone on there in the past few years—the mounting violence by EOKA against the British Administration, the abortive negotiations with Archbishop Makarios, his exile to the Seychelles, the support of the Greek majority in the island by the Greek Government, the equally determined support for the Turkish minority by the Turkish Government, the repeated debates in the United Nations, the release of Makarios from the Seychelles and his return to Athens without any break in the deadlock. Both within the island and in the international dispute there seemed no gleam of light. But I took some hope from my experience in Cyprus six years before. The Greek community in the island had never been given any say in the running of their own affairs. The Turkish community had seemed to me reasonable and moderate. My belief was that if somehow time could be given for the two communities to work out their own salvation without outside interference, a solution on the basis of self-government might eventually be found. The more the dispute became international rather than a problem to be worked out within Cyprus by the people of Cyprus, and the more Athens and Ankara interfered, the further would chances of a settlement disappear over the international horizon.

But these reflections now seemed academic. I had apparently come within distance of an assignment very much after my own heart and I had lost it. Soon I would learn who had been appointed. Another soldier? A retiring Conservative Chief Whip? I doubted if they would send another Colonial Official when they had so unceremoniously removed Governor Armitage to make way for Field Marshal Lord Harding two years before. With these speculations I turned to prepare my speech for the Quebec Branch of the English Speaking Union. Not in itself a very stimulating prospect in an overwhelmingly French speaking city!

Then just before the meeting the British Consul came to me with another immediate telegram from London. They were dissatisfied with my reply. No wonder, I thought. I was instructed to return at once to London to discuss the matter and no one repeat no one must know the purpose of my visit. Now this was awkward. I had a crowded list of speaking engagements ahead of me. I was due back in Jamaica on a date already announced. It was now Saturday afternoon and no offices were open. No planes left for London direct from Quebec. I went at once to the airport, flew back to Montreal, got a flight to London through the Sunday night, saw the Foreign Secretary, the Colonial Secretary and the Prime Minister, flew back to Montreal through Monday night and continued my speaking tour, returning to Jamaica on the date I was expected. Surprisingly no one knew or discovered about my dash back to London.

When I had been in London I had told the Ministers what I had to say about Cyprus and they had made polite, cautious noises; but it was several weeks before I knew that I was, after all, to be appointed Governor of Cyprus, and must arrive there to take up my duties before the end of the year.

In November on my way to Cyprus I again went over my ideas for future policy in Cyprus with Ministers in London. The essentials I thought were four. A period of five or seven years before any final decision. An end to the Emergency and the return of Archbishop Makarios to the island. Negotiations in the island with the leaders of the two communities to evolve a system of self-government. And an assurance that no final decision would be taken at the end of the five- or seven-year period which was not acceptable to Greeks *and* Turks alike.

But though I repeated these ideas to the Foreign Secretary and the Colonial Secretary before I left for Cyprus at the beginning of December 1957 I was careful not to press any detailed plan upon them. A Governor could not carry much weight with the British Government before he had even taken up his duties. Instead I made one request, that I should be permitted to say on my arrival in Cyprus that I had been

WAITING...

Zec. Courtesy The Daily Herald.

instructed to return to London to report when I had made my
first assessment on the spot. This request sounded reasonable,
and it was readily granted. I knew that if I could come back
from Cyprus with definite proposals after a month or so in the
island my recommendations would carry far more weight.
Indeed it would be awkward to reject them. So I set out for
Cyprus well content—and I was back in London with my
recommendations within the month.

As soon as I had taken the oath of office on the day of my
arrival I sat down with General Kendrew and the Deputy

Governor (George Sinclair) and the Administrative Secretary (John Reddaway) to tell them what I had in mind. We discussed the plan day after day and put it into final form within two weeks.

Meanwhile it was necessary to try to shake everyone in Cyprus itself out of the sense of gloomy hopelessness which had descended on the island. I called on the surprised Greek Mayor of Nicosia, Kiki Dervis, at his home; walked through the streets of Nicosia; saw the Turkish leaders repeatedly; rode through the villages; visited the Detention Camps on Christmas morning; went to see the Bishop of Kitium (who was head of the Greek Orthodox Church in the absence of Archbishop Makarios).

On Christmas Eve I broadcast to the people of Cyprus giving explicit assurances to the Turkish community and, at the same time, announced three gestures of good-will to the rebellious Greeks. First one of the principal Greek schools of the island at Larnaca, which had been closed as a punitive measure, would be opened again. Second, I ordered the release of 100 of the 750 in Detention Camps including all the eleven women detained without trial. Third, I gave orders for the removal of restriction on 600 people who had been required under the Emergency Regulations to stay in their villages and report once a week to the police. I went on to say:

"You may say that these actions do not solve anything. Certainly they don't. I do not for a moment suggest that what I have already decided solves any of our problems. I do, however, believe that these decisions give an indication of my desire to re-establish confidence and trust, and I hope and believe that these gestures will be received by the people of Cyprus in a spirit of good-will.

I have spoken everywhere I go of the building of the two bridges of trust. When I was so speaking a few days ago a member of the Turkish community put to me a very shrewd question. He said that he understood what I was trying to achieve but he asked what I had to say about building a third bridge—a bridge of confidence between the Greek and Turkish communities. That is not primarily a matter for me.

It is primarily a matter for the two communities themselves. But in everything I do I shall seek to reduce the tension that has arisen between the two communities. I earnestly call on everyone who occupies a position of influence in either community to help me, to say no word which might increase friction, to take positive action for the full restoration of friendly understanding.

Let the New Year be a new year of new hope. We are beset by difficulty and danger, but we can rejoice in the confidence that we can overcome them. That confidence springs from the deep longing of all the people for a new start. For myself, I must do my duty—to keep public order, to win your trust and to serve you well. I must do all these three things. I cannot hope to do one without doing the others. Peace and confidence and progress must go hand in hand.''

As I left for London on the 1st of January 1958 I said this at the airport:

"On our journey to the promised land we are not yet at the Jordan. We are just about at the Red Sea. The waters of despair may part for us to go over. And when we have gone over they may swallow up the pursuing forces—the fears and animosities of the past. But we still have a long way to go and hard times ahead. We have in December made some limited progress here, but the main dangers and difficulties still lie ahead of us. Our task, as I said last night, must be to find a good road towards an eventual settlement—and we all want to cut out any unnecessary wandering in the wilderness.''

By the end of December I was feeling pretty pleased with myself. I had a positive policy to take home to London. Locally I had at least shifted the log-jam. The Press in England, and even in Cyprus, had been friendly. One night just before I left to fly to London there was a big gathering at Government House. The Commissioner of Police was talking to a senior Army officer unaware that I was within earshot. The Army officer said, "Why do you let the Governor go round in the streets and villages unguarded?" "The Governor," replied the Commissioner, "at the moment he is the safest man in Cyprus." It was true. I was not facing the daily dangers which confronted our soldiers and police—or even British civilians. No Greek or Turk was going to attack the Governor who had just arrived. They wanted to see what I would do. Many of the leaders remembered me from the time when I was in Cyprus before. They had not yet had time or cause to lose confidence in me.

When I arrived in London that was exciting too. Conferences in the Colonial Office and the Foreign Office, meetings with Ministers, a full discussion in the Cabinet, a confidential discussion with Labour leaders, even a talk with the Archbishop of Canterbury. And within ten days all was agreed. My recommendations were accepted in full. The time-table was worked out. I would go first to Ankara to talk to the Turkish Government, then to Athens to explain the new policy to the Greek Government and to Archbishop Makarios, then back to Cyprus to announce the policy and the end of the Emergency. I prepared my speech for the time when the announcement of the new policy would be made in Cyprus on the 23rd of January.

I knew of course that the Turks, who were to be approached first, would strongly dislike some aspects of the policy, and I wrote to the Deputy Governor on the 7th January from London to say that everything would depend on whether the British Government would stand up to the Turks. But I thought that our absolute assurance that no final decision on the future of the island would be made without Turkish approval might outweigh their objections. They were in fact being given an absolute veto on long-term policy. Much more difficult to persuade Archbishop Makarios and the Greeks, it seemed to me. But the return of the Archbishop to Cyprus, the ending of the Emergency, the promise of self-government might be sufficient to sway them. The Turkish veto might stick in their gullets, but surely we should all hope and work for a final settlement agreed by all. We were offering the Greeks immediate advantages, and the Turks long-term assurances, and offering both of them the immediate prospect of finishing with violence and repression and getting on with sensible negotiation and practical work in the island.

The telegram went off to our Ambassador in Ankara (Sir James Bowker) instructing him to explain the plan and the time-table and to seek approval for my immediate arrival in Ankara. The Colonial Secretary, Lennox-Boyd, was to leave London that day to recover from a painful accident which necessitated his arm being strapped at an awkward angle, but he repeatedly put off his departure to wait for the Turkish reply. I waited with him in his house in Chapel Street. We heard in the afternoon that the reply was in—and was long. The pages of the telegram would be sent round to Chapel Street as they came off the machine. We read the telegram scrolls in silence. It was not until later that it was quite clear the Turkish reply was a blank no, but as we read through the long pages of the telegram and handed them to one another I realised with a sick feeling that everything was going to go wrong. On the essential parts of the plan the Turks raised every possible objection. And as to the proposal that I should visit Ankara, they would not hear of it if I were to visit Athens too. Telegrams went back restating our arguments, making it quite clear how strong, indeed complete, was the assurance to be given to the Turks, asking them to think again. I realised it would be no use. On that day of the first Turkish reply everything, all our hopes and all our plans, collapsed.

Now I must return to Cyprus. Already the newspapers were asking what the delay was about. I had to go back with no announcement and no plan, worse still no explanation—and precious little hope. Worst of all was the realisation that Turkish intransigence was such that no conceivable proposal we put to them would be acceptable—short of partition. I realised from that moment that we had reached the end of the road in *asking* the Turks and the Greeks to agree on a plan. Now we must decide what we would do, and not ask them but tell them.

The next few weeks were the worst of all. To have nothing to say, nothing but evasive and vague answers for the Press, no explanation and no guidance and no initiative; that was the worst burden of all. I went with our Foreign Secretary, Selwyn

CYPRUS: OPERATION FRATERNISE

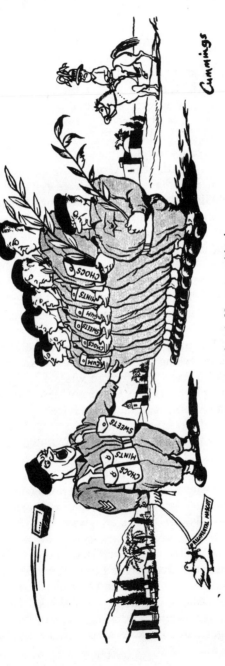

"Private Smithers! No ammunition!
And a dirty olive branch!"

Cummings.   Courtesy The Daily Express.

Lloyd, first to Ankara and then to Athens. While I was in Ankara Turkish riots took place in Nicosia leading to several deaths. The Turks were, as usual, making their stand clear by actions as well as by words. In the discussions with the Turkish Ministers in Ankara, and then with the Greek Ministers in Athens, it became clearer still that no agreement at all was possible. It was difficult to see any way ahead.

There was one special problem which arose in my visit to Athens in February 1958 to participate with Selwyn Lloyd in the discussions with the Greek Government. Archbishop Makarios was in Athens. He had been released from his exile in the Seychelles but was prohibited from returning to Cyprus. Should I meet him when I was in Athens? I was most anxious to do so. Sooner or later he must take part in a settlement. He was a key figure, if not the key figure, in the whole puzzle. To put it at its lowest, if I went to Athens and didn't see him we should be not nearer but further away from any negotiation and any progress. Before leaving for Athens I called a big meeting of all my civil and military advisers. The question whether I should see Makarios in Athens was one of the main subjects we discussed. One after another those at the meeting advised strongly against seeing him. The fierce Turkish riots which had occurred only a few weeks before while I was in Ankara were fresh in our minds. If the Governor saw Makarios, Turkish fury would break out again. The advice was unanimous—and to me deeply depressing.

When I got to Athens I told Selwyn Lloyd of my anxiety to see Makarios, and of the unanimous advice against it amongst those who worked with me in Cyprus. I reminded him of this as our talks with the Greek Ministers proceeded. It was on the last night of our stay in Athens that we turned to discuss it again. He and I were due to fly away, he to London and I to Cyprus, the next morning. The Greek Ministers were guests at dinner at the British Embassy that night. Some time after midnight Selwyn Lloyd decided to give me a break, so he took Mr. Averoff and me aside. The Governor wanted to meet the Archbishop. What did Mr. Averoff think? Mr. Averoff was enthusiastic. He would send a message to Makarios at once. The messenger came back. Yes, the Archbishop would be glad to see me early in the morning at his hotel, the Grand Bretagne. Elaborate arrangements were made on our side to keep the meeting secret. I went to have breakfast in a private room in the hotel and then walked up the stairs to the Archbishop's suite.

I had half an hour's conversation with him. I had no proposal, no plan to discuss, but we were each anxious to get the measure of the other. We imagined that one day we would have to work closely together. We established that morning a personal understanding which was invaluable later.

Our talk over, I avoided the elevators and went down the stairs hoping to make my way unobserved to the airport where the R.A.F. plane was waiting to fly me back to Cyprus. But when I got to the main lobby of the hotel there, as far as one could see, was a flood of Press correspondents and photographers. The Greeks had apparently not shared my views about the desirability of keeping my talk with the Archbishop private. I got away after half an hour's fencing with the newspaper men. My overwhelming concern was to get quickly back to Nicosia. I pictured the Turkish reactions when news of my meeting with Makarios preceded me, and I feared that there would be more rioting. I imagined Nicosia in flames. As we flew on a lovely clear day over the Greek islands I asked the R.A.F. men to get, if they could, reports on the situation in Nicosia. What a relief to hear from the Deputy Governor as I landed that all was quiet. We often used to say that the one thing you could be sure of in Cyprus was that what you expected to happen wouldn't. Another thing we used to say was that anyone who understood the situation in Cyprus had been misinformed.

So after scarcely more than two months in Cyprus, London, Ankara and Athens, we were much worse off than when I first arrived. My proposals had utterly failed. The Turkish riots had put out new danger signals. EOKA was reorganised, and embarked on a new campaign of sabotage and assassination. Nevertheless we had started a new idea. This is how I repeatedly stated our aim throughout the terrible year of 1958:

"The conception is that the people of Cyprus should live in

peace in an undivided island, undisturbed by animosity from outside or inside the island, managing their own affairs, with the two communities working in secure confidence and mutual respect, and with the three interested powers of Great Britain, Greece and Turkey coming together in practical co-operation to give Cyprus all the advantages. I believe that that basic conception is sound and fair. I believe that it offers the only hope of escape from the perplexities and miseries of the existing situation."

That was the basis of the discussion I had with our Prime Minister at Nicosia airport on the 15th of February 1958. If the Greek and Turkish Governments wouldn't come to the conference table, and if we couldn't shift the negotiations back to Cyprus by ending the Emergency and bringing back the Archbishop, very well, we would work out a detailed constitutional programme ourselves. And this time we wouldn't ask everyone or anyone to agree. We would make it clear that whether they agreed or not we would go ahead with our plan. We would not allow violence or anything else to deflect us from it. This time we would ourselves take and keep the initiative.

Within two months we were ready with our new proposals. I went home to London again to discuss them. Then there was infuriating delay, first because of the Parliamentary Whitsun recess and then at the request of NATO. But on the 19th of June at last the Macmillan Plan was announced.

In a broadcast to the troops in Cyprus that night I said:

"What is the new policy? It can be summed up in three sentences. First, we want to give the best possible deal to all the people of the Island. Second, we want to bring the three Governments of Great Britain, Greece and Turkey together in a joint effort to make sure they get it. Third, we believe that this can only be achieved by Great Britain giving a definite and determined lead to break the vicious circle from which Cyprus has suffered so long."

This time we were determined to go ahead with the policy to the utmost extent possible whatever the opposition and violence against it. The Turks didn't even wait for the Plan to be announced. On the night of the 7th of June I was woken in the middle of the night to see from the balcony of Government House what looked like the whole of Nicosia aflame. There followed two months of what we had always most feared, civil war between the Greek and Turkish communities in the island. Most of the killings were isolated shootings, often of old people, lonely shepherds, even children. In those dreadful two months of communal hatred and cruelty 56 Greek and 53 Turkish Cypriots were murdered. Had it not been for the magnificent work of our troops working day and night to protect both sides, the slaughter would have been on a vast scale, for in all the main towns and many of the villages the Greeks and Turks lived side by side.

But the initiative began to have its effect. Within a few weeks of Mr. Macmillan's visit to Athens and Ankara in the summer of 1958, the Turkish Government, which had previously so violently opposed any proposal, came full circle and stated that if in fact the British Government would carry out the Plan the Turkish Government would support it. And then within a few months of the announcement of the Plan, Archbishop Makarios made his statement in favour of an independent Republic of Cyprus. In this all-important declaration he was backed by the Greek Government. The Zurich agreement made by the Greek and Turkish Governments, like the Macmillan Plan, was based on the conception that each community in the island should run its own affairs and that both should come together to run the island, with Great Britain, Greece and Turkey holding the ring to give the island the advantages of both independence and international security. These results would not have been achieved if, having taken the initiative, we had not shown that violence would not deflect us from it.

To bring the people of Cyprus together in constructive and peaceful co-operation, to establish democratic government, to remove the fear of the Turkish Cypriot community that it might become an oppressed and depressed minority, to create an effective guarantee by the joint action of the three Allied Governments for the independence of the island, to make Cyprus a symbol of unity instead of a source of discord, those were the objects we set ourselves from the beginning. Those were the objects which led in 1959 to the Zurich and London Agreements.

The most difficult thing throughout the turmoil and terror and the killing and the burning was to keep one's mind constantly on those objects. Almost every day throughout the worst months of 1958 one of my A.D.C.'s had to attend the funeral of one of our soldiers or policemen. Fury and hatred rose on all sides. But while one grieved for brave young men killed and understood so well the anger of the troops, all the time it was essential to remember that one day we must escape from the mess of malice; one day we must work with Greeks and Turks again. The temptation was to concentrate only on combating violence, improving our intelligence, breaking the terrorist hold on the island. Those things had to be done, and done thoroughly and fearlessly. But somehow, sometime we must come out. Always, all the time, it was necessary to look to that day and to avoid doing things which would make that impossible. Somehow or other we must save the island from going beyond the point of no return.

There were many days in that hot summer and autumn of 1958 when there seemed no hope at all. While I constantly reminded myself that we must find a settlement in the end, we were occupied from early morning till late at night with the full-time business of fighting a rebellion. T. E. Lawrence once said that fighting a rebellion was like eating peas with a knife, slow and messy. So it was. We had on our side fine, well-disciplined troops, every Emergency Regulation imaginable, all the paraphernalia of curfews and restrictions, and death penalties for carrying arms. EOKA had on its side a fanatical master of hit-and-run guerilla warfare in Grivas, a small, able, tough group of district leaders under him, a rebel discipline ruthlessly enforced by killing, the sentimental sympathy of the overwhelming majority of the Greek Cypriot population and the support of the Greek Government.

We were haunted right through the first half of 1958 by the overriding fear that the terrorist campaign against the British Government would turn into something much worse, a civil war between the Greek Cypriots and the Turkish Cypriots.

Ian Scott.
The News Chronicle.

THE BABY SITTER

When that came in the summer of 1958—it started with the Turkish disorders in Nicosia on the 7th of June—we faced an entirely new situation. The troops had to switch their effort from combating Greek violence to saving both Greeks and Turks from the attacks of the other side.

On the evening of the 12th of June amongst all the other reports of attacks by one community or the other I was told that a massacre had taken place not far from the Nicosia–Kyrenia road just beyond the Turkish village of Geunyeli. The exact number of casualties was not known, but it was believed that maybe a dozen Greek villagers had been killed. That night and the next morning we pieced together the facts. The whole of the Nicosia plain with its mixed villages of Greeks and Turks was at this time in a state of ferment and terror. The troops and the police had been working day and night, mainly successfully, to prevent clashes. That afternoon a British Police Sergeant had arrested 35 Greek villagers near Skylloura village. They were armed with clubs and stones and seemed about to attack the Turkish quarter of the neighbouring village. With the help of an escort of the Royal Horse Guards he intended to bring his prisoners to Nicosia to charge them with carrying offensive weapons, but on the way it was learnt that a riot was taking place outside the Central Police Station in Nicosia. There was confusion on what orders were then issued but the upshot was that the 35 Greeks were taken out on the Kyrenia road to a point beyond the Turkish village. There they were disarmed and told to walk the thirteen miles home to their village. They had only just started out on their homeward walk when they were set upon by a crowd of Turks who seemed to come from nowhere. Four of the Greeks were killed outright on the spot, four died later in hospital, five were severely wounded but survived. The rest escaped. I went myself to see the scene of this bloody engagement. There I heard a terrible rumour. It was being said that the British troops and police had conspired to deliver their prisoners to be slaughtered in the Turkish ambush. It was important to establish exactly what had happened. It was essential to kill this rumour. Had it been allowed to persist and grow it would have done lasting, irreparable harm to the reputation of the Security Forces.

As soon as I returned from the scene of the killing I asked the Chief Justice, Sir Paget Bourke, if he himself would undertake a formal enquiry. He readily and courageously agreed. I say "courageously" because any findings in such an enquiry would be subject to fierce and bitter, and maybe violent, reactions from one side or the other, or very likely from both. Then I had to convince the troops that the formal enquiry was essential. There is nothing soldiers dislike more than having to come from the scene of violence to justify their actions before civilian judges and answer for their decisions to hostile advocates. I have every sympathy with their attitude. They are ready to do their duty and take their orders and risk their lives but they rightly hate stepping into the political limelight and being subjected to cross-examination by lawyers whose purpose is often primarily political. But in this case, reluctantly at first, the soldiers came to agree that the vicious rumour which we all knew to be untrue must be scotched and that it could only be scotched by a full judicial enquiry. Eventually the Chief Justice's report was published. It made some criticisms of the actions taken that day, but on the main issue the report was definite and clear and final. This is the statement I made when the report was published:

"The main reason which led me to appoint the Commission of Inquiry was that a terrible suggestion was made and repeated that members of the Security Forces had intentionally contributed to the death of the unfortunate victims. I knew that that suggestion must be untrue. But so serious was the allegation that I considered that it should be immediately investigated by an impartial authority.

The Inquiry has supported my confidence that the suggestion made was utterly unfounded. The Chief Justice has found as follows:

'It is a fact that all concerned acted in the genuine belief that once the prisoners were on their way across country leaving Geunyeli, which was anyway under observation, behind, they ran no risk or danger and the worst they had to suffer was the weariness of the walk home. There was no intention to make these people, so to speak, run the gauntlet, or deliberately to expose them to risk or danger in making their way back; and indeed before this tribunal it has been stated by Counsel appearing for the survivors and heirs of the deceased members of the party that they did not associate themselves with any such wild and horrible suggestion. It has been submitted, however, that there was reckless indifference to the fate of the prisoners. I reject that submission on the evidence. There is no justification for it whatsoever. And I have no doubt at all that the impact of the terrible event that ensued came with almost as great a surprise, shock and horror to the members of the Security Forces engaged as it did to this unfortunate band of released prisoners themselves.'

I myself visited the scene the following day. I heard on the spot accounts given by the Military and Police Officers concerned and saw how shocked they were by the dreadful events of the previous evening. I also know very well that at that time of communal strife their ceaseless patrolling for days and nights on end and their prompt and effective action over wide areas saved hundreds of lives.

Had it not been for their efforts carried out with the greatest zeal the loss of life and damage to property would have been far heavier. I greatly admire the courage and resolution and tireless energy with which they carried out a task of the utmost difficulty and I am very glad that the Inquiry has wholly disproved the 'wild and horrible' allegation made against them."

Throughout the summer and autumn of 1958 the killing on both sides continued. British civilians were shot in the streets. Arrests multiplied. Arms were issued to British subjects. For months the dangers and the horrors increased in numbers and intensity.

On the afternoon of the 3rd of October I was working in my office in Government House when a message came that two British Army wives had been shot in the Greek quarter of Famagusta. They had been shopping in the narrow streets of the town when gunmen had attacked them at point blank range. One was dead, and the other not expected to live. This was the culmination of all the terrible events of the past few months. I knew that it would be impossible to hold our troops. I called for a helicopter and spoke to General Kendrew. We were in Famagusta within two hours of the killing but already the troops had gone wild. It was a wonder that there were not far worse casualties amongst the Greeks of Famagusta that afternoon. By the time General Kendrew and I arrived hundreds of Greeks were being treated for wounds inflicted indiscriminately by the furious soldiers. We had been very proud of the restraint and the discipline of our troops throughout the Emergency. Only on two or three occasions they gave way to fury. But this senseless and brutal crime of attacking the women threatened to let loose worse passions on every side. Our immediate visit to Famagusta helped to stop reprisals, but that night as I drove back late with General Kendrew to Nicosia I could see nothing but hatred and violence ahead.

We were fighting against violence but at the same time we had to deal with false accusation and false rumour. After the killing of Mrs. Cutliffe at Famagusta (the other Army wife later recovered) the rumour-manufacturers over-reached themselves. They tried to put it about that the attack on the women had been carried out by the British in order to put the blame on the Greeks.

During November of 1958 amongst all our local preoccupations we turned to watch what was taking place at the United Nations in New York. The Greek Government had decided to take the Cyprus issue yet again to the United Nations, this time with the popular appeal for independence. In earlier years they had managed to obtain a vote favourable to them. This year they determined to win a two-thirds majority if they could and thus force us off the policy we had declared. We read the long telegrams about lobbying in the world capitals and about resolutions, amendments, interminable manoeuvres in the United Nations Committees. We did not understand all the ramifications of United Nations procedure. In any event we saw no prospect of good coming from these remote discussions. If the Greeks won their two-thirds vote we should be further from an agreed settlement. If they lost there would no doubt be a wave of new violence. We admired the indefatigable efforts of the British delegation in stating our case and in working behind the scenes. As the long debates dragged on in the Political Committee of the General Assembly, we realised that our delegation was making steady progress. This time it had a definite policy to defend. The policy might have faults but it was patently a genuine effort to find a just course. As the final vote in the General Assembly approached we realised from the reports that this time the Greeks, far from winning a two-thirds majority, would not win the vote at all.

Our Ambassador, Sir Pierson Dixon, went down to the United Nations on the 5th of December to a personal triumph. The Iranian resolution which the United Kingdom supported had already been adopted in the Political Committee. Nearly all the votes were pledged. Now a voting victory was certain.

But as Sir Pierson Dixon went down that day to the final vote he could not be content. He could not get out of his mind the situation in Cyprus itself and the desperate need to find some escape from the vicious circle of violence. After the fierce in-fighting in the Political Committee there seemed just an outside chance of some compromise. Was it too late to find some way to ease the tension and make some move towards a settlement? Sir Pierson Dixon told me afterwards that as he went down that day to take part in the final vote a phrase stuck in his mind. "What we want today," he said to himself, "is not a victory but a success."

When he arrived at the United Nations building he asked the Turkish Foreign Minister, Zorlu, and the Greek Foreign Minister, Averoff, to come to see him. Zorlu came first. Couldn't something be done even at this last moment? Couldn't some move be made not merely to score in the vote but in the direction of a solution? Zorlu was not optimistic. He might listen to such a plea but the Greeks, he said, were in a frame of mind of Greek tragedy. It was no use talking to them. Where was Averoff? Why hadn't he come? They discovered that he had gone that day to meet the Greek Queen who had just arrived in New York. They found him on the telephone. Would he come down at once? He came and the representatives of Great Britain, Greece and Turkey spoke earnestly and urgently together while the General Assembly impatiently waited below.

At the end of that conversation Averoff and Zorlu shook hands and pledged themselves to work as rapidly as possible for a final settlement of the Cyprus problem.

What to do? They hurriedly drew up a new resolution. It meant very little—except that no one had won. Who could propose it? It was not possible for any of those who had sponsored either of the resolutions already before the Assembly to do so. The Mexican representative was not amongst the sponsors of the existing resolutions. Could he be found? Would he agree to sponsor the new resolution? Quickly he came and quickly understood and quickly agreed. The two Foreign Ministers and the two Ambassadors went down to the Assembly. To the astonishment of the delegates, nearly all of whom had solemnly promised their support to one or other of the resolutions already before the Assembly, a new resolution was proposed by the Mexican Ambassador which they had never heard of before. Immediately it was supported—more astonishment— by Great Britain, Greece and Turkey. It passed that day without debate, unanimously, a rare occurrence in the General Assembly.

Within three months from that date there was a settlement of the Cyprus issue. Not a victory but a success.

We in Cyprus read the telegrams reporting on the General Assembly's vote without fully understanding. We had had so many false starts and disappointed hopes already. The Foreign Ministers went home. Nothing seemed to happen. We turned again to our local pre-occupations. We had plenty of them.

I had at that time one main anxiety. It so happened that since I arrived in Cyprus a year before I had not had to confirm any death sentence. My predecessor, the Field Marshal, had confirmed a number of death sentences. He had commuted many more to life imprisonment, but he got no credit for that. When I arrived the walls of the Cyprus towns and villages carried the Greek painted insults against "Harding the Hangman". It was wholly unreasonable of course but I knew that if and when I confirmed a death sentence any hope I had of contributing to a settlement, to reconciliation, would be gone. As far as I was concerned that would be the point of no return.

In our colonial system it is the Governor, as representative of the Queen and in exercise of the Royal Prerogative, who must himself take the final decision on death sentences. He hears the advice of his Attorney-General and his Executive Council but when he has heard the advice he must take his decision alone. On this he can take no instructions from Ministers or anyone else. It is for him alone to decide whether the law shall take its course or whether the sentence shall be commuted to one of imprisonment. I had acted as Governor in Nigeria and I had been Governor of Jamaica for seven years. I knew the rules only too well.

There had been plenty of killing since I had arrived in Cyprus a year before but it had so happened that in all that year no murder case had been disposed of through all the judicial stages of trial and appeal. But now a case had been completed. Two Greek Cypriot youths had been convicted of murdering another Greek as he slept. It was no doubt a political murder. The crime had been brutal, the evidence was clear and complete. I examined every aspect of the case. I heard what the Attorney-General had to say and I heard the advice of my Executive Council. With a heavy sense of foreboding I realised that there was not the slightest justification for a reprieve. I signed the death warrants. I realised that as I did so it was the end of any contribution I could make. I remember saying to myself that day that I was signing my own political death warrant.

The warrants were signed on the Tuesday. I carefully went over all the preparations for the executions with the Army and police and prison authorities. There might be an attempt to attack the prison from outside. A whole brigade of troops made a cordon round the prison. We knew that all the other Greek prisoners within the prison would do everything they could to create disorder on the execution day. I told Denis Malone, the Director of Prisons, that I must leave it to him to decide what precautions he took in the prison itself, and what the actual time for the executions would be. I fixed the day—the following Thursday. The hangmen flew out from England (we did not want anyone stationed in Cyprus to invite assassination by carrying out the hangings). Late that Wednesday night I went to my room to lie down. I didn't undress for I knew that we had not long to wait. We knew that that night or very soon afterwards British soldiers, policemen or civilians would be killed by EOKA in reprisal. The next day would certainly be a terrible one. I had been in Cyprus for just over a year. This was the wretched end of all our hopes and efforts. A bloody failure.

Sylvia was up late that night. She happened to go into the Private Secretary's Office. She heard a telephone ring. She picked up one from the forest of telephones. It was a call from London—from Downing Street. It was for the Governor, could she get him? She ran to fetch me. It was from Lennox-Boyd, the Secretary of State. He said that he had spoken to the Prime Minister, and had had some delay in getting through to me. He knew of course of my decision about the executions. He did not doubt that I had been right. But there had been a new development which the Prime Minister and he decided I must know. That evening in Paris after a NATO meeting the Foreign Ministers of Greece and Turkey, Averoff and Zorlu, had come together to our Foreign Secretary, Selwyn Lloyd, and had jointly asked that the executions should not take place. Since their meeting at the United Nations earlier that month they had had little time for discussion but they still hoped to work together for an agreement. They had told Selwyn Lloyd that if the executions took place all hopes of a peaceful settlement would be destroyed. Lennox-Boyd went on to say that he fully realised that the decision was mine alone. He well understood all the difficulties and the arguments both ways too. The Prime Minister and he had decided that I must know of this new development, and they would back me either way.

I put down the receiver. I had no difficulty in deciding. I noticed that it was ten minutes before midnight. I called out for the escort cars—I never moved in those days without the escort of the Royal Horse Guards. I picked up another telephone to speak to Denis Malone, the Director of Prisons. "I'm coming down to see you" I said. He hesitated. In a strange, strained voice he said, "Could you give me half an hour?" "What do you mean by that?" I asked, "It will all be over in half an hour" he said. "No," I shouted, "you don't understand, I am coming down to stop it."

Malone in accordance with the discretion I had given him had decided to carry out the executions as early as possible on the appointed day. He had given orders that the hangings should take place at fifteen minutes after midnight.

I went to the Nicosia Prison. Outside I spoke to the Army Commander on the spot. It was a weird scene in the light of the yellow arc lights. And as I approached the prison entrance I heard the terrible din being made by the prisoners. They were shouting and screaming and banging on the doors and floors of their cells. I went in, saw Malone, the hangmen and the Greek priest, and as I did so the din suddenly stopped. There was absolute silence. By some strange telepathy the prisoners realised that something new had happened.

I went back to Government House that night taking the death warrants with me with a sense of overwhelming thankfulness and rejoicing. Divine providence? I don't know. But it was a near thing.

I was attacked in the British Press. "What happened," people said, "did the Governor lose his nerve?" Worse still, some said it was contemptible play-acting. A publicity stunt. Rushing down to the prison at midnight. Last minute reprieves. Playing with men's lives. I could not speak in explanation or justification of what I did that night. Lennox-Boyd several times asked Averoff and Zorlu to agree that I should be allowed to state the reason for my action. Zorlu thought not— and later when Zorlu was under trial in Turkey for his life I didn't tell the story. I thought that just possibly the joint request which he had made with Averoff might count against him. I didn't tell the story till Zorlu had been hanged himself.

It was hard to be silent under such criticism, and specially hard to know that many of the troops and police working with me were confused and angered by my apparent vacillation. The only consolation was to keep on reminding myself that it is for politicians to give explanations and excuses: an official does not reply to personal criticisms. We take a fierce pride in not answering back.

Now at last it was possible to have some hope. The Foreign Ministers of Greece and Turkey apparently meant business. Surely the reprieves would ease local animosities. God willing

1959 would be a better year. At any rate it couldn't be worse than 1958. Perhaps Christmas would bring back some good-will to the distracted island.

On the 20th of December two R.A.F. men went from their radio station in the Karpass to collect their rations. They turned their truck in the usual place. There was a great explosion. They were both blown to pieces by a land mine.

They were the last Service casualties of the Cyprus Emergency. But we did not know that at the time. On Christmas Eve there was talk of EOKA calling for a truce, but we were by this time too cynical and too hardened to believe it. In fact the rebellion was over.

II

"From that moment, as by a charm, the tumults subsided, obedience was restored, peace, order, and civilization followed in the train of liberty."

EDMUND BURKE

Nineteen fifty-nine was a year of sheer happiness. It was the year of agreement, of reconciliation, the year in which we had to create a Republic from nothing. There had been no representative institutions in Cyprus, apart from the municipal councils, for nearly a generation. But now we could leave killing and curfews and hangings behind us. Now we could give our whole effort to constructive work.

The London Agreement was signed in February. On the Sunday after my return we released everyone from the Detention Camps. Then we had to get Archbishop Makarios back and Grivas out. We announced the terms of an amnesty. We established a Cabinet system of government. We created new Ministries. We reformed the Government Service on a Ministerial basis. We had to set up the whole machinery of an independent State within a year. We organised the first national elections ever to be held in Cyprus on full adult suffrage.

Every week I had a long discussion with Archbishop Makarios. We met one week at Government House and the next at his Archbishopric. Every week too I met Dr. Kutchuk, the leader of the Turkish Cypriots, either at Government House or at his surgery. And every week too I presided at the Cabinet meeting with Greek and Turkish leaders sitting together.

The work hummed. By the end of 1959 we had done the job, and reduced the military garrison and the establishment of overseas police by more than two-thirds. As far as internal government was concerned we were ready to hand over.

But still we were not through. Independence was to have been achieved by February 1960, but only a month or so before the appointed date it became clear that we were still in disagreement with Archbishop Makarios on the subject of the British bases to be retained in Cyprus. For six months more we wrestled with wearisome and infuriating negotiations about the bases.

Julian Amery, the Under-Secretary of State from the Colonial Office, came out to negotiate. He came for a week and stayed six months. Every day I feared that the settlement made in the London Agreement would slip away from us, that the island would sink back into the enmities and bloodshed of the past. Nothing could be worse than to come out of the wood, and then to spend months following tortuous paths which seemed to lead back into the wood again. I can still feel the anguish of those months. At one stage the negotiations were dead-locked without even a meeting for forty-five days on end. It was like a long-drawn-out game of chess, with Archbishop Makarios on one side and Julian Amery on the other. Their skill and their patience and their persistence were well-matched. Makarios took us right up to the last minute. There came a time when, if agreement was not signed that day, it would be impossible to get all the necessary legislation for the establishment of the Republic passed in the House of Commons before the summer recess. If we didn't agree that day we might never come through and the whole structure of the London Agreement would collapse. On that day, having got all he hoped and much more than at one time he expected, Archbishop Makarios signed. The date for Cyprus Independence was fixed for the 16th of August.

On the night following this agreement the Archbishop asked Julian and Catherine Amery and Sylvia and myself and many other guests to a celebration dinner at Kykko Monastery near

MAN IN THE MIDDLE

Illingworth. Courtesy The Daily Mail.

Nicosia. After dinner, without explanation and without any reference to the painful and protracted negotiations we had just concluded, he told us a story:

"You see over there," he said, "my old teacher the Abbot of Kykko. Here it was that he brought me as a boy from my mountain village to study. He had heard from the monks at the monastery of my own village of Pano Panaiya that I had done well at my lessons. I became his pupil. He had confidence that I would become a priest and a scholar and he loved me as he would his own son." As the Archbishop told the story we looked across at the old Abbot of Kykko, a great favourite with us all, with his long grey beard and twinkling eyes. "Then the time came," the Archbishop continued, "when the Abbot told me that as I was going into the Church I must now grow a beard. I decided otherwise, and I told the Abbot that I did not propose to grow a beard until later. He was astonished at such insubordination. 'Then I must beat you,' he said. I replied that it would make no difference. He beat me, and I remember that every time he raised his arm I would turn and say 'No'. The next day he pleaded with me. I must obey him. What would my father, the shepherd, and my poor mother say if I were sent home with all hopes of a career in the Church lost? It would break their hearts. I insisted that in such a matter I must be allowed to decide for myself. The Abbott became beside himself with frustration and grief. If I would not obey him I must go home in disgrace. The next day I was sent to fetch a few belongings from a relative in Nicosia. The Abbot ordered the local taxi from Strovolos. The time came for me to go. He pleaded with me once more to change my mind. I made no reply. Sadly he led me out of his study down those steps over there, out through those great gates. And I remember that I actually put my foot on the step of the taxi before he broke down and threw his arms about me and said, 'My boy, come back, I cannot let you go.' "

All along the Archbishop had known that in the negotiations about the bases he had us where he wanted us. We could not afford to abandon the wider settlement of the London Agreement. He could negotiate up to the very last minute, and win his way.

I greatly admire the Archbishop's nerve and his political skill and his confidence in his own opinion. But I sometimes think that he enjoys to gamble, to go right up to the edge, to pit his wits against everyone else.

Just before Julian Amery left to go home after his long stay, I gave a farewell dinner for him and the Greek and Turkish leaders at Government House. We were then in the happy situation of being able to look forward to Cyprus Independence within a month or so. There were speeches by the Archbishop and Dr. Kutchuk and Mr. Amery. At the end, I said that there was an historical parallel in Cyprus which might give all those present some satisfaction. At one time in the eleventh century the ruler of Cyprus was King Amerie. He was succeeded by King Hugh (I had some difficulty in convincing those present that this was indeed an historical fact). I suggested that all of us could take some comfort from the fact that, whereas the reign of King Amerie had been magnificently long, the reign of his successor, King Hugh, was mercifully short.

The 16th of August came in one of the hottest summers I remember. We signed all the documents at a midnight ceremony. The next day the new President and Vice President came to say their farewells at Government House. Sylvia and I and our three sons drove to Famagusta and said goodbye to General Ken Darling and the Royal Horse Guards and the Black Watch. We sailed away in H.M.S. *Chichester* and heard the salute of guns from the ancient walls of Famagusta. As we looked back I remembered a quotation from Shakespeare I had used in jest when I arrived as Governor two and a half years before. I had referred to one of my predecessors as Governor of Cyprus, Othello, and to the cry which went up from the walls of Famagusta as his ship approached:

> "Bring renewed fire to our extinct spirits
> And give all Cyprus comfort."

Comfort? Perhaps not. But at least the killing was stopped.

The age-old problems of Cyprus were not solved: the animosities and the disputes were not removed. But now there was some hope.

One thing at least we had achieved. We had fought a rebellion, we had prevented a civil war, and there were no hard feelings between the British and the people of the island. Within a week or two of the end of the violence our troops were on terms of easy friendship again with Greeks and Turks alike and welcome everywhere. So it has remained.

It had not been easy to succeed a Field Marshal. Lord Harding was loved and respected by all those who served with him, but I had been specially fortunate to work with two such fine Generals as General Joe Kendrew and General Ken Darling. I remembered General Kendrew from years ago seeing him at Twickenham leading the forwards as Captain of England. He won four D.S.O.s in the war. He was as straight and as honourable and as courageous as anyone I have ever met. General Ken Darling, who followed him, was short, fiery, outspoken, consumed with a fierce energy and determination. We used to meet every day, alone usually, when the worst rush of the day was over. Having compared our opinions and pooled our proposals, we were never once in disagreement on what should be done. And our unity and friendship ran through all who worked with us.

One night when the situation was at its worst I heard a report that in the village of Kythrea where an operation was in progress witnesses under examination were being tortured. I spoke to General Darling. We set out together for the village in an armoured car in the very early hours of the morning. We arrived without warning. We spoke to the witnesses. We saw no evidence of maltreatment. A snap visit like that was not an insurance against brutality, but the fact that we went together that night and the purpose of our visit, was known to every member of the Security Forces. More effective than all the written orders.

We could claim when we finished that we had worked to give the new Republic a good start, and that all through the bad times of violence and bloodshed we never abandoned the purpose of keeping the fight clean on our side.

On the night I left Cyprus I said in a broadcast:

"What of the future? It is for you to answer that question. A few dismal commentators say that the people of Cyprus will destroy each other. They say that you will tear your-selves to bits—Greek against Turk and Left against Right. There are a few who say that the Island will go down in a sea of blood and hate.

It could be—but I don't believe it. People who have been to the brink of hell don't want to go over the edge. I know the difficulties and dangers as well as anyone, but I myself have faith in your ability, and in your good sense too. I believe that the forces of moderation and tolerance and com-passion, and the desire to serve all the people of Cyprus well, and an overwhelming wish for peace, will prevail."

CHAPTER X

The United Nations

"For which I am an ambassador in bonds: that therein I may
speak boldly, as I ought to speak."
ST. PAUL'S EPISTLE TO THE EPHESIANS, VI. 20

I

WHEN I came back to England from Cyprus I went to my
father in Cornwall. I had not yet made up my mind what I
would do next, and I wanted to consult him. But as soon as
I came home the Congo crisis broke and at once I felt that if
I possibly could I would like to help the United Nations in its
tremendous task. I walked up to the Callington Post Office
and sent this telegram:

"Dag Hammarskjöld
United Nations
New York

Respectfully offer to perform any task for United Nations
in Africa or elsewhere Stop Have just finished my assignment
as Governor of Cyprus having completed thirty years
work in Middle East Africa and West Indies Stop All the
countries in which I have worked are now self-governing or
about to be Stop Glad to serve the United Nations temporarily or otherwise in any capacity whatever.

Hugh Foot"

As I walked home I felt ashamed of myself. Dag Hammarskjöld was at that time perhaps the busiest man in the world. He
had performed the astonishing feat of assembling in a few days
and nights an international military force and airlifting it to
the Congo. He faced tremendous responsibilities, great international pressures, almost unbelievable strain. Who was I

to worry him at such a time? I told myself that I was suffering from delusions of self-importance.

To my surprise a reply came back at once from Hammarskjöld himself thanking me for my offer, saying that he would be glad to see me if I could come to New York—but adding that just at that time it might be rather awkward to employ an Englishman in the Congo.

I made my plans to get to New York, but before I could set out Prime Minister Macmillan sent for me, and I went to see him at Admiralty House.

He had been thinking what I, "a Colonial Governor who had run out of colonies," should do next, he said; and he had the idea that I might "follow my sheep to the fold of the United Nations." My main task, he suggested, might be to deal with the subjects of concern to the new nations. His proposal was that I should work in New York, and possibly Washington too, in close association with the representatives of the new nations, specially with the Commonwealth countries, and he told me to discuss his idea with four men—Mr. Iain Macleod, then the Colonial Secretary, Sir Frederick Hoyer-Millar, the Permanent Under-Secretary at the Foreign Office, Sir Harold Caccia, our Ambassador at that time in Washington, and Sir Patrick Dean, our Ambassador to the United Nations. I said that I was intensely interested in the new nations, that I had already hoped to work at the United Nations and that to undertake the kind of work in New York and Washington which he had outlined was exactly what I would most wish to do. I would go at once to see the four men he had named.

I did so, and the upshot was that I went in 1961 to join the United Kingdom Delegation to the United Nations. I was to serve under Sir Patrick Dean, the Head of our Mission to the United Nations. I was to have the personal rank of Ambassador and I was to be the principal adviser to the United Kingdom Mission on problems affecting the "emergent and newly emerged countries". I was also to be available to advise our Ambassador in Washington on these subjects, and was to be the representative of the United Kingdom in the Trusteeship Council and the Fourth Committee of the General Assembly. And, lest I should find time heavy on my hands, I was also instructed "to undertake speaking engagements throughout the United States".

My terms of reference were somewhat different from those of my predecessor, Sir Andrew Cohen, but in effect I was to take over from him. When I had been in Nigeria I had worked closely with Sir Andrew who was then at the Colonial Office and the main assistant to the Secretary of State on African affairs. I had followed his subsequent career, first as Governor of Uganda and then as British spokesman on Colonial questions at the United Nations. I had an admiration for him. I had not always understood or agreed with all he did, but I respected his fertile brain and his unrivalled experience of African affairs. He is an extraordinary man, restless, impatient, apparently absent-minded, the despair of his secretaries, and the terror of anyone foolish enough to be driven by him on any public highway. He is now the Director General of the Department of Technical Co-operation (what a wretched name!) which is mainly responsible for directing British assistance to overseas countries. I knew that his knowledge and originality and conviction had won him a fine reputation at the United Nations, and I was proud to follow him in New York.

The peak of the work at the United Nations comes during the main Annual Meeting of the General Assembly which starts in September and goes on till Christmas. Sylvia and I arrived in New York well before the 1961 Assembly began and were lucky enough to install ourselves at once in a little house in 52nd Street belonging to our old friend, Edward Molyneux. Most people in New York live in huge blocks of apartments but we were fortunate to have a house with a front door and a back garden of our own, furnished by Molyneux himself with some of his own paintings to remind us of him. We were within ten minutes' walking distance of the United Nations' building and only a little further from the United Kingdom Mission, then at 99 Park Avenue. Sylvia and I had none of the heavy social responsibilities of a Head of Mission but several times a week we would have small lunch parties for eight—and United Nations delegates were happy to escape for an hour or so from the bustle of the crowded Delegates' Lounge and the din of the Delegates' Dining Room.

I was soon immersed in the hectic life of a delegate to the United Nations. I have never worked longer hours. Any research or careful preparation had to be done very early in the morning. Then we would get to our Mission offices at 8 o'clock, or soon afterwards, and our first duty was to read the telegrams which had come in during the night. All the troubles of the world eventually come to the United Nations, and our Ambassadors and High Commissioners and Governors round the world repeat many of their reports to our Mission in New York. Action was not required on all of them, and in any event I was concentrating on the new nations and their problems. I did not have to follow in detail the interminable discussions on disarmament, for instance, or all the complicated financial and economic questions which are dealt with in the United Nations. I was not directly concerned with such subjects as Kuwait or Cuba or the United Nations' budget, or the activities of the United Nations' Agencies such as the World Health Organisation or the Food and Agriculture Organisation or with the work of the United Nations for refugees. But many of the morning telegrams on such subjects as New Guinea, Singapore, Aden, British Guiana and Malta, as well as the problems of the African countries, did very much concern me. And in any event it was well to have a passing knowledge of everything likely to lead to some sudden United Nations crisis.

So we started the day by reading rapidly through reports of scores of difficulties and disputes and disasters and dangers—a substantial breakfast of all the worries in the world.

Scarcely had we finished this disturbing task when we would assemble for the early morning Mission meeting. Nearly all the one hundred and thirteen Missions find such morning meetings essential. The senior members of the Mission come together to review the events of the day before and plan for the day ahead. In the United Kingdom Mission about twenty of us would meet for the daily Mission meeting, and while the General Assembly was in session that number would be doubled, usually during the Assembly with a Minister in the chair. This exercise had to be done at the gallop. Half an hour was the absolute limit. We would quickly run over the current work before the various Committees. Each of us would be called on to give an account in a sentence or two of the difficulties we were facing, the objects we had in mind and the subjects on which we would welcome support in the corridors from our other delegates. We were mainly dealing with daily tactics—all at a great pace. For by half past ten, many of us must be down at the United Nations' building ready for the meetings of the day. And those of us who dealt with Trusteeship and Colonial matters sat with very little break all through the year, in the Fourth Committee or the Trusteeship Council or the Colonial Committee of Seventeen (now the Committee of Twenty-four).

The Committees usually started rather later than the declared time of half past ten but we continued, with a break for lunch, till six o'clock, occasionally with a night session to follow. Often the long debates in the Committees were dull, and sometimes it was possible to read reports or draft telegrams as they proceeded. But the United Kingdom representative had to be on the alert all the time. He had to be ready to reply or to protest or to intervene in the debate. And when the day's debates were over he had to be prepared to report at once to London.

Later in the evening there would usually be at least one reception to attend—sometimes as many as three or even four—and often a dinner after that. These receptions given by the Delegations on national days or for visiting Foreign Ministers could scarcely be described as social occasions. Most of the wives refused to come knowing that the men would talk only United Nations' business, and indeed the receptions were opportunities to do much of the day's work. To seek out other delegates, try to find out what they intended to say and how they proposed to vote, endeavour to persuade them by some fresh argument, suggest some compromise, try out a new idea, communicate some information just received, argue, propose, urge, threaten—the work often went on far into the night.

There was an interval between the end of the debates in the Committees at six o'clock and the first reception, and that was the most important time of the day. Each delegate would dash back through the rush of the evening traffic in New York to his Mission office. His duty was to report by telegram to his Government on the day's proceedings and most important of all, to make proposals and recommendations for the future.

The recommendations made by United Nations' Delegations were not always accepted in the capitals of the world—as I later had good reason to know—but they had to be taken into account. No country can afford to disregard the weight of United Nations' opinion.

Not all the Delegations kept in as close touch with their capitals as we did with London, but Delegations cannot act on any matter of importance without instructions from their Governments. Every night during the session of the General Assembly, and most other nights too, the stream of telegrams goes out reporting and recommending.

The recommendations vary of course according to the subject and the country concerned, but generally they have a common purpose. To avoid a deadlock or a clash, to escape from an isolated position, to find some common ground, to search for a compromise, to initiate some new proposal likely to win a wide consensus of support, to reach agreement—these are the purposes which usually dominate the recommendations.

I sometimes felt, as we dictated our evening telegrams and thought of all the other Delegations doing the same with the same purposes at the same time, that New York was like a heart pumping out conciliation to every great capital of the world. New York has become the diplomatic centre of the world, and the daily flow of telegrams from the United Nations constitutes a new and powerful influence in world affairs.

We Europeans, by the way, had one advantage in our communications with our capitals. We would send off our telegrams at any time during the evening or the night making our recommendations and asking for instructions. Our telegrams would be in London first thing the next morning and the Foreign Office would have the whole morning to study the reports and recommendations and (owing to the five-hour difference between London and New York time) could still get us a reply before we left our Mission office to go down to the United Nations' Committees at half past ten New York time that morning. I sometimes wondered how the Far Eastern delegations managed.

A delegate's life at the United Nations is rushed and ha-

rassed, requiring unlimited patience. Much of his time is spent
in reading reports and listening to long speeches. He must
endure the specialised and pompous jargon in which many
United Nations' documents are written—too often a succession
of woolly clichés. The speeches are often uninspired and usually
read from a prepared script, for the delegate is in effect merely
reading the detailed instructions of his Government. Often the
speech is intended more for the newspapers in the speaker's
home country than for the United Nations. So many of the
debates are tiresome and tedious. I must admit too that sometimes I found the lobbying distasteful, though I recognised the
need for it.

These are the chores of United Nations' work. But suddenly
the crises come. A dull debate will in a moment jump into life.
Quite unexpectedly some quick decision will be essential. And
just beneath the sometimes oily surface the swell of feeling and
the tide of opinion are always moving.

Once when Foreign Minister Paul Henri Spaak of Belgium
was with us in the Fourth Committee, he became infuriated
by our untidy methods and our strange procedures. I answered
him then:

"The distinguished Foreign Minister of Belgium has been
puzzled by the procedures of the Fourth Committee. He is
not alone in that predicament. He suggested that we should
proceed in our discussions step by step from one decision and
conclusion to another. Such a reasonable progress would
appeal to his orderly and logical mind. But we in the Fourth
Committee don't work like that. Our way is a slow cooking
process, with more than a hundred cooks. And our method
of cooking in the Fourth Committee is to put everything into
the pot. Reports, statements, questions, answers, explanations, they all go into the pot. Flavouring material is then
added—some nationalist relish, and a plentiful supply of
Russian vinegar and occasionally, Mr. President, some spice
of humour. Then it is all mixed up together. We all stir the
pot vigorously and bring it to the boil and serve it piping
hot to the Assembly, in the form of a resolution.

These are our methods, Mr. President, as we well know,

and we are unlikely to change them. But let me assure the distinguished Foreign Minister that the final dish is nearly always much more attractive than the original mess.

These procedures may not be logical. But let me also, with affectionate respect to the Fourth Committee, assure the distinguished Foreign Minister that in this Committee there is much good sense and much good-will. There is, moreover, in this Committee a ready response to sincerity and a genuine respect for outstanding ability, and we all deeply appreciate the way in which the distinguished Foreign Minister has with great patience and thoroughness and understanding set before us the reasons for the actions of his Government and for the new proposals which his Government has made. What he has said has carried great conviction and if, as we greatly hope, a sound solution is found for the grave problems of Ruanda-Urundi, we all shall know very well that that result has been due to the character and efforts of the very experienced and very distinguished Foreign Minister of Belgium."

Foreign Minister Spaak showed us all what can be done in the United Nations by the personal influence of one man. Belgium had previously infuriated the Africans by its actions in the Congo. So when we had to deal with the last of the Belgian colonies in Africa, Ruanda and Burundi, he had a particularly difficult task to win the support of the United Nations for the Belgian proposals. He came and sat for three weeks in the humble Fourth Committee. He met the Afro-Asians and with infinite patience listened to them and tried to meet their views. Sometimes I thought that he would explode in anger, but he just managed to keep his temper. And in the end agreement was reached. The final overwhelming vote was taken in the General Assembly. The Russian delegate was unwise enough to attempt a parting crack at Belgium. M. Spaak replied in a brilliant unprepared speech attacking the Russians as troublemakers, wreckers, instigators of chaos in Africa. As he warmed to his theme he was repeatedly cheered by the Afro-Asians. The Russians sat glum. And finally one of the French-speaking Africans rose to congratulate Belgium on leaving Africa "with flying colours". It was a triumph for M. Spaak's persistence and patience and eloquence.

It was the influence of individual personality that made the work of the United Nations so fascinating.

Presidents and Prime Ministers and Foreign Ministers came to the United Nations. They came for many reasons, but mainly because no country can neglect the United Nations now. When they came they were subject to new ideas and new pressures and new contacts. They sometimes failed to judge the temper or the mood of the General Assembly. Some of them looked puzzled, in the unfamiliar glare of the Assembly, by these new influences in world affairs, influences which they could not control and could not yet fully assess or understand.

But, while the great world figures came and went, it was the permanent delegates who carried the constant strain and kept up with the pace of the crises, big and small, which somer-saulted over one another in daily succession. The personalities of the main delegates became factors of vital importance. A powerful nation can quickly lose influence by reason of a weak delegate, and a small country can become powerful in council when represented by a man who commands personal respect. Delegates tend to judge a country by its United Nations' representative. The only woman Ambassador to the United Nations, Agda Rossel of Sweden, for instance, was a worthy representative of a country with the best United Nations record and reputation in the world. She set a high standard of informed and effective initiative. She knew very well the first rule of success at the United Nations, which is that you cannot carry others with you unless you give your whole mind and effort to the job in hand. Foreign Ministers or Heads of Mission who hope to descend on the Assembly and impress by super-ficial speeches without preparing the ground by the hard work of discussion and persuasion in advance soon learn their lesson. Another outstanding United Nations' personality is Ambassador Boland of Ireland, an ex-President of the General Assembly, who is always at the centre of events, shrewd, genial, fully familiar with every new development. His special strength lies in his independence of action, and his influence with his own Government—a rare asset which distinguishes a few principal Ambassadors from those who merely carry out their instructions. Omar Lufti of the United Arab Republic, whose death a year or two ago was such a loss, was universally liked and greatly respected. He later became a United Nations' Under-Secretary under U Thant but even when he was Head of the Egyptian Mission he was first and foremost a United Nations' man—and not a worse delegate of his country on that account. The Commonwealth representation was strong and influential with men like Sir Zafrullah Khan of Pakistan, Sir James Plimsoll of Australia, Jha and later Chakravarty of India, Quaison-Sackey of Ghana and Adebo of Nigeria in the first rank at the time when I was there.

Most of the Heads of Missions are experienced diplomats. Some, like our own Sir Patrick Dean, are also lawyers trained in presenting a case and able to bring a barrister's concentration to one subject after another. All are men of wide experience in world affairs. Some of them affect a superior cynicism, but I have not met one of them who does not believe in the United Nations as an increasingly powerful, indeed an essential, instrument for world progress and international understanding.

Amongst all the turmoil and pressures and conflicts close personal friendships sprang up. I had a special respect and affection for Oberemko, my opposite number in the Soviet Delegation. He was fierce and damaging in debate, but his quickness and his eloquence and his wit made him an opponent worth fighting. Almost daily we would go for each other in the Committees. Sometimes I could score by making him laugh. When he referred to me as "Mr. Foot, a subordinate colonial official" I replied that it was interesting to watch the Russians, with an insistence on rank and status, becoming snobs. One day if he stuck carefully to the party line he would, I felt sure, become Sir Valentine Oberemko or even, perhaps, Lord Oberemko of Turtle Bay. Once he was due to go back to Moscow on leave. That evening there was a specially bitter exchange in the Trusteeship Council. I asked to say a personal word to the Council at the end. I said that I felt an affection and admiration for the distinguished delegate of the Soviet Union. Angry members of the Council glared. I added: "The sort of admiration and affection felt by the toreador for the

bull". Oberemko laughed, and the tension was broken. I
wished him a happy stay in his own country and a speedy
return to the free world.

I had no difficulty in speaking about the British colonial
record. This extract from a statement I made in the Committee
of Seventeen in August 1962 sums up the argument which I
repeatedly pressed and elaborated (and I persuaded the
Committee to agree to include this extract from my statement
in its formal report to the General Assembly).

"The aims and, to a large extent, the methods of our general
policy have been the same in the three main areas of Africa:
first in West Africa, comprising Nigeria, Ghana, Sierra
Leone and Gambia, with a population approaching fifty
million; second, in East Africa, comprising Tanganyika,
Uganda, Kenya and Zanzibar, with a population of about
twenty-three million; and thirdly, Central Africa, comprising
Southern Rhodesia, Northern Rhodesia and Nyasaland, with
a population of about eight million. With all the striking
differences which exist between the varying problems of these
diverse territories, we have followed the same main policy
and the same system of administration.

Representative Government
We created in each of the territories separate governments
so that the people should gain experience in the management
of their own affairs and so that the transition from bureaucracy to democracy could take place as quickly as possible by
progressive and natural stages. With the people we worked
out systems of representative government, and established
parliaments in every territory under our administration.

Career Civil Services
We created public services owing allegiance not to a party
and not to a tribe, but to all people of the country they serve.

Impartial Courts
We established impartial courts, free from interference by

the Executive, dispensing justice without regard to party or race or politics, without regard to anything except the necessity to administer equal justice.

Local Security Forces

We created local security forces, both military and police forces, so that, when these countries attained independence, they had their own means at their own disposal to maintain law and order without recourse to outside assistance or intervention.

Education

We gave special attention to the problems of education — first, by building up the basic structure of primary and secondary education, and also by giving early access to higher education so that the political and professional leaders of these new countries would be progressively and rapidly enabled to take over the leadership of their own countries. We are proud of our tradition by which one out of every ten students of higher learning in England comes from overseas; two out of every three of them from the Commonwealth. We have in my country a much larger proportion of university places allotted to men and women from Asia and Africa than any other country in the world, and we followed this up by the establishment of one university after another in Africa itself. Not the least of these advances has been in East Africa where, following the fine tradition of Makerere in Uganda, branches of the new university of East Africa have been established in Kenya and Tanganyika too.

Economic Aid

On the economic side, it is well to recall that British aid and investment for developing countries since the war amounts to about £3,000 million, and that a higher proportion of our national income has been directed in such aid to underdeveloped countries even than that provided by the United States.

National Unity

While we have given ourselves through recent decades to these tasks our over-riding purpose in all these territories has been to bring people together in constructive effort. We recognise the value of diversity but whether it was in Ghana or Nigeria or Sierre Leone or Tanganyika or Uganda or Zanzibar or Kenya, our purpose has been to overcome racial and sectional and tribal differences, and to foster a true national patriotism.

Often we hear in this Committee the old worn-out phrase 'Divide and rule'. In fact, the record shows that our purpose throughout has been to unite and to set free."

I had ample opportunity to state our case in the various Committees dealing with colonial affairs. My difficulty was not with the case but in getting permission to present it. I had to persuade my own masters that "we should be prepared to discuss, justify and defend the policies we follow". I went to London to urge this course and in the end it was accepted. Not without a fight. Our first instructions were to claim that all discussion on our individual colonial territories was *ultra vires*, and we were told to speak on our policy in individual territories only with special advance authority from London and then only "to correct briefly any glaring misstatements". In the memorandum I took to London I said:

"The question is whether we join in discussion seeking by vigorous and confident justification to influence debate, or whether we are to enter the Committees with our tongues tied behind our backs. If we follow the latter course we shall get the worst of all worlds. We shall play into the hands of our enemies and make it difficult or impossible for our friends to help us."

Looking back I am amazed that there was so much pressure from London to let our strong case go by default, to adopt an attitude of superior silence, to refuse to speak, to threaten to walk out of the Committee and not to participate in the debates or the votes. But had we accepted our first instructions without making strong and repeated protests that was the course we would have followed.

It took more than a year to get approval that we should speak up, answer back, justify, defend, confidently adopt an aggressive attitude. Some high officials and some Ministers in London took exactly the opposite view, but in advocating a positive and militant course I was backed by my own delegation and by the Foreign Office, and finally by Mr. Duncan Sandys and Mr. Iain Macleod.

I have spoken so far about work in the Trusteeship Council, the Fourth Committee and the Committee of Seventeen. It was not normally my duty to speak in the General Assembly itself. That was the function of the Foreign Secretary or other Ministers or the Head of my Mission, Sir Patrick Dean. But any delegate to the United Nations looks forward to the day when he will speak for the first time from the rostrum in the great chamber of the General Assembly.

My first opportunity to do so came unexpectedly. The Fourth Committee one day had for some reason finished early and I casually wandered into the General Assembly to watch what was happening there. I sat down next to the Head of our Chancery, Alan Campbell, and idly tried to follow what was taking place. Apparently a well-supported resolution had just been introduced expressing sympathy with Algerian prisoners in Paris who were on hunger strike. Alan leant across to me and said that I would have to speak. I was appalled. I didn't know the subject and I hadn't been present when the resolution was moved. But apparently Sir Patrick Dean was occupied in a Committee elsewhere and there was no one else from our Delegation available at the moment. What was I to say? Alan told me it was quite simple. All I had to do was to protest against the introduction of a snap resolution without warning and with no time allowed to Delegations to obtain instructions from their Governments. As he was speaking to me to my utmost relief I saw in the distance Sir Patrick Dean approach. I hastily made room for him and whispered to him that he would have to make the protest. No, he said, he had to get back at once to his own Committee. So I was left again with the depressing prospect of making an unpopular protest on a subject on which I knew nothing. I made my way to the rostrum. I explained that I was speaking not to the substance of the resolution but solely to a point of procedure; but in the name of my Government I must register a protest. I miserably returned in the silence of general disapproval to my seat. My great moment of addressing the General Assembly had come—and shamefully gone. My depression was not lessened by hearing Ambassador Boland of Ireland speak immediately after me. He too was objecting to the rushed resolution, but he coupled his objection with an eloquent and moving reference to the historic sufferings of Ireland and Irish sympathy with all prisoners, all hunger-strikers, all oppressed people. He was going to abstain on the vote for the same reasons as we were, but he resumed his seat to a murmur of appreciative applause.

I had a happier opportunity in the General Assembly soon afterwards. The annual debate on colonialism had been going on for days in the Assembly. This was my subject but I expected the Minister, Mr. Godber, to make the reply for the United Kingdom Government. Then he had suddenly to leave for London, and I was left to hold the fort. The final day of the debate dragged on into a night session. We had to listen to long, dreary, offensive speeches first from the representatives of the Byelorussian Soviet Socialist Republic and then from Mr. Lapin, the representative of the U.S.S.R. Their speeches went on till well after midnight. As Great Britain had been the main object of their attack some reply was essential. It was a quarter to one when I made my way to the rostrum. In the vast Assembly there were only a few weary delegates left—an occasional head bobbing about, so it seemed, in a wide sea of emptiness. But this time I had no inhibitions and no notes, and no instructions. It was good to keep the Soviet representatives longer in their places. I attacked them on what they had said on Nigeria, India, Kenya, Tanganyika. I enjoyed myself that night. I went on:

"The representative of the Soviet Union speaks about slavery, and certainly slavery has a shameful record in the history of the human race. He is speaking about a very long time ago, in which many people were concerned in the trade of slavery. But we are more interested in the slavery, the neo-slavery, of our own age when great numbers of people have been brought in our own times and in our own generation under foreign domination. It is the neo-slavery of the Soviet system which we condemn.

We come to a specific case. We talk about the islands of the Pacific. The Soviet representatives in the Trusteeship Council and elsewhere concentrate their interest on what is taking place in the islands of the Pacific, in New Guinea, for instance, and in the tiny island of Nauru. But what happens in the Soviet Islands? What happens in the Kurile Islands? This question was raised specifically by my Minister, but not a word of answer has been given by the Soviet representatives. These islands, also in the Pacific, remain in the sinister silence of Soviet domination. Not a word—no information whatever is provided. They are not made Trust Territories. We know nothing about what goes on in them. They are treated as part of the Soviet empire, and from the time they entered the Soviet empire not one word has reached the outside world.

We are experts in enfranchisement. We have brought to enfranchisement and into the councils of the world three times the population of the Soviet Union in the last sixteen years. I am not surprised that the Soviet representatives are ignorant of this process. They are not experts in enfranchisement; they are experts in suppression. We are the people who, particularly in these last few decades—the decades with which I myself have been familiar—have worked to bring people to the full stature of independence, and we are proud of our record.

The new countries of the Commonwealth have come forward into freedom while the satellites of the Soviet Union have gone backward into neo-slavery.

We sometimes feel, when we have been listening to these old accusations time after time, as if we had been listening to a worn-out gramophone record, a cracked record. We listened earlier in this debate to Mr. Kiselev. He said 'the fight for independence in Tanganyika continues'. The fight for independence continues in Tanganyika—that is what he said. Two weeks from today, Tanganyika will celebrate its independence. At this very moment, when according to our Soviet friends the struggle, the fight, continues in Tanganyika, the people of Tanganyika are in fact preparing the celebrations to mark the time, when, with the full approval and co-operation of the United Kingdom, they reach their independence. So much for the cracked record of the Soviet Union.

And the same progress goes forward in our other territories. One after another the territories of the British Commonwealth are brought forward to self-government, self-determination, independence. One after another they join this Assembly. It is a record which we justify, a record which we defend, it is—and I say it again—a record of which we are proud. All my life I have been devoted to the preparations which the Soviet Union representative so much scorns. And all my life I have worked with the people of these countries to build parliaments, to create civil services, to the task of training and education . . .

Finally I would say one word about the subject of nationalism. I believe that nationalism, one of the great forces of our century, of our generation, is a force for good. I believe that the new nations which have been brought on the tide of nationalism to this Assembly may save the world. I believe that their influence may be decisive in the future. No country —neither the Soviet Union nor any other country—can disregard them. They are going to have a vital influence in the future. I thank God that it is so. I believe that they are in many ways the hope of the world. They came here on a tide of nationalism. Nationalism, I agree, can turn to racialism, can turn to evil; but nationalism can be the source of patriotism and the source of pride and constructive effort. Does the Soviet Union believe in nationalism? I have taken some trouble to discover what was the latest pronouncement of the Soviet Union from the highest quarter on the question of nationalism. They say one thing here; they say different things at home. And, on nationalism, shall I read to the Assembly this section of the party declaration issued in the Soviet Union very recently? This declaration of the all-

powerful party calls for 'a relentless struggle against manifestations and survivals of nationalism of all types'. That is
the Soviet Union speaking to its own people at home—not
the way it speaks here. It goes on:

'The liquidation of manifestations of nationalism is in
the interest of all nations and nationalities of the USSR.'

I believe, we all believe, that one of the great movements
of this generation, of this age, is the creation of new nations.
And I am glad and proud that I have been, all my life, able
to associate with some of the peoples concerned in creating
those new nations.

I reject the accusations which have been made, and I am
very glad to have this opportunity, even at this late hour, of
rejecting in particular the accusations made by the Soviet
Union."

II

"We rejoice with you that the difficult transition from colony
to self-government can be accomplished in the great British
Commonwealth not violently, but peacefully, not with obstruc-
tion, but encouragement, preserving with it those priceless bless-
ings of British justice, education and public responsibility."

ADLAI STEVENSON, SPEAKING IN JAMAICA IN 1953

When I had survived my first session of the General Assembly
the opportunity came early in 1962 to visit a part of the world
quite new to me. All my overseas service had so far been in
Arabia and Africa and the West Indies. Now I had the chance
to go to the Pacific. I was elected by the Trusteeship Council to
be Chairman of a United Nations' Visiting Mission to Australian New Guinea and Nauru.

I was glad to go for many reasons. It was good to escape for a
while from the diplomatic centre and go back to the more
familiar administrative circumference. I would be travelling
east of Arabia for the first time in my life. I would have the
chance to stop for a few weeks on the way to the Pacific to visit
Ceylon and then Malaya. I would be able to go to Canberra
to talk with the Australian Government—and since I worked
with the Australian sappers on the desert railway in the war I
had always hankered after a chance to get to Australia. I would

be going with two of my best United Nations friends, Ambassador Carlos Salamanca of Bolivia and Ashok Bhadkamkar of India. The fourth member of our Mission was to be an American, Delmas Nucker, who had been for many years High Commissioner in the American Pacific Islands, so I had a strong and experienced team with me.

I already knew a little about the strange problems of New Guinea and Nauru. Amongst the last of the territories under United Nations supervision (all the United Nations Trust Territories outside the Pacific have already attained independence) they presented, in their entirely different ways, unique problems. Moreover I thought that our task had a special importance and significance for the United Nations. We were not merely a mixed committee going to visit and comment on two remote territories. We would be able to show that the United Nations in action could be fearless in criticism but fair in its judgment and positive in its recommendations. The enemies of the United Nations direct their criticism particularly to what they call irresponsibility in colonial issues. They like to give a picture of United Nations debates as exhibitions of wild emotionalism and intemperate rhetoric. They speak of the "interference" of the United Nations as something to be feared. Now we in our Mission had an opportunity to show that the United Nations could do a sound, sensible, constructive job without for a moment forgetting the principles for which the United Nations stands.

I knew enough about previous discussions in the Trusteeship Council on Australian New Guinea and Nauru to realise that our task would be a delicate one. The Australians were rightly proud of their work in the two territories. They are very sensitive to criticism. Could we gain their confidence as well as the confidence of the people of New Guinea? Was it possible to reconcile United Nations' anxiety to see rapid steps to end colonialism with Australian insistence on solid preparation for self-government? If we could succeed we would have served the people of New Guinea and the Australians and the United Nations well. If we failed, Australia would become vulnerable to anti-colonial attack and, at the same time, those who wished to discredit the United Nations would be encouraged in their contention that the United Nations is unrealistic, unpractical and unreasonable. Our success or failure would have repercussions elsewhere in the Pacific, and beyond.

Our Mission went first to Nauru. We flew for a night and a day from Sydney out over the Pacific with one stop in the Solomon Islands. When we landed at Nauru we were told that our aircraft was the first to use the landing ground on the island since the last United Nations' Visiting Mission had arrived three years before. After several days in Nauru we went on to spend more than a month in Australian New Guinea and then returned to Canberra. Our duty was to visit these two territories, consult with the people and with the Australian administrators and the Australian Government and then report with our comments and recommendations to the Trusteeship Council in New York.

If three professors in sociology and economics and political science came together to think of a single mythical territory containing for examination purposes a maximum number of textbook problems they might imagine something like the island of Nauru. For Nauru, although it has a total population of less than 5,000, presents many social, economic and political conundrums of special difficulty and complexity. There are less than 2,500 Nauruans on the island, the remainder of the population being people imported from other South Sea Islands and from Hong Kong under work contracts. But the Nauruans have their own language and pride in their own traditions and a determination to maintain their national entity. They have their own elected leaders and a Head Chief, a man of grave wisdom and intense public spirit, who combines the role of a national figure-head and a very practical Prime Minister. The islanders have a temperate climate, a comfortable life, highly developed communal services, two good hospitals, excellent schools and an efficient system of Police and Courts. Everything is free—schooling, electric light and water, and even cinema shows. There is no unemployment and no illiteracy. And there are no taxes.

But it is a false paradise. For these gentle people are dominated by the knowledge that the present happy state of affairs cannot continue. The dilemma of the future casts a dark shadow over the sunny scene. They have one economic asset, and only one. That asset is phosphate. A large part of the island is made up of phosphate, and the phosphate is being exported to Australia and New Zealand. In two or three decades the phosphate will be entirely exhausted. The great cantilevers which feed the phosphate ships are, in effect, rapidly draining away their security, their happiness, their future. As we looked down from the aircraft on our arrival we saw the derelict worked-out phosphate lands—acres of barren, sharp coral pinnacles like huge, jagged, crowded gravestones—a forbidding reminder that about a third of the phosphate had already been extracted.

When the phosphate has gone how can the Nauruans live? Where can they go? Is the export of the phosphate by a British monopoly for the benefit of Australian and New Zealand agriculture a classic example, as the Russians claim, of colonial exploitation? Are the islanders being paid enough for their sole asset? Are they being adequately consulted and taken into Australian confidence about their future?

These were the questions we discussed with the Nauruan elected Council and at a long public meeting attended by nearly everyone in the island, then with the Australian Government in Canberra, and later in debates in the Trusteeship Council and the Fourth Committee of the General Assembly in New York.

We made two main recommendations. First we recommended that specific plans for a new settlement for the Nauruans should be worked out, the settlement to be either in another island or in Australia itself, and that these plans should be put as a definite proposition to the Nauruan people for their decision. We also recommended that the elected representatives of the people of Nauru should participate more fully both in the administration of the island and in the phosphate enterprise itself.

Since we reported an island near Australia has been found which might provide a future national home for the Nauruans. Even if this island proves suitable there will of course be many awkward problems of resettlement and readjustment and compensation to be solved. These problems are absorbing and urgent. I trust that they will be dealt with wisely and generously. I believe that they will be. For what impressed me most during this expedition was the effectiveness of the combination of three factors—the good leadership of the democratically elected Nauruan leaders, the constant concern of the Australian Government to find a just solution, and the salutary effect of supervision by the United Nations. It seemed to me that the whole exercise in constructive co-operation provided an outstanding example of the practical effectiveness of the United Nations Trusteeship system.

Let me also say, in passing, that the problems of a tiny territory are often no less difficult than those of a large one, and surely no less important. When I was Governor of Jamaica I was also responsible for the administration of the Cayman Islands and the Turks and Caicos Islands each with a population of about that of Nauru. I sometimes felt that I spent almost as much time in dealing with these dependent islands as I did in dealing with the problems of Jamaica itself.

When I presented the report of our Mission to Nauru to the Trusteeship Council I said:

"I have heard it said that Nauru is so small that it can scarcely justify the attention devoted to it in this Council. No one who has been to Nauru can have any patience with any such contemptuous references.

In Nauru there is a concentration of problems just as exacting and just as important as there is in much larger countries. Here in this little island there are perplexities which demand our undivided and earnest attention.

As we discuss the needs and the future of these people we shall show that the United Nations can devote just as much sympathy and just as much concern to the few as to the many. I am sure that we approach our task in this Council today determined to do our utmost to serve the best interests of a small people who face great anxieties. And may their Head Chief return to Australia and to Nauru fortified in the confidence that at the United Nations we take special pride in our concern for small peoples, and special pride, too, in the fact that justice and freedom are infinitely more important to us than size and power."

We went on from Nauru to an entirely different set of prob-

lems in New Guinea, an island of 230,000 square miles with a
population of approaching three million.

The island provides a striking example of the continuing
complications caused by colonialism. The Dutch colonised
Western New Guinea, the Germans North-East New Guinea
and the Australians South-East New Guinea (Papua). Then
after the First World War the Australians took over the administration of North-East New Guinea from the Germans. It was
this, the Trusteeship Territory of New Guinea, with which our
Mission was concerned. And, since we were in New Guinea, the
Indonesians have taken over Western New Guinea from the
Dutch. The result is that the island is now run half by the
Indonesians and half by the Australians. Small wonder that
the inhabitants have been confused by the succession of different
masters, and small wonder too that they look on foreigners with
a mixture of envy and distrust.

We were surprised to hear so many references, particularly
in the coastal districts, to the famous cargo cult—another odd
result of colonialism. The cult still has some influence on the
minds of the people. They had seen foreigners come, Germans
and Australians and Japanese and Americans, they had seen
the material things which these foreigners brought in their
ships, and they imagined that they could acquire these products
of foreign civilisations for themselves by some supernatural
intervention. In the past whole communities would fast, burn
their huts and canoes, and work themselves up into a frenzy
of expectation, hoping for a dream ship to come over the sea
bringing to them all the good things which foreigners enjoy—
like expecting to win a football pool or prizes at a Bingo session.
It may be that few New Guineans now actively practise the
cult in anything like its original form, but it is clear that the
attitude of mind which created the cult persists. The people
associate the material benefits of civilisation with the coming
of the foreigners from overseas; they dream of obtaining these
worldly goods without any effort of their own. It is an association of a something-for-nothing materialism with a belief in
miracles.

There is nothing very new about such materialism. It is
perhaps neither more selfish nor more sordid than the material-

ism of the modern world elsewhere. Indeed by comparison it may be less contemptible, for its greed is touched with the light of belief in miraculous salvation. But there could scarcely be a more damaging influence on a people who must now strive to create a new nation by their own enterprise and effort.

Nowhere is there wilder country—and nowhere wilder people—than in New Guinea. Through the middle of the island runs one of the greatest mountain ranges in the world, the highest peak reaching 16,500 feet. On either side of this mountain mass the country falls steeply in huge cliffs and gorges down to the swampy lowlands. As we flew over the mainland we had the impression of patches of habitation and cultivation separated not only by ravines in the highlands but also, lower down, by stretches of almost impenetrable rain forests and, even more difficult to cross, the huge swamps into which the mountain rivers disgorge their muddy water.

To match the obstacles and divisions which nature has created—and mainly as a result of those divisions—the people of New Guinea have lived in the past in isolated pockets of population, each clan with its hand against its neighbours. There are hundreds of quite different languages some of them spoken by only a few hundred people. It is this division of the population into tiny groups, until recently feuding and fighting amongst themselves, which has presented the principal problem of New Guinea—the problem of creating a single people with a common purpose. I had seen isolated, backward people untouched by any outside influence in some parts of Africa but I had never seen people living in wilder conditions than those I saw in the mountains of New Guinea.

The Japanese occupied this part of New Guinea during the last war and when they surrendered the Australians faced a task of tremendous magnitude. They tackled it with the courage and enterprise and drive of a pioneering people and soon there were remarkable results. Perhaps the finest examples of Australian effort were in the patrol posts where young men created order and carried a message of progress and new hope to people living in the most primitive conditions in the world. Again typical of Australian enterprise was the way in which airstrips were built on spurs of the precipitous mountains, and extensive bush air services were provided by young pilots who cheerfully and daily faced sudden danger. The administration and the supply and the trade of large stretches of Australian New Guinea are still undertaken solely by air. Now administrative stations, schools and medical aid posts have been built in these wild mountains. Behind the initial effort came roads, towns, bigger schools, training centres, large new hospitals, some of them costing a million pounds each, and agricultural centres and demonstration farms. The record of Australia in New Guinea in practical development has been a record of pioneering enterprise carried out with magnificent devotion and enthusiasm.

While the thrust and the momentum came from a fine team of Australian administrators in the territory, the planning and the direction came from Canberra. For the past decade, Mr. Paul Hasluck has been Australian Minister for the Territories, and he has brought to his task outstanding qualities of administrative ability. His headquarters have been in Canberra but no local detail has been too small, no problem too complicated, no area too remote to escape his all-pervading intervention. He has been the District Officer of New Guinea. I at once recognised in him the characteristics which I knew so well in District Officers elsewhere, a passionate devotion to the well-being of the people under his charge, a dedicated determination to serve them well—and an intense suspicion of interference from any outside authority. We were specially grateful to him for the great effort of patience and forbearance which he made in dealing with us.

In our report, we suggested that there were three main needs. Firstly to undertake a full review of the economy of the territory; secondly to find and train and guide potential leaders as a matter of maximum urgency; thirdly, by developing representative, democratic government at the centre to overcome the divisions which have so far bedevilled the territory.

In stating the case for a representative parliament we said in our report:

"We are convinced from our public discussions in every district of the territory that the people have leaders well competent to speak for them and to represent them in a thoroughly responsible way in a central parliament. Indeed, wherever we have been in the territory—in patrol posts and country centres as well as in district and sub-district headquarters— the leaders of the people (often presidents or members of the local councils) have spoken out for those they represent, often with vigour and eloquence and nearly always with an impressive steadiness of judgment and a sense of constructive responsibility . . .

We believe that the establishment of a central representative parliament will, more than anything else, give to the territory that national sentiment and that sense of political unity which has so far been so noticeably lacking. The constituencies for which the present six New Guinea members are elected are far too big to give the people a sense of direct representation through their own elected leaders. The attitude will be considerably different when each sub-district elects its own parliamentary representative (with the larger sub-districts being divided into two or more constituencies). Then the House of Representatives will at once become a political reality in the minds of the people and a true centre of political opinion and political activity. It will come alive and help to provide that living unity which has so far failed to emerge."

In many countries a single national legislature has helped to create a sense of national solidarity and unity. It is not only a matter of bringing people of different racial origins and religions and tribes into constructive co-operation; a central Legislature also gives representation to both rich and poor, and country people as well as townspeople. It prevents a country being split by different racial and social and economic interests. A parliament is not only the mirror of nationalism; it can also be the creator of unity.

There are generally excellent relations between the people of New Guinea and the Australians, partly coming from the days in the last war when Australians and New Guineans shared hardships and dangers and fought together side by side. I shall not forget one magnificent bearded, naked chief speaking for a vast concourse of thousands of his followers who had come from their mountain villages to meet the United Nations Mission at Mount Hagen. Speaking in a bold, confident voice which carried to the neighbouring heights he said that he had one question to put to us. Did we come as friends of the Australians? If so the conference might proceed. If not they did not want to talk to us; we could go on our way.

As we travelled from outstation to outstation we heard everywhere in the wild countryside evidence of admiration for Australia and gratitude for what Australia had done for the people. The same spirit exists in the towns, though there sometimes we saw indications of some restlessness and dissatisfaction with anything which discriminated against "the natives". Even if it were only a question of good administration I felt strongly that no time at all should be lost in mobilising the racial good-will which exists in New Guinea. An effective outlet and an expression of the views of the people should be provided while there was still time. Even looked at solely as a local question there was no time to be lost in confidently admitting elected representatives of the people to a full share in the management of public affairs.

But it is not solely a local affair. Elsewhere colonialism in its old form will probably not outlast the present decade. The danger is that Australia as perhaps the last colonial power will become the butt of intense anti-colonial feeling. Such a development would, to put it at its least, do damage to Australia's position and influence in the Pacific and elsewhere. No great effort of imagination is required to foresee more immediately menacing dangers as long as Australia can be represented as a foreign power in New Guinea. Free elections and fully democratic representative government are necessary in New Guinea not only for local administration but for international defence. The best and perhaps the only effective shield against aggression in New Guinea, as elsewhere, is the free will of the people openly expressed not only in local councils or to interested visitors but through the well-tried processes of parliamentary election.

When our proposals were considered in Canberra the Australian Government and the Australian Parliament went most of the way with us. Our recommendations for an economic survey by the World Bank and for a new programme of university and higher education were readily approved. And, although the Australian Government did not fully accept our recommendation for a representative parliament, it was agreed that the existing Legislatuıe should at once be enlarged and made much more representative.

I believe that the substantial measure of agreement represented an achievement of all-round advantage. The wishes of the people, the invaluable leadership and assistance of the Australians, and the hearings and proposals of the United Nations Visiting Mission all contributed to the result. There had been consultation and there had been compromise and there had been co-operation. Not a victory for anyone, but a success.

III

"At all events, I must have some consciousness of being some-where near right; I must have some standard of principle fixed within myself."

ABRAHAM LINCOLN

Not long after I returned from this expedition to the Pacific an event took place in the United Nations of far-reaching consequence. For the first time a resolution was passed in the Fourth Committee on Southern Rhodesia. The United Kingdom maintained that Southern Rhodesia was self-governing in its internal affairs and had been since 1922, and that in any event the whole question of Southern Rhodesia was for the United Nations *ultra vires*. In spite of our strong objection the resolution was passed by a vote of 57 in favour, 21 against and 24 abstentions.

The first shot had been fired in a long campaign likely to drag in the whole of Africa, and the rest of the world too. From then on I became increasingly concerned that we would throw away all the good-will we had earned in the world by enlightened and progressive colonial policies. I feared that we should find ourselves in African affairs isolated with Portugal and South Africa in opposition to intense and unanimous African and Asian opinion.

By June 1962 a more serious step was taken. A resolution calling on the United Kingdom to summon a conference of all concerned to work out a new constitution for Southern Rhodesia was carried in the General Assembly by 73 in favour, 1 against (South Africa), with 27 abstentions. The United Kingdom and Portugal refused to participate in the vote.

Before I go on to tell of these events which led to my resignation from the United Kingdom Mission in October 1962, I should stop to deal with an important matter of principle. I have been an official for nearly a third of a century. I know the rules very well. When an official takes the extreme step of resigning his post he has no right, without permission, to publish information which he acquired in the confidence of his official position. The rule is important. I do not question it. Were this not well understood all confidence between Ministers and officials would be destroyed. And so, when I faced a crowded Press conference in the United Nations on the day after my resignation I refused to say anything at all about Southern Rhodesia. Again, I refused to say anything about the reasons for my resignation on my arrival back in England. But this well-established rule does not prevent me, now that I am no longer an official, from expressing my own opinions. I have very strong views on the problems of Africa in general and on Southern Rhodesia, the Portuguese territories of Angola and Mozambique, and South Africa in particular. I have been free to state them in America and in England. I have not hesitated to do so. And I was given permission after my return to say why I had resigned. I shall consequently tell my own story. I shall continue to state my own views. But I shall be careful to avoid any disclosure which would be a breach of any confidence extended to me either by Ministers or by the officials who were my colleagues. I shall limit what I have to say to facts already publicly known and to my own opinions and my own actions.

I had served in West Africa and North Africa but I had never been to Central Africa. Now, however, I found myself having to speak at the United Nations for the United Kingdom on Southern Rhodesia, and I did all I could to become informed about it. I had two sources of information. I had of course access to all official information put out by the Southern Rhodesian Government. But the African majority in Southern Rhodesia had no representation in that Government. So I had long conversations with Joshua Nkomo and the other Southern Rhodesian African leaders who came to the United Nations to state their case. It seemed to me in the summer of 1962 as I studied the contentions of the two sides that there was a chance of avoiding a clash between the white minority (230,000) and the African majority (3,690,000) provided Great Britain would take a new initiative.

The Government of Southern Rhodesian white settlers under their Prime Minister, Sir Edgar Whitehead, held very different views from those of the South African Government. He had declared against racial segregation and had agreed to give the Africans fifteen seats in the Southern Rhodesian Parliament of sixty-five members. This didn't seem to me to go far enough, but it was at least a move in the right direction. On the other hand, many of the African leaders seemed to me able men, by no means extremist and genuinely anxious to find a sound solution. Many of them had been supporters of the Capricorn Society and other movements working for racial understanding. Surely if a new initiative could be taken in time it should be possible to bridge the gap. But the timing seemed to me all-important. The Southern Rhodesian Government was engaged on rushing through new repressive legislation. As soon as the new legislation was through it was expected that the African party, ZAPU, would be banned and action would be taken against its leaders. Moreover the British Government had undertaken to introduce a new constitution which removed the British veto-power on Southern Rhodesian legislation (the British veto had in fact never been used though its existence had undoubtedly acted as a check on Southern Rhodesian actions) and to allow new elections to take place on the basis of the continuation of white majority rule. These new elections were due to take place in the spring of 1963. There was for the moment a lull, an interval, but very soon a train of events would start which could make a settlement rapidly more and more difficult.

Was there not still a last hope of avoiding deadlock? If we

could prevent the open conflict which seemed so near I thought that we might save Southern Rhodesia from ruin and bloodshed. We might also give a lead and a hope to all the oppressed African peoples of southern Africa. I set myself to try to work out what the new initiative might be.

First some time was necessary. So when the General Assembly's vote was cast in June 1962 calling for a constitutional conference in Southern Rhodesia (with only Great Britain, South Africa and Portugal in opposition) I told the Afro-Asians that in my opinion it was unwise for the United Nations to intervene at that time. I spoke accordingly in the Fourth Committee (and later in the Committee of Seventeen). I went myself to a full meeting of the Afro-Asians (such a thing had never been done before by any member of our delegation) and strongly argued that the attempt to intervene at that stage should not be pursued. I did this because I felt—and I knew that a number of friendly delegations felt the same—that more time should be given to the United Kingdom to deal with the complicated and difficult issues in Central Africa in general and Southern Rhodesia in particular. Certainly I did not feel that we would be justified in taking no action at all. We needed some time to manoeuvre, to find a way to avoid the approaching dangers, not merely to procrastinate and drift. I could not imagine that the British Government intended to do nothing about Southern Rhodesia, and that the resolution calling for a conference was to be altogether ignored. It seemed to me that if we took no action, conflict in the United Nations with all the Africans and Asians would become certain, and that even our friends would not be able to stand with us. A last opportunity of a settlement would be lost. I asked to be allowed to go to London to discuss the whole question urgently with the Government Departments concerned. I explained my concern and my misgivings in the Foreign Office, the Colonial Office, the Commonwealth Relations Office and the Central Africa Office.

I was very well aware of all the difficulties. I had to accept that the assurances already given by the British Government would be honoured. I realised that, with elections coming, Sir Edgar Whitehead could not be expected to risk votes by any drastic new action. But some gesture, if no more, from the Southern Rhodesian Government was necessary. I recommended that the Southern Rhodesian Government should be pressed to do three things—to release the very few Africans then under restriction, to withhold the new repressive legislation then being prepared and to grant at least some relaxation in the restrictions on the African franchise. But whether the Southern Rhodesian Government could or could not be persuaded to take these steps, the important thing was for the British Government to give the Africans some hope and some assurance. My recommendation was that the British Government should state at once that *after* the elections a conference of all concerned, including of course the Africans, would be called, and that it should also be clearly stated that no change in the constitutional status of Southern Rhodesia would be approved by the British Government until a new course had been worked out and agreed at such a full conference. I maintained, and still strongly maintain, that such action was fully within the competence of the British Government. There was nothing to prevent the British Government stating its intention to call a full conference and there was equally nothing to prevent the British Government making it quite clear, as indeed it apparently has since done, that independence will not be granted to Southern Rhodesia on the basis of continued white domination.

When I went to London I took with me a memorandum summarising my own views and recommendations. I left the memorandum with all the Government Departments concerned. Here is what it said:

Colonial Questions at the United Nations

It is the future that matters, particularly the future in Africa. It will be useless to continue patting ourselves on the back for past achievement and winning debating points against the Communists if we are on the wrong side in the struggle between African nationalism and white domination in Africa. We would then throw away all the good-will and influence which we now enjoy in Africa and Asia.

In this all-important question of the future in Africa we are already dangerously vulnerable. More and more we are coming to be regarded as the champions of the *status quo*. We speak of peaceful change, but we can point to no effective action to bring it about in the southern part of Africa. We show no concern for the subject African peoples, and no indignation at their continued suppression. We are looked upon as the supporters, if not the friends, of Tshombe, Welensky, Salazar and Verwoerd. We may soon be regarded as accomplices in a policy of repression in Southern Rhodesia. We have made no positive proposal about the Portuguese territories or about South-West Africa.

We may soon find ourselves on the wrong side in a losing battle. All that we have done in preparing colonial territories for independence will then count for little or nothing in our favour. Our many African friends will turn against us. Instead of discrediting the Soviet Union we shall play into its hands. We shall be divided from the Commonwealth. The Americans will not stay with us. We shall be isolated with Portugal and South Africa.

The proposal that a general declaration of colonial policy should be made has not yet been pursued. The dangers which now threaten render it the more necessary to make a declaration now, and the declaration should clearly apply to all Africa. The coming General Assembly is the time (possibly following discussion at the Commonwealth Prime Ministers' Conference) to make our positive position clear on the principles which we have applied in the past and which should equally guide us in the future.

Then in regard to the Portuguese territories and South-West Africa we should agree with the United States and Commonwealth countries on practical steps which we consider should be taken in preparation for eventual self-government and self-determination, and jointly urge the Governments concerned to take such steps, first of all by private representation and then, if necessary, by public pressure.

It is in Southern Rhodesia, however, that there will be the greatest test both for the future of Africa and for British policy, and if things go very wrong there no general declarations or advice which we can offer will carry any weight.

Many of the new nations understand the peculiar difficulties which we face in Central Africa and in Southern Rhodesia in particular. Some of them recognise that the new Southern Rhodesian Constitution and measures already taken by the Southern Rhodesian Government to remove racial discrimination were sincere attempts to move in the right direction. But even those who are prepared to see the difficulties and give us credit for the right motives cannot be persuaded that Great Britain could justify standing aside and leaving full control in the hands of the white minority. They are alarmed to see Great Britain give up its reserve powers. They fear that Southern Rhodesia will be granted or will seize independence while the minority still exercise political domination, and they believe that once the minority have secured full power they will not give it up. To them Southern Rhodesia is the central and critical issue in Africa, and they regard it as the testing point in our policy.

What can be done to save the situation? Unless something is done very soon non-co-operation and violence on one side and repression on the other are likely to rule out any hope of a peaceful settlement, and then all the forces at present moving in Africa will come into conflict. There is perhaps still time to avoid such a calamity, but to do so some practical gesture is required from the Southern Rhodesian Government and some reassurance from Her Majesty's Government.

Could the Southern Rhodesian Government be persuaded to release the political detainees and to declare that the new repressive legislation will not be brought into effect if violence is avoided? At the same time could the Southern Rhodesian Government be persuaded to make substantial improvements in the franchise? (At least the qualification for the B roll could be simplified and extended without adding to the number of African members of the Legislature.)

Might not the British Government at the same time declare that we are in favour of progressive steps towards full participation of all the people of the territory in the Government, and that following the forthcoming elections we shall invite the leaders of all parties to participate in a conference on future constitutional advance? Above all could we not now make it plain that independence will not be granted to Southern Rhodesia until a new constitution has been worked out at such a conference?

Neither Her Majesty's Government nor the Southern Rhodesian Government would be abandoning the course already set. Both Governments would be confirming that course but also offering hope for the future and confounding our enemies. We should have regained the initiative both in Africa and in the United Nations.

New York,
22nd August, 1962.

I had made it plain in London that if no new initiative were to be taken I could not continue to speak on Southern Rhodesia in the United Nations, and when I returned to New York I wrote this to the Head of my Mission:

It is the question of Southern Rhodesia which, as far as we are concerned, must dominate the "colonial" debates during this Assembly.

There may well be several weeks debate on Southern Rhodesia (with petitioners being heard) in the Fourth Committee.

There is certain to be a long debate in the Plenary too. For as far ahead as we can see (that is not only at this Session of the Assembly) the question of Southern Rhodesia will be the main subject on which we shall have to defend our position.

Consequently I should at this time be preparing to take my full part in that defence, both in the Fourth Committee and elsewhere.

I have most anxiously considered this prospect, and my conclusion is, I greatly regret to say, that I do not feel able to speak in the U.N. or elsewhere in defence of our position in this matter. I simply cannot do it.

If this were an isolated or minor disagreement my feelings would not matter. But, as I have emphasised, this is the main African question before the U.N. in which we are directly concerned, and no other subject I deal with now has anything like comparable importance. If, therefore, on this issue I am in disagreement and consequently unable to defend our policy I fear that I must become a liability to the delegation.

I realise that if I drop out now there is likely to be some public comment, but my continued presence in the delegation when I was unable to speak on this main issue would, I am afraid, be interpreted as an indication of disagreement in our delegation—and that would be worse.

I am most sincerely sorry to create this difficulty, and to cause inconvenience at this time to our delegation in which it has been a privilege and a joy to work, but in view of what I have said I think that it would be best for me to be replaced as soon as possible.

Meanwhile the drift was continuing. The new repressive legislation was passed in Southern Rhodesia. As we had expected, it was at once followed by the banning of ZAPU. Nkomo was sent to a remote village and kept under police supervision. The Africans boycotted the elections (only a few thousand Africans voted). The drift to deadlock went on.

Even at that late stage I thought that the British Government might still intervene to give some hope and some assurance for the future. Lord Home was in New York and I went to him to urge that the drift should be stopped. I flew to London and had a long talk with Mr. Butler. I thought at one time that I had convinced them. Lord Home went back to London and told me I could expect a quick decision. I repeated that if there was to be no new initiative someone else would have to take my place. But the word came back within a week that nothing would be done. I resigned, and it only remained to decide on the date and form of the announcement. A week or two ahead might be the best time.

I was sitting in my place in the Fourth Committee on the 11th of October 1962, when Sir Patrick Dean came to speak to me. Could I slip out for a word with him? I moved with him to the back seats. There had been a leak, he said. The news of my resignation would be published in an English paper the next morning. We went to our small upper room in the United Nations building and we were joined there by Minister Godber and some members of our delegation. I apologised lamely for all the trouble I was causing. They spoke to me more in sorrow than in anger, with the embarrassed restraint of visitors to a prisoner on the day of his execution.

There was now only an hour before the London papers would go to press. Could we get the announcement out in time to beat the leak? We spoke to the Foreign Office in London by telephone. All the Ministers were at Llandudno attending the Conservative Party Conference. A Minister was called out of the Conference. I pictured his irritation. Yes, the announcement could go out. With only a few minutes to spare Robin Haydon, our Public Relations Officer, went out to give it to the correspondents. It was all over.

A few weeks after I got back to England I said this to the Press:

"I should like to say that there is no truth at all in suggestions that I was at loggerheads with those who worked with me in the United Kingdom Mission to the United Nations. It was a great privilege to work with such a fine team. I had every respect for all those I worked with and specially for my chief, Sir Patrick Dean. They have throughout shown me outstanding kindness, and have always given me the fullest opportunity to state my own views and to make representations when necessary to the responsible Ministers of the British Government.

Secondly, I should like to deny any suggestion that I have been in disagreement with our policy in colonial territories over recent years. On the contrary, I have been glad and proud to speak in defence of that policy. I myself have been engaged for more than thirty years in working with colonial peoples to give them a good start in self-government and independence, and all the countries in which I have served are now governing themselves.

It was only in respect of Central Africa and, in particular, Southern Rhodesia, that I was in disagreement.

There is another accusation made against me which I am specially anxious to deny.

The suggestion has been made that I care only for the Africans and that I disregard the interests of the white people of Southern Rhodesia. I strongly resent that. Certainly I understand and share the African alarm and African aspirations to take a full share in the government of their own country, but I have throughout been specially concerned about the future of the white population.

In advocating that we should urgently take a new initiative to save the situation by giving some hope and some assurance for the future, my concern all along has been to prevent a dreadful calamity for everyone in Southern Rhodesia.

That calamity would be worst of all for the white population. Surely their future must depend not on suppression but on reaching a working understanding with the great majority of the people of the country.

I have learnt two principal lessons in my overseas service. First that self-government must be built on consultation and co-operation: it cannot be built on the dictatorship of one race, or the domination of one people over another. The second lesson I have learned—and this lesson applied in such widely different territories as Nigeria, Jamaica and Cyprus—is that the initiative is all-important. To find the way out of difficulties and disagreements you must take and keep the initiative.

Within the obvious limitations, which I well knew, I thought that the British Government in co-operation with the Government of Southern Rhodesia should take a new initiative last summer. I made my specific proposals accordingly at that time. When these proposals were not accepted I reluctantly came to the conclusion that I could no longer speak as an advocate of a policy which I didn't agree with. That was no hasty decision; I had made my views and my proposals and my position clear over a period of months.

That brings me to my last point. Some people have said that an official should not resign. I have been an official for a long time, and the work of which I am most proud has been the work of training civil servants in the Near East and Africa and the West Indies.

I told the civil servants who worked with me that it is the

duty of an official fearlessly to advocate the policy he thinks right. And when a final decision is taken by the highest authority the official must carry it out—and he must carry it out whole-heartedly. Only one exception is possible. If the question is one of main principle, and is a continuing major issue, and one in which he himself is directly involved, he has the right to say 'I am sorry, I cannot do it.' I maintain that that is not only a right: it is a duty.

I could not go on for month after month speaking to a policy which I didn't believe in and I have no doubt that I was right to say so."

I have told this story at some length and quoted from what I wrote at the time not because I think that my own resignation was of any public importance, but because it did raise interesting questions of whether and when an official should resign. Some people maintained that an official should never resign on a question of policy. There was a correspondence on the subject in *The Times*. A letter from Mr. Kenneth Younger brought the discussion to a conclusion. He said:

"Quite apart from the holders of this special kind of post, civil servants are likely to take the extreme step of resignation only if deep convictions are at stake. If one denies them this elementary right, where can one stop, short of condoning Eichmann's sustained obedience to high political authority?"

When Sylvia and I left New York we were most kindly treated by the other members of my Mission. By dropping out in the middle of the session of the Assembly I had put them in some difficulty. It would be harder for them to speak to a case which their own representative had publicly refused to support. But they made no complaint or reproach. Sir Patrick Dean and his wife came to see us off at the boat. Ralph Bunche told me before I left that, quite apart from the reason for my resignation, what had impressed people in the United Nations was the way it was done. That was a compliment more to my friends in the United Kingdom Mission than to me.

Mr. Duncan Sandys was asked by newspapermen what he had to say about my resignation. He replied that he was not interested in the private opinions of civil servants. Nor should he be. He was quite right. I have no doubt that he would go further and agree that he would not wish his Government to be represented in a world assembly by a spokesman convinced that that Government was drifting to disaster.

*   *   *

The Central African Federation has now been dissolved. Mr. Butler has rightly taken credit for this achievement. He has also rightly paid tribute to the African leaders whose moderation and restraint made an orderly dissolution possible. But what has been done is merely to agree to dismantle and terminate the Federation which was forced through against the opposition of the Africans concerned. The British Government gave, and the British Government hath taken away: blessed be the name of the British Government.

The ship of federation is being broken up, but the rock on which it foundered—the rock of white domination—remains in Southern Rhodesia. If the rock had been removed the ship could have been saved. The British Government has given its attention to the destruction not of the rock but of the ship.

IV

"Contending for an imaginary power we begin to acquire the spirit of domination, and lose the relish of honest equality."
EDMUND BURKE

Southern Rhodesia is the outpost of white control in southern Africa. Behind it lie the great Portuguese territories of Angola and Mozambique and the stronghold of South Africa. The forces of African nationalism have swept down through West Africa and East Africa and into Central Africa. Now the Africans control their own destiny in all Africa right down to the River Zambesi. But south of the Zambesi no African has any effective say in the Government of his country. Power is held by the white minorities, and ruthlessly maintained. They will not give it up without a long and fierce fight. The Africans, supported by the Asians, will never be content to leave the African majorities in political slavery. Who can imagine that the struggle in southern Africa between these two forces—African

227

nationalism and white domination—will be resolved without a long, bitter, bloody convulsion?

It is a struggle which cannot be quickly won by one side or the other. The military strength of the Governments in power in southern Africa is overwhelming. It will not be a matter of battles between armies. It will be the beastly business of a war between civilians, of guerilla warfare on one side using the weapons of assassination and sabotage, and fierce repression on the other, with mounting hate on both sides.

When I have been speaking in America and trying to describe modern Africa as I see it, I have spoken of Africa as a great house of many separate rooms. We look into one room and see encouraging constructive work going forward. We look into another room and we are uneasy and disturbed by what we see. In another room what we see going on seems dangerous, misguided, wrong. But in all the separate rooms the effort goes forward. Meanwhile down in the cellars— in the southern States of Africa—the fuses are already lit. They are likely to cause explosions which will blow not only the cellars but the whole house sky high.

In 1961 I was speaking in Chicago and a woman came up to me afterwards who was disturbed by what I had said about dangers in Africa. She had a friend going out to work in Africa—in Lagos, Nigeria. Was it safe? "Well," I said, "you can never be sure, but I was in Nigeria only a few months ago and I have never seen better relations than at that time—the time of the celebration of Nigerian independence. I would say that Lagos is the safest place in Africa." I went back to my hotel. The next morning I switched on the television news, and heard the report of Lumumba riots in Lagos, with indescriminate attacks on white people. What did they know about Lumumba in Lagos? Very little. But they knew that an African leader had been murdered. When blood flows in Africa, all Africa is involved. And as the struggle in southern Africa develops all African States will be dragged in. So surely will the rest of the world. A race war in Africa will involve everyone.

Can nothing be done to prevent such a horrible clash? Can no one do anything in time to stop the world being involved in a colour war? Will the Americans be able to intervene, or the British or the French? Will the Russians step in? Or will the Chinese pursue their claim to be the champions of the coloured people everywhere? No one can believe that one great power could intervene without bringing in the others. Sooner or later, probably when others have failed, it is to the United Nations that the world will turn.

When I was in New York on the 25th of September 1963, the Danish Foreign Minister made a speech in the General Assembly on South Africa. It was a speech of outstanding honesty and originality and, I have no doubt, of far-reaching effect. The record of the Danes and the other Scandinavian countries in the United Nations gives them the right to be heard with respect. Unlike the Soviet countries and the French (and sometimes, alas, Great Britain) they have been anxious to increase and not to restrict the capacity and authority of the United Nations. The Danish Foreign Minister made four main points. First, he made his country's position quite clear on the question of principle. Denmark and the other Scandinavian countries were utterly opposed to apartheid. They were in favour of "a truly democratic multi-racial society of free men with equal rights for all individuals irrespective of race." Secondly, his country supported a ban on arms shipments to South Africa and in regard to economic sanctions "supports this line of action and feels that it should be pursued and pressure gradually increased". But the Foreign Minister went on to say that those who advocated an unconditional policy of sanctions carried special responsibilities. Pressure of bans and sanctions must be directed to a positive plan not just to destruction. His third point consequently was that "it is our duty to prove that there is an alternative to catastrophe". His fourth point was that the United Nations would have to play "a major role to avoid a tragic disaster". It was for the United Nations to formulate a "supplementary policy" and "make clear to the world what should take the place of apartheid". And during the transitional period he said that it would be for the United Nations "to contribute to the maintenance of law and order and the protection of life and civil rights of all individuals".

Such courageous, constructive speaking may not be welcome to the extremists. But it opens up new possibilities of positive action. It also adds force to the contention that the future obligations of the United Nations will be far greater than any so far undertaken. The greatest danger of all is that when the need comes the United Nations will be too weak to meet it. If that time comes the greatest responsibility will rest on those whose policy towards the United Nations has been negative, those who have sought to limit its powers and diminish its authority. It will be too late then to blame the South African Government or the Afro-Asians. The burden of blame will rest on those who have neglected over many years to support and strengthen the United Nations, who have formulated no positive policies, who have been content to watch the drift to disaster.

CHAPTER XI

The Future

"O Lord God, when thou givest to thy servants to endeavour any great matter, grant us to know that it is not the beginning but the continuing of the same unto the end until it is thoroughly finished which yieldeth the true glory."

SIR FRANCIS DRAKE

I

I WAS caught up in my last few months as a delegate to the United Nations with the dangers in southern Africa in general and Southern Rhodesia in particular. These are growing and pressing dangers and likely to involve the whole world, but there are of course many others.

The greatest danger for us of the Western nations, so it seems to me, is that in our affluence we shall become soft and selfish and self-centred, so superior in our attitude to the rest of the world that we forfeit respect and abandon our influence, and so complacent that we fail to see the dangers of the wider world in time.

We in Great Britain seem to be sinking into a new kind of suburban isolationism. Many people fail to see the potentialities of the Commonwealth: they are too busy regretting the loss of an Empire. We sulkily turn inwards on ourselves. We no longer speak with the pride of an imperial governor. A very good thing too. But now we speak with the petulance of a retired governess.

We lecture but we no longer lead. The Nigerian Ambassador to the United Nations said to me recently that the things he once learnt from England he hears now from Africans, but scarcely ever from Englishmen. Now we seem to be guided not by patriotism but by pique. We show no indignation when we see political slavery or economic exploitation or social injustice. When subject people talk about freedom we call them "emotional". When they urge some positive policy of liberation we call them "reckless". When resolutions are passed in the United Nations with the overwhelming support of the world we call them "utterly lacking in responsibility". In a world full of explosive danger we seem to have no higher ideal than the maintenance of the status quo. It is in fact a hankering to go back to a world which no longer exists. Our leaders accuse others of "the double standard". But some of them become more excited about Goa than Angola. They lay themselves open to the accusation that they are more anxious to preserve a little colony than to liberate a large one. They support the Russian thesis and speak of getting back to the United Nations Charter "as it was meant to be". What they really mean is that they still wish to see the United Nations a machine for preserving the privilege of the haves rather than an effective instrument for helping the have nots. Our danger is that in world affairs we become conservative in the worst sense of the term—negative, defensive, cowardly, sterile.

The charge against our leaders is not only that by sneers and jibes they have carried out a campaign to denigrate the United Nations. Certainly that campaign has done harm, particularly because in this country there have been so few people with first-hand knowledge of the United Nations who can answer back. The poison has gone deep and wide and many people who are not narrow or reactionary have half-accepted the accusations which have often been hinted and implied rather than openly stated. Better the forthright denunciation of Lord Sandwich who spoke of the United Nations as "a monster of iniquity" and Britain's "principal enemy" than Lord Home's lofty lecturing on "serious falling away from the principles of the Charter" which places Britain in "an appalling dilemma".

The charge is much more serious. It is that we have failed by every means and at every opportunity to strengthen the United Nations. We have paid our standard contributions but we have not followed a definite policy of building up the organisation to face the coming dangers. If when new crises come the United Nations is too poor and powerless to take the strain the responsibility will not rest with the United Nations organisation. It will rest with those who were content to smear rather, when there was still time, to support and sustain and reform.

But was not the Soviet bloc the main opponent of a stronger United Nations? True. We can hope that on this as on other matters the Russians will be ready to reconsider and to change their views. But whether they are prepared to alter their attitude or not the Communists, both the Russians and the Chinese, have set themselves to win the leadership of the Afro-Asian world. We have had plenty of evidence to show that they do not propose to abandon that aim. If the Western powers had sided with the new nations in a steady, persistent, determined endeavour to support and strengthen the United Nations the Communists would have hesitated to isolate themselves on such an issue against the overwhelming weight of the opinion of the whole of the rest of the world. The open opposition of France and the British double talk have encouraged the Soviet attempt to make the United Nations impotent. Even those who think in terms of cold war tactics must see the tactical opportunity which has been lost. But it is far more than that. The case for supporting and strengthening the United Nations is the case for providing an effective alternative to the division and destruction of the world.

*   *   *

Meanwhile the new nations face immediate dangers. The greatest of all arises from the fact that the population of the world is increasing so rapidly that it will double in less than fifty years. That means that the two thirds of the population of the world which lives near the starvation level may drag down the prosperous third into chaos. "I begin to wonder," says Barbara Ward, "whether there are any forces inside our comfortable, cosy, complacent Western World that will make us accept this challenge and see that we now face thirty or forty years of world-building on a scale never known in human history." "World building" indeed. The phrase shocks us into the realisation that we have scarcely started to think of such a task. It is not in our affluent third of the world that these ideas mean very much. It is in countries beset by ignorance and superstition and disease and poverty that the extent of the effort required is recognised. Without capital of their own, often with few natural resources and with only a handful of men with professional and scientific experience, the new nations face the Herculean task of endeavouring to raise their people from economic degradation.

At the same time they face both external and internal dangers. In many parts of Africa the forces of tribalism threaten to bring down the new States in bloody disintegration. We see that danger in the Congo. That has been the danger in Kenya too. Ghana and Nigeria faced the same possibility of tribal dissolution. Tribalism does not die quickly; it is only in the past few decades that the new forces of wider nationalism have prevailed.

More immediate and more explosive still are the dangers arising from the old colonial frontiers—the evil legacy of colonialism. Not long ago I was in Somalia and Ethiopia and Kenya. The most pressing danger in that area is the danger of conflict between the Somalis on the one hand and their Ethiopian and Kenyan neighbours on the other. The Somalis claim that they have been robbed of their great grazing grounds of the Ogaden now in Ethiopia, and that their brother Somalis in the Northern Frontier District of Kenya are denied the right of self-determination.

There are frontier problems wherever colonialism existed. We see the dangers arising from the old colonial frontiers in the Far East, for instance in the angry friction between Indonesia and Malaysia.

It is well that we should remember that it was not the Africans and the Asians who made these frontiers. The frontiers between Indonesia and Malaysia were made not by the Indonesians or the Malaysians but by the British and the Dutch in their scramble for eastern territory. The frontiers of Somalia were created not by the Somalis or the Ethiopians or the Kenyans but by the colonial penetrations of British, Italian and French long ago, and were finally drawn as they now exist by the great powers after the last war.

The era of colonialism is almost over, but the frontiers which arose from European competition and domination will long remain a curse to the people of Asia and Africa.

On tribalism, too, it is not for us, the colonial powers, to adopt a superior attitude. Policies of indirect rule which strengthened and perpetuated the power of feudal chiefs were continued too long. In Kenya we delayed the development of political associations which transcended tribal allegiancies. The separatist tendencies in the Congo which still threaten to bring down the whole country in ruin directly arise from the refusal of the Belgians when they ruled the Congo to encourage or allow the development of political parties on a national scale.

Where in Asia and Africa there is appalling poverty and where there is ignorance due to lack of education and where there is narrow tribalism and where there are frontier disputes let us remember that until recently in most of those vast areas we exercised full authority.

It is the complacency and superiority of so many people when they speak about the new nations which seems to me so intolerable.

We should make a sufficient effort of imagination to put ourselves in the position of an African, for instance, who is told that he should imitate the enlightened, civilised, Christian example of Europe. When the African hears such admonitions and reads modern European history he is perplexed. He is bewildered by what he hears and sees. He may well make the old reply, "What you do speaks so loud I cannot hear what you say." He knows that twice in living memory Europe has engaged in mass slaughter which makes his tribal clashes look like child's play. He sees a great proportion of our national wealth being spent on instruments of mass destruction. He hears of bitter disputes and harsh despotisms. He sees enmity, and tyranny too. Is he to imitate East or West? Is he to imitate Salazar of Portugal or Franco of Spain—or de Gaulle? We may possibly get some satisfaction in the thought that one cannot duplicate de Gaulle. Is he to imitate Hitler or Chamberlain? Stalin, or Khruschev? Albania, or Yugoslavia? In England and America he hears of many things unlikely to excite his admiration. Who can blame him if he concludes that it is we who may be misguided, if he decides to think for himself and make his own mistakes?

Most Africans grew up in a world in which the European was

in full charge—in Government, in commerce, in education, in the churches. The Europeans exercised complete authority. Their standards were at one time unquestioned. As Africans gained in knowledge and experience they first questioned and then rejected our infallibility. Ndabaningi Sithole, one of the African leaders of Southern Rhodesia, trying to describe the Africans' sense of disillusion with European leadership quotes Calaban:

> "What a thrice-double ass was I,
> To take this drunkard for a god
> And worship this dull fool!"

We cannot be surprised if the Asians and the Africans decide to go their own way. The surprising thing about both Asians and Africans is not how much they reject of so-called Western standards and methods but how determined they are to take the best we have to offer in ideas and institutions and to make full use of them. I am constantly amazed that having endured so many humiliations and injustices they are so free from malice, so ready to co-operate with us and so anxious to preach and practise equality.

Lord Home said not long ago that the greatest danger today is from racialism. It is the Africans who are opposing racialism: it is the white people who perpetuate it. While no African is admitted to the white cabinet of Southern Rhodesia, the Minister of Agriculture in the African Government of independent Tanganyika is an Englishman. The Minister of Agriculture in the African Government of Kenya is a Scotsman. The African leaders repeatedly denounce racialism and show by practical example that they mean what they say. President Nyerere of Tanganyika says "What we fear are the evils of racialism on the minds of majorities and minorities alike." I am not so optimistic to believe that this moderation will last. When the race struggle gets hot and rough there will be no more "moderate" leaders in Africa. The good-will still existing will be thrown away. There will be no neutrals in a colour war.

* * *

The Future

We should not forget the principles we ourselves taught in Asia and in Africa. We of the Colonial Service were sometimes criticized for imposing, so it was said, the Westminster model of parliament and the Whitehall system of administration on peoples who had not the advantages of our history and our heritage. We imposed nothing. We taught and gave the people what they wanted. If we had taught them some second-rate substitute they would rightly have rejected it.

We taught what we knew, what we believed in. Were we to teach something else, or something less? Would the peoples of Asia and Africa have thanked us if we, in condescending superiority, had taught them something which we could not have accepted ourselves? Certainly we were right to teach what we knew.

We taught the principles of representative government and the rule of law and impartial and incorruptible civil services, and I believe that where the people have known those things they will not for long be content with anything less.

No one suggests or expects that the new nations will maintain exactly what we created. They are rightly determined to develop their own institutions and their own economies in their own way. They will no doubt make mistakes. There will be failures, dictatorships, civil wars and frontier wars. But the principles of free government will not be forgotten. I believe that they will survive. I trust that they will at least fare better in Africa in the second half of this century than they did in the first half in Europe. In any event we can be sure that we shall not see elsewhere in Africa any racial tyranny so thorough or any minority domination so ruthlessly maintained as we see now in South Africa.

There are many people ready to jeer at the new nations, and anxious to see them fail. Such people will have plenty to gloat over. But, though there will be set-backs and obstacles, there are many encouraging factors too—lively African parliaments and African Ministers determined to succeed in improving the lot of their people, and African civil servants of the highest quality —men like Adu of Ghana, chief executive of the East African Common Services Organisation, and Robert Gardiner, also of Ghana, who is head of the United Nations Economic Commission for Africa in Addis Ababa, or Michael Ani of Nigeria, who came over to East Africa while I was there recently to advise the East African Governments on the problems of a federal civil service. These are men of outstanding ability by any test anywhere in the world.

What of the political leaders? Most of them are young men and many have exceptional ability and courage and originality. There is also of course a proportion of self-seekers and crooks amongst them, but the proportion is not higher, I would judge, than the European average.

In 1961 I was going to Tanganyika to take part in the celebration of the initiation of the new Republic. Our flight from England was held up by fog for three days. The passengers spent the day waiting at the airport and at night were carried off to an hotel in Worthing of all places. Amongst them was Kenneth Kaunda the leader of the Africans in Northern Rhodesia. I had not known him before and I was glad to have this opportunity to talk with him during our long wait. At last the fog cleared and we set out. The air hostess offered us tea or coffee. Kaunda who was sitting by me refused. I had already noticed that at the airport and in the hotel he had not eaten meat or fish. I asked him the reason for such a list of prohibitions. He didn't reply. Strange, he was usually so cheerful and forthcoming. I thought that he might be a vegetarian but why the ban on tea or coffee? A little later on I turned to him again. "We know each other fairly well by now," I said. "I don't want to irritate you with personal questions but I should really be grateful if you would tell me why you refused tea and coffee just now." Again he shut up. But I pressed him, and half-angry he replied, "It was all a long time ago. When I started out as a very young man in politics one of my first activities was to help in organising a strike against European butchers. We Africans opposed a regulation under which we could obtain certain meat supplies only through the European butchers. And during the strike I naturally had to make sure that in my own household the ban on eating meat was carefully maintained. I have forgotten the details about the strike; it was soon over. But when it was finished I said to myself that it had been good for me to do without something for a while. I decided to maintain the ban and, to make it a little more difficult, I added fish and tea and coffee. That was many years ago. The reason? I had made a small start in politics. My people had put some trust in me, and I wanted to remind myself several times a day that I was not in this game for myself. And, you know, when you make a rule like that it is difficult to give it up."

There are all kinds of leaders in Asia and Africa. But with all their variety and with all the diverse difficulties and dangers they face they have some characteristics and some strong views in common.

They are good judges of us. A subject people has to be expert in its so-called masters. When I was a District Officer the people knew within a week or two of my arrival in a new post what I was worth. The qualities of their governors were important to their daily lives. I have had to write hundreds of confidential reports on Government officials in my life, but I always knew that I could write a much better report on my superior than on my junior. Most Asians and Africans have been long trained in understanding us. They had to be good judges of us. And many of the leaders have been educated in Europe or in America. They got to know us then. Prime Minister Nehru of India was at Cambridge, Premier Norman Manley of Jamaica was at Oxford. President Nyerere of Tanganyika was at Edinburgh. President Nkrumah of Ghana and President Azikiwe of Nigeria were educated in the United States. These leaders know Great Britain or America very well—too well I sometimes think. They are not likely to be fooled by the Americans or the British or the French—or the Russians or the Chinese for that matter.

The Asians and the Africans showed their good judgment in their dealings with their British and French masters. Those who lived in French territories accepted and copied French culture and French social custom, but they were never impressed by French institutions. In the territories administered by Great Britain they accepted and adapted British institutions —parliaments, courts, universities and civil services—but they never attempted to imitate the social habits of the British. When I remember the great dull, official suburb of Ikoyi outside Lagos where hundreds of British officials lived an exclusive suburban existence, I certainly do not blame them.

Another characteristic common to all the Asian and African leaders is a determination to think for themselves. That may sound obvious enough. But not so long ago such an attitude was officially regarded as "dangerous neutralism". They are not prepared to become mere pawns in a game of international chess played by the two great power blocs. They do not believe that they achieved independence merely to be told that they had only one decision to take—which side they are to support in the cold war. They are determined to think for themselves, make up their own minds, state their convictions and make their own distinctive and independent contribution to world affairs.

The Asian and African leaders are also at one in their passionate belief in national independence. Having achieved self-government and independence themselves they are determined to end colonial and racial domination everywhere. It may be difficult for us who have not lived under foreign rule to understand their strong feeling on this, but we should be making a grave error to under-estimate its intensity. The Asians and the Africans regard this as a crusade for which they are prepared to make great sacrifices.

The Afro-Asian leaders have another main aim in common. They are fully convinced of the necessity for a strong international organisation in the form of the United Nations. The big powers will support the United Nations when it suits them. When it does not, as we have had frequent evidence, they will do their best to hinder and hamper it. And in any event they have been reluctant to see it grow strong. When the Soviet Union sought to destroy any possibility of effective initiative by the Secretary-General by introducing the "troika", in effect the big powers' veto, into the United Nations Secretariat, the proposal was opposed by the United States and the United Kingdom. If that had been all there would have been just one more disastrous deadlock between East and West. But the new nations rallied as one to make their opposition clear. They simply would not have it. And twice the Russians had to withdraw the whole proposal. If it had not been for the firm stand of all the new nations the initiative of the Secretary-General would have been destroyed. The United Nations would be now merely an international debating society.

So when we think of the new nations and all their faults and failures and difficulties and dangers it is well to think of nations representing the majority of the peoples of the world determined to exercise their own judgment, believers in national independence but at the same time firm supporters of international co-operation. Their influence may yet be decisive in saving the world both from mass misery and wholesale destruction.

*　　*　　*

The respect which these new nations feel for British methods and British institutions is still immense. Most of the new nations have been under British administration. Most of the leaders of the new nations have been educated in British schools and universities. Great Britain has an unrivalled opportunity for understanding the peoples of Asia and Africa, for co-operating with them and helping them.

They do not forget that we led the world in building free parliaments. They know that we have set the pattern for advance in freedom. They remember that we have given one country after another round the world a good start in self-government and independence. They find it difficult to believe that we should forget what we stood for and abandon what we ourselves used to teach. As the dangers increase and the challenge comes nearer, they cannot bring themselves to believe that we shall content ourselves with timid lecturing and show ourselves more concerned about profits than about justice.

What a betrayal it will be if we throw away all the influence and respect and good-will we still enjoy, if we lose our lead, and betray the trust placed in us. What a disaster if we run out of initiative and cut ourselves off from our Commonwealth and from America and find ourselves isolated on the side of racial domination.

A Start in Freedom

"We have it in our power to begin the world over again."

THOMAS PAINE

Now I work for the United Nations. I have been a consultant to the United Nations Special Fund and I have recently been several times to Africa to discuss with the African Governments their plans for economic development, to discover how the United Nations can help them to formulate their economic programmes and projects and then give them practical assistance in carrying them out.

My assignment is limited in scope and in area, but I have the exciting feeling of being amongst the first of the few who work for a new cause. We bring to our task a new motive and a new spirit.

When I arrive in a new country I go first to report to the United Nations Resident Representative. These Representatives act for the United Nations Technical Assistance Board and the Special Fund, but they are increasingly recognised as United Nations ambassadors. They are drawn from many different countries. In Ethiopia, for instance, the Resident Representative is a Canadian, in Somalia a Trinidadian, in Uganda an American of French extraction, in Tanganyika an Australian assisted by a New Zealander, in Kenya an African Southern Rhodesian. These men of so many different origins are building up a new international foreign service. Other Ambassadors and High Commissioners are primarily and naturally concerned with the interests of their own countries. But the United Nations Representatives all have the one clear purpose—to give disinterested help to the Governments of the countries to which they are posted. The African Ministers and officials increasingly turn to them for assistance and for advice too. They have no national interest. They are not trying to sell anything. They represent a new departure in world diplomacy.

Before I went to Africa recently I went to talk over my assignment with one of the chief executive officials of the Special Fund, Paul Marc Henry. He is a Frenchman. It struck me as I walked down the corridor after our conversation that it had never occurred to either of us in talking about United Nations work to allow any consideration of national interest to enter our heads. It was unthinkable that either of us should do so. We were concerned only with the interests of the people of East Africa and how the Special Fund could help them. We would have been ashamed to allow any French or British motive to influence us.

Early in 1963 I met General Rikhye of India in New York on his return from Western New Guinea. There he had had to deal with Pakistani troops sent under United Nations auspices to maintain order in the difficult period of transfer of power. Not easy for an Indian General to give directions to Pakistani troops. I asked him how he had got on. "No difficulty at all," said General Rikhye. "We had an awkward job to do together but we were all on United Nations work and the Pakistani Brigadier and I never had the slightest disagreement."

The fact is that any of us who have the privilege to work for the United Nations instinctively and automatically leave our national differences behind, and work with a new will to a new standard of international co-operation.

This new will and new purpose may be the most hopeful thing in the world. We have grown used to the "balance of terror". For a long time now it has seemed that the best we could hope for was that the balance would be maintained. The bomb and the balance were becoming the symbols of our security and the guarantee of our survival. It was a miserable prospect—a sort of deification of defeatism.

But now we can have new hope in the independent initiative of the United Nations. Some people speak and dream of world government. Perhaps I do not fully understand what they mean, but the idea does not yet attract me. Somehow world government suggests to me too many civil servants. But the idea of the new independent initiative of world leadership by the Secretary-General backed by the overwhelming opinion of the world and drawing its authority from the General Assembly, the parliament of the world—that is a child already born. We must not expect too much of it too soon. But if we can persuade proud and powerful nations not to starve or smother or strangle it in its infancy, then soon it will grow strong.

The new men who work for the United Nations are not airy idealists. They have to be severely practical. They cannot afford to be perfectionists. Problems are not brought to them until others have failed. Usually they have to make the best of a bad job. Ideal solutions are often far out of reach. In the Congo, in Western New Guinea, in the Yemen, in Cuba, in Malaysia, in the question of the future of the Palestine refugees, for instance, they have no power to achieve all they would wish. But it is motive that matters. Now there is a band of able men constantly searching for an impartial initiative to keep the peace and, more important still, to find positive remedies for problems which if left will fester into conflict.

Those of us who work for the United Nations have no illusions. We realise that the Secretary-General and those who work with him high on the 38th floor of the United Nations building are human and fallible. No doubt they make mistakes. It would be amazing if they did not. They work under terrific pressure, usually far into the night. They have to turn hurriedly from one crisis to another. They have no large staff of career experts like the Foreign Offices of the great powers. They have no adequate military organisation and no intelligence service. Above all, there is the desperate shortage of money. They are badgered and buffeted and threatened by all and sundry.

At the lesser level of organisation there are grave weaknesses. The necessity for preserving some balance of employment in the Secretariat between the officials of all the member nations, the difficulty of securing adequate liaison and co-operation between all the U.N. agencies, the need to curb the arrogance and self-importance of inexperienced officials and to cut down the red tape in which any official machine delights, the object of giving to the whole ungainly world-wide organisation cohesion and leadership—all these requirements create constant problems.

The extraordinary thing is that the men at the top can stand up to the strain, and that the whole family of United Nations agencies and departments in fact works so well together.

Some thought that no one could fill the great gap left by Dag Hammarskjöld. His brilliant analytical brain and clear sense of high purpose and almost superhuman endurance seemed irreplaceable. But now U Thant, so different in temperament and method, has already established himself with dignity and courage in a personal position of great influence and authority.

He can never refuse to see any visiting Foreign Minister or any Head of Mission. He is constantly subject to every world pressure. Always calmly and courteously he listens—and then he has to judge and to decide and to act. He is abused, jostled and harassed. But within the narrow limits of his authority, coolly and carefully and courageously he and his team pursue their steady purpose to the best of their judgment in the international interest.

The organisation he leads has faced great trials. There are much greater tasks ahead. What a tragedy it will be if the organisation is kept so weak that it will be incapable of acting when the greatest tests come, when the United Nations may well be the sole hope of saving mankind.

But now there is at least a new hope, a new idea, a new ideal. The Secretary-General is the personification of that new force. He and his team are the new men. Now when there is an international dispute there are, as ever, the adversaries snarling at each other, seeking to outwit, to, weaken, to defeat, to destroy each other. But now in every dispute there is also a new initiative. Now there is the effort of the new men. They apply a new test and pursue a new purpose. They are not influenced by national greed or national pride. They apply the test of international advantage and the test of the interests of the common people concerned. That is a new thing in the world.

I have always believed that the forces of conciliation are potentially stronger than those of conflict. The trouble is that the forces of hatred and conflict are so often well organised and well led while the forces of conciliation are ill organised or ill led, or not organised or led at all. Now in the United Nations we have a permanent organisation for promoting international understanding and co-operation. It is this new initiative which gives us new hope in a divided world. It is above all motive that matters, and the strength of the Secretary-General is that he and his team bring to every problem the best motive of all, the motive of disinterested service.

The old barons of greed and pride and hatred and racial domination are as strong and proud and confident and well-mounted as ever. But now a new and hitherto unknown champion has entered the lists. He faces immensely powerful opponents, and his company is small. But the heavier the odds and the smaller the army the greater the honour. I for one am proud to ride behind him.

*   *   *

As I finish writing this at the end of 1963 world tensions seem to mount and multiply. Whichever way we look we see old dangers and new failures and disappointments—in Indonesia, in Arabia, in Ghana, in Somalia, for instance. In Cyprus, after five years of uneasy peace, suspicion and distrust and hatred have boiled over again in ferocious violence. In southern Africa the greatest danger of all, the danger of a colour war which must involve all Africa and the whole world, comes closer. The forces of conciliation and co-operation seem to falter while the forces of disruption and despotism flourish.

The extent of the dangers is a measure of the need for new effort and for a new sense of urgency, and for new methods. Increasingly we must seek solutions not by old national means but by new international action. The dangers should surely intensify a determination to win freedom from racial discrimination and domination, to settle disputes before violence takes over, to make a new assault on the poverty of more than half the world and, for all these purposes, to support and strengthen the authority and the capacity of the United Nations. Few people will dispute that the dangers exist. The question is whether we understand and care enough to act while there is still time, and time is terribly short.

I think that my father's text was better than mine. Perhaps we should not "glory in tribulations" but we can rejoice in facing and overcoming adversity in the confidence that "we are troubled on every side, but not distressed; we are perplexed but not in despair".

Index

247

Index

Index

Index

Index

Jamaica—*cont.*
119; Nonconformists of, 120; Hotel Association of, 122; and adult suffrage, 125–7; and constitutional changes, 127–8; and full independence, 128; economic problems of, 128; population of, 129, 131; slavery in, 129–30; economic progress of, 130–1; and Commonwealth Sugar Agreement, 130; and Agricultural Development Corporation, 130; and Industrial Development Corporation, 130; Legislature of, 131; and W. Indian Federation, 131–2; Independence Celebrations of, 132; public service in, 133; parliamentary tradition of, 134; Parliament of, 134; Banana Growers' Association of, 134; People's National Party of, 135, 138; Democratic Party of, 137; and Bauxite negotiations, 139; Government of, 139

Jebel el Akhdar, 79
Jenin, 48, 49, 50, 51, 55, 56
Jerrash, 68
Jerusalem, 13, 18, 19, 36–7, 38, 40, 42, 43, 46, 51, 56, 68, 77, 84, 85, 88; American School of Archaeology in, 73
Jewish Agency, 40, 41
Jews, 13, 35–6, 37, 38, 40, 42, 47, 48, 54, 99, 149; and Arabs, 19, 36; from Cyrenaica, 81–2; nationalism of, 57
Jezreel, 42
Jha, 197
Johnson, Brigadier Jimmie, 83
Johnson, Mrs. (sister of Col. Keyes), 83
Jordan, 13, 63, 64, 67, 77, 147; valley, 68, 88
Judea, 18
Judeida, 93

Kaiser company, 139
Kano, 18, 100; Emir of, 107
Kantara, 18
Karamanlis, 150, 151
Karpass, 181
Katsina, Emir of, 107–8
Kaunda, Kenneth, 111, 238–9
Kendrew, General, 160, 175, 186
Kenya, 53, 111, 198, 199, 200, 202, 234, 235, 236, 242

Kerak, 68
Keyes, Colonel, 82–3; sister of, 83; brother of, 83
Khan, Sir Zafrullah, 197
King Edward's Horse, 58
Kings House, Jamaica, 18, 30, 31, 114, 115, 120, 121, 122, 123, 136, 141, 149
Kingston, Jamaica, 115, 124, 136, 141; Harbour, 18, 115, 141; Ward Theatre Incident, 137
Kirkbride, Sir Alec, 17, 64, 65, 66, 67, 68, 88
Kiseler, Mr., 203
Kitium, Bishop of, 161
Knibb, William, 129
Krushchev, Mr., 235
Kufra, 79
Kurile Islands, 203
Kutchuk, Dr., 14, 181, 185
Kuwait, 191
Kykko Monastery, 182; Abbot of, 184
Kyrenia, 144
Kythrea, 186

Labour Party, 24
Lady Margaret Boat Club, 27; First May Boat, 28
Lagos, 107, 109, 110, 228, 239
Larnaca, 161
Latin, Mr., 202
Lawrence, T. E., 65, 66, 67, 70, 74, 170
Leathem, John, 33
Lebanon, 68, 69, 90, 92, 93, 97
Leighton Park, 27
Lennox-Boyd, Alan, 150, 152, 153, 155, 156, 164, 179, 180
Liberal, cause, 28; Club, 31; Land Campaign, 31; principles, 24
Libya, 13; King of, 84
Limassol, 149
Liskeard, 25
Litani, gorge, 92; river, 91
Llandudno, 224
Lloyd, Selwyn, 31, 150, 151–2, 159, 164–6, 179
Lloyd George, 28–9, 32
London, Agreement, 170, 181, 182, 184; mentioned, 17, 18, 28, 61, 62, 150, 151, 152, 155, 159, 160, 162, 163, 167, 168, 179, 192, 193, 200, 222, 223
Lufti, Omar, 197

Index

Luke, Sir Harry, 39, 40–2
Lumumba, 228

Ma'an, railway at, 73–6, 98
Macaulay, Lord, 110
Macdonald, Ramsay, Coalition Government, 25
MacGillivray, Donald, 18
Macleod, Iain, 189, 201
Macmichael, Sir Harold, 85
Macmillan, Harold, 150, 151, 155, 156–7, 169, 189, *see Prime Minister*
    Plan, 155, 156, 168
Macpherson, Sir John, 84, 85, 103, 104
Mafrak, 68, 69
Magloire, President, 123
Mahnes, brothers, 47
Maiduguri, 107
Makarios, Archbishop, 14, 149, 150, 156, 158, 159, 161, 163, 166–7, 168, 169, 181, 182–4, 185
Makerere, 199
Malaya, 46, 51, 53, 205
Malaysia, 234, 244
Malone, Denis, 178, 179, 180
Malta, 18, 41, 77, 191
Manley, Norman, 32, 135, 137, 138–40, 239
Margaret, H.R.H. Princess, 123
May, Erskine, *Parliamentary Procedure*, 134
Mazar, 50
Mboya, Tom, 111
Meiklejohn, Sir Roderick, 59
Menderes, 150–1
Mexican Ambassador, 177
Milverton, Lord, 103
Moffatt, 55
Molyneux, Edward, 190
Montgomery, Field Marshal Lord, 42, 78
Montreal, 94
Morocco, 135
Mozambique, 216, 227
Munoz, Marin, Governor, 123, 132
Mustapha, Turkish Kavass, 143

Nabatiya, 191
Nablus, 42, 43, 45, 48, 49, 51, 52, 54, 87, 148; Mayor of, 52
Nathanya, 47, 48

National Liberal Club, 25
NATO, 168, 179
Nauru, 203, 205, 206, 207–9
Nazareth, 42, 44, 49, 50
Ndabaningi Sithole, 236
Nehru, 239
New Guinea, 76, 191, 203, 205, 206, 207, 210–15, 243, 244
Newman Missionary School, 43
New York, 14, 33, 133, 148, 175, 189, 190, 192, 193, 207, 208, 222, 226, 229, 243
New Zealand, 208
Nicosia, 18, 89, 143, 144, 150, 156, 161, 166, 167, 168, 169, 172, 184; Prison, 180
Nigeria, 100–12; Legislative Council of, 14, 104, 105, 106, 107, 109; problems in 1947, 100–1; Northern Region, of, 76, 100; Federation of, 101; first Parliament of, 101–2; achievement of, 102; Regions of, 102–3; and preparation of new constitution, 104–5; and General Conference on constitution, 105; and Secretary of State's despatch to Governor, 105–6; Administrative Service of, 106; new constitution of, 106; diversity of, 106–7; and Yorubas, 108; and the N.C.N.C., 109; and ban on Dingle Foot, 111; and integrity of courts, 111; assets of, 111; first University of, 112; Delegation to U.N., 112; leadership of, 112; mentioned, 17, 18, 22, 32, 120, 148, 178, 190, 197, 198, 200, 202, 225, 228, 234, 238
Nkomo, Joshua, 217, 223
Nkrumah, President, 239
Northamptonshire Regiment, 42
Nyasaland, 198
Nyerere, President, 111, 236, 239

Obas Council, 108
Oberemko, Valentine, 197, 198
Obote, Prime Minister of Uganda, 111
Omar, Mosque of, 19
Ottawa, 157, 158
Ottoman Empire, 40, 78
Oved ben Ami, 47
Oxford, 22, 27, 31, 33, 239; Union, 33, 152
Oyo, Alafin of, 108, 109

253

Index

Pacific, 205, 206, 214, 215; Islands, 203, 206

Pakistan, 197

Palestine, mentioned, 13, 17, 18, 21, 22, 28, 35, 36, 37, 39, 42, 43, 51, 53, 55, 56–7, 58, 64, 69, 73, 81, 93, 95, 96; Arab rebellion in, 35–7; British Mandate in, 36, 37, 57; Emergency, 54; Gendarmerie, 37, 40; Jewish State in, 36; Jewish national home in, 36; refugees, 244

Partisides, 149

Patch, Air Marshal, 89

Pavlides, Stelios, 149

Peake, Pasha, 64, 67

The Pen and the Sword, 26

Petra, 98

Plimsoll, Sir James, 197

Plumer, Field Marshal Lord, 37, 38

Plymouth, 18, 25

Port Royal, 115

Port Said, 18, 55, 148

Portugal, 215, 216, 218, 220, 235

Press, the, 88, 155, 162, 164, 167, 181, 216, 224

Prime Minister, 157, 159, 168, 179, *see Macmillan*

Quaison-Sackey, 197

Quatana, 97

Qubeia, 92

Quebec, 158

Queen, H.M., 101, 124, 134

R.A.F., the, 80

Ramallah, 42

Ramsey, A. M., 29

Reddaway, John, 161

Renison, Patrick, 60

Reynolds Company, 139

Rhodes, 143

Rhodesia, Northern, 111, 198, 238; Southern, 198, 215–27, 231, 236; Government of Southern, 217, 219, 221, 222, 225; Constitution of Southern, 221

Richards Constitution, 103

Rikhye, General, 243

Robertson, Sir James, 103

Rommel, 82, 83

Rossel, Agda, 196

Royal Horse Guards, 172, 179, 185

Ruanda Urindu, 195

Ruhi Bey Abdul Hadi, 40

Said Idris Es Senussi, 84

St. Andrew Dinner, 41–2

St. Cleer, 24

St. Hilarion Hill, 144

Salamanca, Ambassador Carlos, 206

Salazar, 220, 235

Samaria, District, 36, 42, 43, 45, 46, 55

Samoza, President, 123

Samuel, Sir Herbert, 37, 38

Sandwich, Lord, 232

Sandys, Duncan, 201, 226–7

Seaforth Highlanders, 48, 49

Security Forces, 172, 173, 174, 186

Senussi, the, 13, 78–80, 83, 84

The Seven Pillars of Wisdom, 65

Seychelles, 149, 158, 166

Sherlock, Hugh, 119

Shubaa, 93, 94, 95, 96; Mukhtar of, 94–5

Shuna, 88

Sierra Leone, 198, 200

Simon, Sir John, 25

Sinai, 73, 85

Sinclair, George, 161, 163, 167

Singapore, 191

Sirte Desert, 82

Spaak, Paul Henry, 32, 194, 195, 196

Spain, 235

Spain, Nancy, 30, 31

Spears Ambulance Unit, 73

Speeches on American Independence, 34

Spicer, Colonel Roy, 52

Solomon Islands, 207

Somalia, 234, 242 and postscript

Stalin, 235

Stevenson, Adlai, 123, 205

Stevenson, Sergeant, 115

Sudan, 46; Political Service of, 27–8, 78, 87

Suez, 123

Suleiman Bey Toukan, 53

Sokoto, Sultan of, 107

Soviet Bloc, 233; Delegation to U.N., 197; islands, 203; Union, 202, 203, 204, 205, 220, 229, 240

Supreme Moslem Council, 40

Syria, 17, 48, 64, 68, 69, 72, 73, 90, 97

Tanganyika, 198, 199, 200, 202, 203, 204, 236, 238, 239, 242

254

Index

Index